JUNG
A Complete Introduction

MW00460670

Dr Phil Goss is a Jungian analyst (member of the Association of Jungian Analysts, London, and of the International Association of Analytical Psychology) and a UKCP-registered psychotherapist. He is course leader for the masters programmes in Counselling and Psychotherapy at the University of Central Lancashire. Phil's publications include *Men, Women and Relationships, A post-Jungian Approach: Gender Electrics and Magic Beans* (Routledge, 2010), journal papers and chapters on a range of themes in edited collections.

Praise for *Jung: A Complete Introduction*

'This is a lucid and refreshingly innovative introduction to the complex thought of C.G. Jung. Its splendid mix of rich information and accessible presentation means it will be valuable to anyone from a whole range of disciplines, from Cultural Studies through to Psychology. I would not hesitate to recommend this genuinely helpful introduction to students and general readers alike, while analysts, too, will welcome Phil Goss's thoughtful presentation of Jung's theories.'

Paul Bishop, William Jacks Chair of Modern Languages, University of Glasgow

Phil Goss combines dexterity in writing and clarity of thinking to create a goldmine of knowledge in this eminently readable book that transcends the constraints of a set formula. The ideas of two towering figures in the contemporary Jungian world, Wolfgang Giegerich and Sonu Shamdasani, are skilfully elaborated as are the developmental stages of Jung's thought. The latter culminates in Jung's all-important contribution to the history of ideas, viz. the psychological application of alchemy. The author brings to life the first meeting between the neurologist, Freud, and the psychiatrist, Jung, in the course of which the more mature Freud grounds the fiery stream of Jung's outpourings. Goss goes on to spell out the similarities in their thinking as well as the differences that led to their tragic split, the consequences of which continue to reverberate in the psychoanalytic world. Among the highlights of this far-ranging book is an account of the intellectual forerunners of Jung's thought that include the genius of Schopenhauer. The book is studded throughout with insightful quotations and dreams from Jung, and the acknowledgement of his paramount importance as a religious thinker, the application of which is exemplified in appropriate clinical vignettes. Questions for the studious reader, definitions of key notions, and further references for deeper research make this book a supremely useful tool for teaching Jung in the academy and training institutions. It should also find a wide circulation among lay readers as well as experienced psychoanalysts and psychotherapists.'

Ann Casement, Licensed Psychoanalyst; Fellow of the Royal Anthropological Institute

'Of the many introductions to Jung's work, I find this one not only the most comprehensive but, importantly, very readable for the non-Jungian. It will appeal to those in the arts as well as to those working in the psychological therapies and complementary disciplines – whether they are a seasoned practitioner, a student or a lay person who wishes to learn more about the man who challenged Freud's reductionist theories. Those not familiar with Jung's ideas, terminology or life will find this a coherent guide to what otherwise might be a maze. Each chapter focuses on a different aspect of his intricate thinking about human psychology and is written in a style that is both erudite – with serious scholarship behind it – and accessible. There are parallels for me with Jung's own autobiography, *Memories, Dreams, Reflections*, which, unlike his scientific writings, offers poetic observations about life and how we psychologically negotiate the world. Phil Goss has written a work that not only celebrates his subject but also asks important questions. This work will endure, as it succinctly maps the remarkable contribution of Jung's distinctive approach to a wide number of subjects, principally psychology, psychotherapy, philosophy and the human condition.'

Steve Mitchell, Dramatherapist / Director Pathfinder Studio; former Course Director of Dramatherapy, Roehampton Institute, London

JUNG
A Complete Introduction

Phil Goss

First published in Great Britain in 2015 by John Murray Learning. An Hachette UK company.

Copyright © Phil Goss 2015

The right of Phil Goss to be identified as the Author of the Work has been asserted by him in accordance with the Copyright, Designs and Patents Act 1988.

Database right Hodder & Stoughton (makers)

The Teach Yourself name is a registered trademark of Hachette UK.

All rights reserved. No part of this publication may be reproduced, stored in a retrieval system or transmitted in any form or by any means, electronic, mechanical, photocopying, recording or otherwise, without the prior written permission of the publisher, or as expressly permitted by law, or under terms agreed with the appropriate reprographic rights organization. Enquiries concerning reproduction outside the scope of the above should be sent to the Rights Department, John Murray Learning, at the address below.

You must not circulate this book in any other binding or cover and you must impose this same condition on any acquirer.

British Library Cataloguing in Publication Data: a catalogue record for this title is available from the British Library.

Library of Congress Catalog Card Number: on file.

Paperback ISBN 978 1 473 60176 5

eBook ISBNs 978 1 473 60178 9; 978 1 473 60177 2

1

The publisher has used its best endeavours to ensure that any website addresses referred to in this book are correct and active at the time of going to press. However, the publisher and the author have no responsibility for the websites and can make no guarantee that a site will remain live or that the content will remain relevant, decent or appropriate.

The publisher has made every effort to mark as such all words which it believes to be trademarks. The publisher should also like to make it clear that the presence of a word in the book, whether marked or unmarked, in no way affects its legal status as a trademark.

Every reasonable effort has been made by the publisher to trace the copyright holders of material in this book. Any errors or omissions should be notified in writing to the publisher, who will endeavour to rectify the situation for any reprints and future editions.

Cover image © Getty

Typeset by Cenveo® Publisher Services.

Printed and bound in Great Britain by CPI Group (UK) Ltd, Croydon CR0 4YY.

John Murray Learning policy is to use papers that are natural, renewable and recyclable products and made from wood grown in sustainable forests. The logging and manufacturing processes are expected to conform to the environmental regulations of the country of origin.

John Murray Learning
Carmelite House
50 Victoria Embankment
London
EC4Y 0DZ
www.hodder.co.uk

Contents

To all colleagues and friends in the Jungian community, for their support and the constant flow of stimulating ideas; and to the memory of Carl Jung who set a ball rolling that continues to gather pace one hundred years on. To the efforts of all colleagues who work to get Jungian and post-Jungian ideas seen and heard in psychotherapeutic, academic and cultural contexts.

Introduction

'... it is the function of consciousness not only to recognize and assimilate the outside world through the gateway of the senses, but to translate into visible reality the world within us.'

Jung, C. G., *The Structure and Dynamics of the Psyche*, CW8 para. 342 (London: Routledge, 1970)

When Carl Jung began to explore the unconscious, he soon came to realize its power. As a boy, he was privy from a young age to its mysteries through powerful dreams. Later, as a student and then doctor of psychiatry, he came face to face with its capacity to overwhelm fragile minds. He also came to recognize its potential for healing when the energies locked away within it could, first, be released and, second, channelled in a healthy way. The 'world within us' for Jung was a living reality and he saw it as our responsibility to notice and explore it, before applying the implications of what we had found to our understanding of the external world, and more importantly, to ourselves.

What does Jungian analytic thinking and practice – or, more accurately, in Jung's own words 'analytical psychology' – have to offer us in our twenty-first-century interconnected world of increasing globalization, multiplying diversity of cultural identities, fast-developing technologies and high-speed living? Could his somewhat esoteric interests, such as synchronicity and alchemy, and his unusual perspectives on areas such as the place of religion in psychology, really have anything to contribute to scientific and postmodern perspectives on the human condition?

This book gives you the material to form a view on this question. We will explore the full gamut of Jung's thinking – not to mention the ideas and applications of some of the more eminent thinkers and analysts who have followed in his wake. After all, one thing Jung cannot be securely criticized for is a lack of ideas. His reach in this respect was breathtaking: in areas from psychiatry to particle physics, from the analytic relationship to our experience of the divine, from archetypal influences to personality typology, Jung applied his considerable intellect and intuitive gifts. He did this to strong effect in order to generate insights, theories and visions about who we, as human beings, might be and how the healing powers of the unconscious can quietly transform us individually – possibly even collectively.

You might have got an idea already of how broad (and deep) Jungian theory and its applications are. The book is laid out to reflect this but also to help you to navigate your way through the material in a manageable and engaging way. This means you have a choice: either you can read the book through chronologically (if your objective is to get as full an overview as possible), or you can dip into specific chapters which will help you understand a particular theme or concept, or help you find the information you need for your studies (or an assignment you need to write).

The book has four sections, each working to a clear theme:

▶ **Section 1, Introducing Jung and his discoveries,** sets the scene for the model Jung developed (and others further modified). There are chapters on Jung's discovery of archetypal influences in the psyche (1), a portrayal of his early life and formative influences (2), his early career and the philosophers who deeply influenced his thinking (3), and his momentous collaboration and then schism with Freud (4). This section will provide you with a clear picture of the man and his way of approaching human psychology.

▶ **Section 2, The world within: Jung's model of the human psyche,** applies a magnifying glass to his key theories. This takes us on a journey into the human psyche and the archetypes within it as he named them. Chapter 5 explores the crucial relationship between *ego* and *self* for the *individuation* process (or 'becoming more fully who we are'). Chapter 6 includes a foray into our dark side with *shadow*, followed in Chapter 7 by an exploration of Jung's theories about the feminine and masculine (*anima* and *animus*). In Chapter 8 we consider the way in which *archetypal* influences in the human psyche (situated deep in the unconscious and ubiquitous to the human condition) can generate difficult states of mind (*complexes*). These dominate our way of dealing with life and can take some overcoming in therapy. Finally, in Chapter 9 of this section, Jung's model for understanding personality types will be explained and critiqued. This section thus provides a picture of key influences in the human psyche, which will inform your understanding of how Jungian analysis is practised.

▶ **Section 3, Jungian analytic practice,** explains analysis as a concept and reality (Chapter 10), before we enter the fascinating world of dreams and dream analysis (in Chapter 11). Chapter 12 develops this theme of working with material from the unconscious by explaining what is meant by 'active imagination' and how it is worked with in analysis. Chapter 13 covers Jung's exploration of the work of the medieval (and older) alchemists as they attempted to turn base metal into gold, something Jung came to see as a valuable metaphorical framework for understanding the therapeutic process in Jungian analysis. In Chapter 14 we consider an important development in the field after Jung's initial model was established – the work of Michael Fordham and his developmental approach to Jungian analysis and thinking, something which complemented Jung's predominant focus on adulthood and the second half of life. The final chapter (15) in this section describes valuable and innovative applications of Jungian thinking to mental health issues such as working with addiction, trauma and personality disorders – a fitting way to conclude a section that illustrates the relevance and creativity of the Jungian analytical approach.

▶ **Section 4, Jung's legacy: culture, spirituality and therapy,** considers to what extent his ideas have influenced academic, cultural and religious thinking in the modern and postmodern world. We examine the relevance of Jung's ideas to the contemporary world. The breadth of his ideas about the individual and the collective – and the wider influences on human history and 'progress' – comes across as we look at culture, arts and science (Chapter 16); religion and spirituality (Chapter 17); politics, ecology and education (Chapter 18). In Chapter 19 we then stand back to look at further developments in the Jungian analytic approach, and in particular consider how Jungian ideas and tools may be integrated into theory and practice in psychotherapy and counselling generally (as reflective of the growth in integrative approaches). We also look at research on the 'effectiveness' or otherwise of the Jungian approach. Finally, the concluding chapter lays out how the Jungian field has evolved after Jung and the discussion includes some interesting critiques of his fundamental tenets.

I hope this overview of the content and structure of the book has whetted your appetite, even if some of the terms described are unfamiliar, or seem a bit weird and wonderful. The key thing about Jung and his ideas is that they have a life of their own. He once famously said he was 'not a Jungian', meaning that it is a mistake to try too hard to pin down what being 'Jungian' is, since we are all unique individuals. In that regard, you are invited to see this book as a reflective tool as well as an academic one. Do try to apply the concepts to yourself – though this works best where you feel motivated and engaged, as well as in a stable state of mind (working with the unconscious is not advisable if you are feeling distressed, markedly low, anxious or disturbed). One way to do this is to keep a journal in which you can write and draw, or stick words and images, in response to the ideas in this book. If you follow this approach, you will find that this book offers a rich resource for your personal development as well as a deeper understanding of the Jungian model and its applications.

However you choose to read, or use, this book, I hope you enjoy the experience and take away ideas and insights that enhance your studies and enrich your experience of life – principles which echo Jung's intentions when he set out on his voyage of discovery in and around the unconscious.

Phil Goss

How to use this book

This Complete Introduction from Teach Yourself® includes a number of special boxed features, which have been developed to help you understand the subject more quickly and remember it more effectively. Throughout the book, you will find these indicated by the following icons.

 All chapters include a few **quotes** from Jung, Jungian thinkers, or commentators on analytical psychology, which you can draw on for your academically assessed or examined work.

 Each chapter includes a **case study** to help you situate the theories within the living experience of analysis (including the use of a fictional character 'Jolanta' and her experience of the Jungian therapeutic approach).

 The **key ideas** and **key terms** are highlighted throughout the book. The key ideas explain one interesting aspect of, or influence on, the theme being discussed, to get you thinking further. Key terms used in the book are listed with their definitions at the end of each chapter for ease of reference.

 The **spotlight** boxes in each chapter should grab your attention and lighten the mood: they focus on less obvious details and quirky perspectives or anecdotes. They also include some reflective exercises.

 The **dig deeper** boxes give recommendations for further study so that you can explore the topics in more depth.

 The **fact-check** multiple-choice questions at the end of each chapter are designed to help you ensure that you have understood the most important concepts from the chapter. If you find you are consistently getting several answers wrong, it may be worth trying to read more slowly, or taking notes as you go.

Please note that, for ease of referencing, where Jung's collected works are referred to, the abbreviation 'CW' is used with the volume number, e.g. CW7.

Section 1

Introducing Jung and his discoveries

1

Creative madness? Confronting the unconscious

What is 'the unconscious'? Why is it such an influential idea? What part has the thinking of Carl Jung and his followers played in promoting its significance for understanding who we are, for dealing with human suffering, and promoting healing and growth? We will begin to consider these questions in this chapter as well as describe how Jung approached the unconscious himself. We will also start to unpick some crucial Jungian terms such as individuation, archetypes and shadow.

Working with the unconscious

'The unconscious is the ever-creative mother of consciousness.'
Carl Jung, 1966, para. 207

The proposal underpinning this statement by Carl Jung (1875–1961) is a crucial aspect of psychoanalysis, and depth psychology generally. This proposal is that much of what informs our thinking and behaviour as human beings occurs beyond our conscious awareness. When we get irrationally angry, for example, it is because of something influencing us that is beyond our rational capacity to control.

Whatever this 'something' is – a repressed hurt from our early childhood, perhaps, or an underdeveloped capacity to mediate our primitive rages, or an aspect of our potential which has somehow not been 'allowed' to develop or express itself healthily – it has a lot of power. When we are not conscious of the source of this power to make us mad with someone else, we are *unconscious* of what the 'something' is and, until we become more conscious of it and how it operates, we will remain vulnerable to its influence. When we fall in love, or when we dream – these are other examples of the unconscious at work. This 'discovery' (Ellenberger, 1970) of the unconscious can be found earlier in the work of philosophers such as Schopenhauer (1788–1860) and Carus (1852–1919), as well as in the attempts by pioneers in the world of psychiatry such as Charcot (1825–1893) and Janet (1859–1947) to uncover and address unconscious influences on their patients.

The term 'depth psychological' refers mainly to the approaches in psychotherapy that stemmed from the initial model of psychoanalysis developed by Sigmund Freud (1856–1939) (Storr, 1989). Jung's work is one such approach, and a hugely influential one, not just in counselling and psychotherapy, but stretching out into fields of study and popular interest such as cultural and religious studies, politics and identity, and film studies, to name but a few. (These areas and more will be explored in Section 4.)

For Jung, the notion of the unconscious was much more than an idea. For him, it was a living reality that requires us to pay heed to what may be going on within it, as a fundamental part of becoming fully human. Many of his key theoretical ideas arose from his own encounters with the unconscious. Here he wrestled with his personal demons, and experienced influences arising from the pool of human experience (stretching back over a million years), which he said we all carry around within us.

Encountering the unconscious

A man sat still at his desk, his eyes closed and his hands resting on his knees. He had placed his glasses and pipe on the desk so that he could really concentrate. However, what he was trying to do was, in a way, the opposite of concentrating. It was more like letting go of concentration. He was trying to allow all his thoughts and worries to fade into the background: his worries about his job as a psychiatrist at the local hospital, about his family – his wife and four children – and about his professional relationships, including one connection which meant so much to his hopes for promoting his ideas and developing his practice, which had soured and ended recently.

Instead, the man was clearing a space in his mind. He opened his eyes and began to stare at the wall, a blank space on the wall, his eyes glazed over. Then he let himself 'drop' – his mind was falling, falling into the unconscious, or as near as he could get to into it. It felt as if he was dropping through the floor and into an abyss that was opening up beneath him; there was nothing to stop his fall and nothing for him to reach out and grab as he descended, at speed. He had chosen to do this, but now he was wondering what had driven him to take such a risk with his own sanity. Then the man found himself standing on soft but sticky ground, in the dark. After a while his eyes adjusted to the darkness and he could just make out what looked like rocks and the opening of a cave. There was a short figure standing in the entrance. The man wondered where he was, who this character might be, and what the figure might say (or do?) to him.

Key idea

There are around 2,500 qualified Jungian analysts practising around the world, and more than 30 training institutes approved by the International Association of Analytical Psychologists, the organization that governs Jungian analytic practice and training. There are training institutes in Austria, Belgium, Brazil, Canada, Denmark, France, Germany, Israel, Mexico, Switzerland, the UK and the USA.

Carl Gustav Jung was a psychiatrist and psychotherapist. He was a scientific thinker but also a dealer in visions, dreams and imagination. He came to believe that who we are as human beings is powerfully influenced, even determined, by unconscious forces outside of our awareness. At the same time, he strongly promoted the vital task of the individual to find out who they are, and become that person as fully as anyone can become within the three score years and ten of an average human lifespan. Jung saw this as our central task in life, our task of **individuation**.

That is the term Jung used to describe this task to become (Jung, 1953 para. 266) 'a psychological "in-dividual," that is a separate, indivisible unity or "whole."' The challenge life throws up for us, according to Jung, is to become more completely who we are, through integrating our unconscious influences and conscious minds. Jung was convinced it is the individual human being rather than the popular masses, or God, who held the key to humanity's development. Our task in this respect is to get to know all key aspects of ourselves, including our **shadow** (Jung, 1968) (which holds the darker, hidden aspects of us), and integrate these so we can be more authentic and complete. Jung did not see this as an 'ultimate' process where we achieve some kind of perfected wholeness, but rather as a 'work in progress' that we get as far as we can with in one lifetime.

Jung was a thinker in the field of psychotherapy for whom **paradox** was key. He came to understand that two (or more) principles, which may seem antithetical to each other, can both be real or 'true' at the same time. His approach to understanding the human psyche and its journey through life was hallmarked by an attitude not of 'either/or' but rather 'and/both'. Opposites that we are familiar with, such as 'good vs bad', 'love vs hate', 'war vs peace', 'arts vs sciences', are two sides of the same coin. This was a key aspect of Jung's theory of **archetypes** (Samuels et al., 1986) where these refer to 'essences' which do not concretely exist themselves but which strongly influence our experiences and behaviour. An example would be the archetype of love. It exists everywhere in human history and activity but has to be manifested in a feeling or relationship (or breakdown of relationship) to find its form.

Also, as implied above, archetypes are *bipolar* – not in the sense associated with mental illness, but more in the sense of 'two opposite poles', within which there is a continuum of possibility, such as all the shades of grey which operate within the relationship between, say, 'good and bad', or, 'love and hate'. The concept and applications of *archetypes* in therapy are explored in Chapters 8 and 12, and applications to social and cultural developments are described in Section 4.

This principle informed his work with his 'analysands'. He coined this term for people who came for analysis, which was his term for psychotherapy. Freud's term was the more medically conventional 'patient'. When Jung split from his professional alliance with Freud, he wanted to make this distinction to reflect his new 'analytic' approach to working with the psyche, an approach he also termed 'analytical psychology'.

Spotlight: 'Analysand' – does it still work?

Jungian analysts today might still use this term but they may also use the term 'patient' to indicate they are working in a psychoanalytic way. They may also use a term more commonly used in the wider counselling and psychotherapy field: 'client', especially if they practise in a more humanistic way – a point we will return to in Chapter 19 when we consider how some Jungians integrate aspects of other therapeutic approaches. However, 'analysand' is still the official Jungian term in use.

As you work through this book, you will become familiar with an archetypal approach to reality. It is a way of recognizing that people are complicated and life is full of contradictions. In Jung's way of describing this, these are **archetypal polarities** – in other words, these contradictions and tensions crop up everywhere and are a part of being human. They also provide an opportunity to work on different aspects of ourselves, to help us get to know these and integrate them as part of the process of individuation.

As well as deriving his ideas about the unconscious and archetypal influences from thinkers in philosophy and psychiatry, Jung also found that his work at the Burgholzi mental hospital in Zurich seemed to confirm the presence of these influences. He noticed how similar images and reactions would come up in the responses and associations of the patients he worked with, suggesting that there might be patterns in the human psyche we all share – though they will manifest themselves in an individual way, such as in the dream described here.

What is the horse trying to tell its rider?

A young man had a dream in which he is trying hard to control a horse he is sitting on. The horse is large and strong and keeps rearing up, seeming to try to throw the man on to the ground. This man had had a rollercoaster of a time recently – he had moved around jobs, and countries, for the previous three years, and his partner had recently rejected him, saying he was too obsessed with himself and not able to commit properly to the relationship.

When he came for analysis, he easily saw the parallel between the horse trying to throw him on to the ground and what had recently happened to him. But he found it harder to accept that there might be something about the way he was going about his life which could be represented by the struggle he was having in the dream to control the horse. He and his analyst explored what associations or meanings the horse might have for him. The analyst was aware that a horse had certain archetypal associations – as an animal it can represent the more instinctual side of the human psyche but, more specifically, the horse can be seen as something instinctual that can serve us if we can master it – and masculine, phallic sexual instincts can be represented in this symbol.

Many tales from ancient traditions and stories of the Wild West illustrate how the horse can represent a strong, loyal 'carrier' of a person, of the psyche. For the man in this case study, though, the 'carrier' did not want to carry him at the moment. Rather than trying to explore this archetypal context with the man, his analyst waited for him to find his own way to the connection. This came about through his ruminations on what had gone wrong with his ex-partner. He knew that unless he could 'rein in' his own tendencies to wander – through jobs, places and sexual dalliances with women – then his impulsiveness would make a long-term relationship very difficult to attain or sustain. He understood when the analyst observed that we cannot control a horse unless we can control ourselves. Although the man struggled to find a new long-term relationship for a while, he began to moderate his impulsiveness and find a better balance in his life.

Making sense of the unconscious

Returning to the earlier narrative, let's see what Jung, in his own words, did with what he found in his unconscious:

'I was sitting at my desk once more, thinking over my fears. Then I let myself drop. Suddenly it was as though the ground literally gave way beneath my feet, and I plunged down into the dark depths... [before]... I landed on my feet in a soft, sticky mass.'

Jung, 1963, p. 203

After going into the cave, past a dwarf with 'leathery skin' (the figure he could just see in the cave entrance) he 'waded knee deep through icy water to the other end of the cave where, on a projecting rock, I saw a glowing red crystal.' Jung lifts the crystal, and in the hollow underneath he sees a dead body in the water:

> '... a corpse floated by, a youth with blond hair and a wound in the head. He was followed by a gigantic black scarab and then by a red, newborn sun, rising up out of the depths of the water. Dazzled by the light, I wanted to replace the stone upon the opening, but then a fluid welled out. It was blood.'
>
> Jung, 1963, pp. 204–5

Reflecting on these powerful images, Jung makes an 'archetypal' interpretation – that is, he looks for a template for what he has seen from the vast collection of myths, stories and images from the cultural heritage of humankind. In his view, these templates are not available to us just in their concrete narrative form (as stories in books and films, for example). Rather, we actually carry them around inside us, in a shared layer of the unconscious below the individual **personal unconscious**. Jung agreed with Freud that we each have this repository of repressed instinctual material, which would otherwise overwhelm our conscious mind. However, the layer Jung saw as underneath that, which he termed the **collective unconscious**, would become a central tenet of his theoretical model (and one that would contribute to his painful break with Freud).

In this case, Jung noticed an archetypal template from Egyptian mythology:

> 'I realized, of course, that it was a hero and solar myth, a drama of death and renewal, the rebirth symbolized by the Egyptian scarab. At the end, the dawn of the new day should have followed, but instead came that intolerable outpouring of blood... [which] I abandoned all further attempt to understand.'
>
> Jung, 1963, p. 205

Through *active imagination* – the conscious allowing of a string of images to come through, and then engaging with them before trying to understand what they mean and applying them to one's life and self-awareness – Jung recognized that he had been privy to a version of an Egyptian myth of rebirth.

However, while the scarab, or beetle, confirmed this link, the outpouring of blood was a mystery. This is where the unconscious can take a very old archetypal template like this myth and give it a currency for the time the individual is living in. Jung gradually came to see the relevance of the bloodied corpse of the blonde hero and the outpouring of blood. With other linked fantasies, the possibility became clearer that the bloody disruption at the end of the mythological sequence connected with real events. First, there was the huge, and difficult, change going on inside him following the distressing split with Freud. Secondly, there was the impending outbreak of the First World War.

However one views Jung's speculations, it is hard to deny the power of the images he uncovered, and the way the unconscious can throw these up in our dreams – or in the kind of work with free imagination that Jung experimented with. The experiment at times threatened his sanity and he had to make sure he had one foot firmly planted in the real world (helped by his wife Emma and their children, as well as his professional life at the Burgholzi). His ego could have been overwhelmed by all this, and at times, reading his accounts, one might say it was. But he was able to pull himself back from serious fragmentation and, instead, his brave – or foolish (depending on how you look at it) – efforts reaped a dividend.

He was able to build a model for understanding what goes on in the human psyche that still stands up well today, although those who have come after him within the psychotherapeutic and theoretical approach he initiated have inevitably questioned, modified and built on his initial model. However, his encounters with various figures and dramas arising from his unconscious, alongside the insights he derived from his work with psychiatric patients and his anthropological studies of different cultures, gave him his 'archetypes of the psyche': ego, persona, self, shadow, and *anima* and *animus*. Jung used what he would see as the most valuable resource for our learning and research – ourselves – and, in this case, what his own unconscious seemed to be trying to tell him.

Key idea: Alienist?

When Jung began practising as a psychiatrist in the early twentieth century, the term used for this role was 'alienist'. When he gave his most famous interview, with John Freeman for the BBC in 1957, Freeman still used that term, which has now passed out of usage in English-language references to psychiatry. However, in France, where the term originated, it remains the official term. Jung as 'alienist' is not to be confused with his interest in UFOs (see Chapter 17).

Jung's 'Red Book'

Jung recorded, and graphically illustrated, his innermost experiences from the period when he explored his unconscious, in his 'Red Book'. This book is written as a description of a series of fantasy journeys, arising from a realization that in

A mandala drawn by Jung, featuring masculine and feminine figures (*The Red Book*, p. 105)

serving the spirit of the modern age (which he saw as being all about how much 'use' or 'value' we can be to human society), he had lost his soul…. He then encounters his own soul and embarks on a journey in which figures emerge from his unconscious and guide him towards his individuation task: to integrate the different, sometimes seemingly contradictory influences in his psyche, and to find a new worldview which encompassed older religious and cultural influences as well as fresh psychological and wider scientific understanding.

A central example in the 'Red Book' of seemingly opposed or antithetical influences is the encounters he describes with Elijah and Salome. While the male prophet Elijah represents ancient, serious and persistent truths, the young woman Salome represents new possibility, sensual youth and movement. Jung's journey in integrating these opposites to get to a new post-Christian worldview unfolds through the manuscript. The figure of Elijah also provided Jung with the template for an 'imaginal' figure in his psyche (imaginary but psychologically real and autonomous) that he would often meet in his journeys of active imagination (see definition below and Chapter 12 for a fuller description). This was Philemon, a wise prophet who guided him into understandings and insights about himself, the human condition and archetypal influences.

Jung also had a 'Black Book', a set of notebooks where he recorded his fantasies before transferring them to his 'Red Book', in which, as he puts it: 'I tried an aesthetic elaboration of my fantasies, but never finished it' (Jung, 1963, p. 213). He did not finish it because:

'I became aware that I had not yet found the right language, that I still had to translate it into something else. Therefore I gave up this aestheticizing tendency in good time, in favour of a rigorous process of understanding. I saw that so much fantasy needed firm ground underfoot, and that I must first return wholly to reality. For me, reality meant scientific comprehension. I had to draw concrete conclusions from the insights the unconscious had given me – and that task was to become a life's work.'

Thus his 'Red Book' provided the wellspring of experiences and ideas that Jung then took and fashioned into a theoretical framework based on grounded scientific principles. This book was not published until 2009 (48 years after his death), because Jung's family and some of his followers wanted to keep it out of the public eye until it was felt that enough time had passed for its unusual imagery and text to find general acceptance. Jung was a controversial figure, as we will explore in greater detail later in this book, and his vivid exposition of his encounters on his inner journeys may have reinforced perceptions in some clinical and academic circles that he and his ideas were too wayward from Western scientific and secular principles to be taken seriously. He and his ideas had made some enemies, and so to release *The Red Book* too soon may have brought more trouble than appreciation. When the book was published, the general response was one of curiosity and excitement, not just in the analytic community but also across the psychotherapeutic field and beyond, with some writers, artists, filmmakers and media commentators picking up on it as a significant cultural and intellectual moment.

Spotlight: *The Red Book* causes a storm

When *The Red Book* was published in 2009, it caused considerable interest around the world, not least in the United States, where a special series of dialogues were set up at the Rubin Museum in New York. As it says on the museum website, 'personalities from many different walks of life were paired on stage with a psychoanalyst and invited to respond to and interpret a folio from Jung's *Red Book* as a starting point for a wide-ranging conversation'.

Those involved, alongside the analysts, included Twitter co-founder Jack Doursey, novelist Alice Walker, musician David Byrne, composer Meridith Monk and *Mad Men* creator Matthew Weiner. Podcasts of all discussions can be found on the website: http://www.rubinmuseum.org/redbook

Key terms

Active imagination: A technique Jung developed in order to engage with the unconscious more fully. Images are allowed to form spontaneously through a kind of 'daydreaming' and, after dialogue with them, new insights can be derived.

Analysand: The term Jung coined for people who came for analysis, to distinguish the Jungian approach as distinct from Freud's use of 'patient'.

Anima: The feminine influence and image in men.

Animus: The masculine influence and image in women.

Archetypes: The essence of phenomena which crop up everywhere in the world and in human experience. They generate instinctual responses and images that can strongly influence our perceptions and behaviour, especially when we are not conscious of this. They are 'bipolar': the opposites within an archetype (such as night and day in the archetype of the earth's cycle around the sun) sit at either end of an 'archetypal pole', with many variations on these at points in between.

Depth psychology: A general term used to encompass approaches that focus on the importance of working with the unconscious. It includes psychoanalysis, Jungian analysis, object relations and more recent developments such as relational psychoanalysis.

Individuation: The task to realize our unique selfhood. This is a 'work in progress' which lasts a lifetime and involves facing aspects of ourselves we do not like (the 'shadow') and integrating these and other aspects.

Psyche: From Greek mythology, 'soul'. In psychology it refers to the mind's overarching 'container' of thought, emotion and behaviour – all that is conscious as well as unconscious. In Jungian terms, the psyche is also seen as having a life with a sense of purpose.

Shadow: For Jung (1968), 'the thing a person has no wish to be, but is': aspects of ourselves we deny, cannot see or try to hide from others. Sometimes this also refers to healthier aspects that have got lost in shadow and that we therefore cannot utilize.

Dig deeper

Ellenberger, H., *The Discovery of the Unconscious: The History and Evolution of Dynamic Psychiatry* (New York: Basic Books, 1970)

Jung, C. G. (1963), *Memories, Dreams, Reflections* (Glasgow: Fontana, 1995)

Jung, C. G. (1966), *The Practice of Psychotherapy*, CW16, 2nd ed. (London: Routledge, 1993)

Jung, C. G. (1968), *Aion: Researches into the Phenomenology of the Self*, CW9ii, 2nd ed. (London: Routledge, 1991)

Samuels, A., Shorter, B. and Plaut, F. (eds.), *A Critical Dictionary of Jungian Analysis* (London: Routledge, 1986)

Shamdasani, S., Introduction, in Jung, C. G., *The Red Book* (Zurich: Philemon Foundation, 2009)

Storr, A., (ed.), *Jung: Selected Writings* (London: Fontana, 1986)

Storr, A., *Freud: A Very Short Introduction* (Oxford: Oxford University Press, 1989)

Fact-check (answers at the back)

1 What is 'depth psychology'?
   a Psychology that explores deep issues in a range of disciplines
   b Jungian ways of exploring the depths of the unconscious
   c All established theoretical and therapeutic approaches stemming from psychoanalysis, including the Jungian approach
   d A way of understanding phobic responses to physical depths and heights

2 Why did Jung confront his own unconscious?
   a He was fascinated by his dreams
   b He thought this might provide him with a way of understanding himself, and the nature of the unconscious, better
   c Freud recommended he do so
   d He thought it might provide inspiration for his writing

3 Why did Jung use the term 'analysand' for his patients?
   a To help distinguish his approach from Freud's
   b To help reinforce how analytical his approach was
   c To help people analyse themselves
   d To reflect his critically analytical attitude to his patients

4 According to Jung, why are archetypes 'bipolar'?
   a They are like the magnetic influences of the north and south pole
   b In some cases they create a serious 'bipolar' mental health condition
   c They have two opposite poles with a continuum of possibilities in between
   d They help you see things from both sides

5 What does 'individuation' mean?
   a To be different from everyone else
   b To grow up via different developmental stages
   c To confront the unconscious
   d To integrate aspects of ourselves so we are more completely ourselves

6 What is 'active imagination'?
  a Letting your thoughts run wild
  b When others activate images for us, e.g. in films or on TV
  c Noticing images arising from our unconscious (e.g. via daydreaming) and actively engaging with them
  d Unhelpful fantasy

7 To what did Jung relate the scarab in his vision?
  a The end of an era
  b An Egyptian myth of rebirth
  c The coming world war
  d An archetype of beetles

8 Why did Jung write *The Red Book*?
  a He wanted to record his experiences of confronting his unconscious
  b Red was his favourite colour
  c He wanted a break from writing psychological theory
  d It helped him stay sane rather than get lost in his 'active imagination' work

9 What are the six archetypal figures inhabiting the inner world?
  a Persona, psyche, anima, animus, ego, self
  b Persona, shadow, individuation, ego, anima, animus
  c Persona, ego, shadow, psyche, anima, animus
  d Persona, ego, self, shadow, anima, animus

10 Where did Jung practise psychiatry while engaged in confronting his unconscious?
  a In various psychiatric hospitals
  b In his private practice
  c At the Burgholzi hospital, Zurich
  d Nowhere – he did not practise during this period

2

The dreamer awakes: Jung's early life

This chapter provides an overview of Jung's childhood and adolescence, with an emphasis on his inner development. It is important to know something about what influenced Jung as he grew up in Switzerland in the late nineteenth century, to help us understand what drove him into psychiatry and psychoanalysis in his adult life. It will also help us make sense of how Jung's ideas were able to grow and flourish in later years; to 'analyse the analyst', one might say.

A child of the unconscious?

> 'Who spoke to me then?... Who but the alien guest who came
> both from above and from below?... What happened then was a
> kind of burial in the earth, and many years were to pass before
> I came out again. Today I know that it happened in order to bring
> the greatest possible amount of light into the darkness ...
> My intellectual life had its unconscious beginnings at that time.'
>
> Jung (1963), *Memories, Dreams, Reflections*, p. 30

Chapter 1 conveyed a clear sense of how important Jung's inner
life was to him. The notion that the unconscious has a life of
its own, an idea germane to his thinking, sprang from a series
of powerful dreams and imaginary encounters in Jung's early
life. In the book about his life, *Memories, Dreams, Reflections*
(1963), Jung described some dreams from his childhood that
can seem astonishing to the 'average dreamer' because of their
rich symbolism and vivid imagery.

Spotlight: Who really wrote *Memories, Dreams, Reflections*?

It is fair to describe this book as more *biography* than
autobiography. Aniela Jaffé, a Swiss analyst, was asked to take
charge of the task as Jung approached the end of his life, and
she wrote much of the book, drawing on conversations with him.
Jung did, however, provide a good deal of direct material about
his childhood, which he felt impelled by his unconscious to record
before it was too late. The first three chapters are his, as is some
of the material on his journeys abroad, and the final chapter.
Otherwise, the book was put together by Jaffé, who had to re-edit
more than once due to worries about the portrayal of some of the
more controversial aspects of his life, before its publication.

Beginning with this vivid encounter with the unconscious at
an early age, this chapter explores some key early influences,
such as his 'two personalities', his wrestle with religion and the

influence of his father's beliefs, plus other important dreams he had. Reflections on Jung's development through childhood and adolescence will be brought to bear on the discussion, including one or two voices from writers who have raised questions about Jung's mental health...

Formative influences: family

Carl Gustav Jung was born on 26 July 1875 at Keswill, a village on the banks of Lake Constance in Switzerland. His father, Paul Achilles Jung, was a priest in the Swiss Protestant Church, and had studied Oriental languages and Theology. His mother, Emilie Preiswerk, adopted a conventional female role in this most conservative of nineteenth-century societies – although there was, unsurprisingly, more to her than this. It is important to bear in mind that, as Brome puts it (1978, p. 27): 'Switzerland in 1875 was a country where women wore skirts which almost swept the ground, the family was sacred..., religion penetrated all areas of life... and sex was regarded by some as an unfortunate prerequisite of reproduction.'

Spotlight: 1875

The year of Jung's birth also featured the establishment of the anti-slavery union in New York, the invention of snooker and first recorded hockey game; and Matthew Webb became the first person successfully to swim the English Channel to France.

Within the straitened social context of Switzerland, what could not be spoken about easily – deeper instincts as they related to sexual, aggressive and self-interested drives and wishes – became all the more powerful for not being expressed. This observation corresponds to Sigmund Freud's conclusions in Vienna at this time about the manifestations of 'hysteria' he treated in his women patients. Freud came to the view that the fainting, paralysed limbs and uncontrolled weeping involved were directly linked to the oppressive social climate which thoroughly censored female sexuality, although he also diagnosed a more direct link to the effects of repressed memories of sexual abuse (1896).

Within the inhibiting atmosphere described, the young Carl Jung became aware there was rather more to life than what could be consciously explained or understood. The power of his unconscious to generate dreams was one example of this that fascinaied him. Another was the occult. He came to share with his mother a curiosity about unexplained phenomena, which apparently occurred in their home (then in Kushnact, in the Zurich suburbs). According to Jung (1963), this included a sudden crack which split the dining room table across the middle, and a shattered bread knife inside a sideboard, which they were sure had been placed inside the kitchen drawer a few minutes earlier. Both incidents left them wondering whether their home was haunted.

From such apparent mysteries, Jung's interest in spiritualism grew, and would eventually lead him to attend weekly séances where his cousin, Helene Preiswerk, appeared to channel the spirit of a woman named Ivanes. In turn, this would lead Jung to focus on occult phenomena in his 1902 doctoral thesis ('On the Psychology and Pathology of So-called Occult Phenomena').

Formative influences: Jung's 'big' dream

In his thinking on dreams, Jung identified what he simply termed 'a big dream' (1964, p. 42). As implied, this refers to dreams we may have now and again which really make an impact on us, leaving us affected by the emotional and symbolic power of what we have experienced, and pondering what the meaning may be for us. They also have a *collective* meaning: the 'message' of the dream emanates from the collective unconscious, the reservoir of shared human images, instincts and experiences, beneath the personal unconscious where archetypal influences have their source. Jung's dream at the age of three, which he described in *Memories, Dreams, Reflections* (1963), falls into this category.

In this dream, the little boy sees a large hole in the ground of a meadow near the vicarage where he lives with his family. Carl goes down the stone stairway inside the hole. He makes his way through a heavy green curtain in the archway at the bottom, and finds himself in a long room with a 'wonderfully rich throne' on a raised platform at the far end. He then goes on to describe what he can see standing on the throne:

> 'Something was standing on it which I thought at first was a tree trunk twelve to fifteen feet high and about one and a half to two feet thick. It was a huge thing, reaching almost to the ceiling. But it was of a curious composition: it was made of skin and naked flesh, and on top there was something like a rounded head with no face and no hair. On the very top of the head was a single eye, gazing motionlessly upwards.'
>
> Jung, 1963, p. 27

Jung reports being afraid that this 'thing' might at any moment crawl, worm-like, towards him. But then, he hears his mother's voice from above ground shouting: 'Yes, just look at him. That is the man eater!', before he wakes up, terrified.

Jung himself came to see this dream as signalling a key theme of his life's work: to uncover the fuller picture around some crucial archetypal polarities – between light and shadow, God and flesh, masculine and feminine. Jung reported, much later in his life and after extensive studies, how 'a passage in a study of religious ritual burned into my eyes, concerning the motif of cannibalism that underlies the symbolism of the Mass' (Jung, 1963, p. 29). He then saw the parallel between the church symbolism of eating the bread (Christ's body) and drinking the wine (Christ's blood), and the signalling of the 'man eater' in the dream.

For Jung, this was the activation of the same archetypes of ritual, cannibalism and phallus, just represented in different forms. The phallus in the dream was in some respects a dark or *shadow* Jesus Christ (like the black-garbed Jesuits Carl reported seeing going about their solemn business); what Jung described as 'a subterranean God "not to be named"'(Jung, 1963, p. 29).

There is also a strong hint in the dream of what would be a long-term area of concern to Jung – the relationship between the archetypal feminine and masculine. Here his mother is heard describing a 'man eater', and in later works, notably *Symbols of Transformation*, Jung (1966) explored symbolism which suggested how the archetype of mother, or 'the Great Mother' becomes symbolized in religious and other myths, postulating a 'battle of deliverance' from the 'devouring mother'. This stands in archetypal counterpoint to the notion of 'God the father' of the Abrahamic religions (Judaism, Christianity, Islam), which place the heavenly Father as the ultimate power. Jung came to see this counterpoint as part of the struggle between the feminine and masculine in human history, and something that plays out in individual psyches.

How might we make sense of this kind of dream more generally? The older Jung saw it, in a way, as evidence of the influence of the collective unconscious on individual human beings. This line of thinking goes:

1 Some dream imagery, when it is as heavily symbolic as in this dream, has meanings that extend beyond (but still include) the individual's constructions of image and meaning.

2 This is the dream of a three-year-old: how could the psyche of such a young child generate this kind of dream and the symbols in it? Could this not suggest a deeper reservoir of archetypal imagery and influences that can apparently break through the membrane between collective and personal unconscious in such circumstances as this?

3 Jung takes this argument a step further: if this dream conveyed symbolic connections to much deeper and bigger process at work in the human psyche than a little child could have learned or heard about, then there must be some kind of 'superior intelligence' (Jung, 1963, p. 29) operating in the unconscious.

This was the dream that set the tone for Jung's relationship to the unconscious, which he saw as a living force within. For him, we have a responsibility to translate the often disguised messages dreams present to us into active ways of thinking, being and doing. The task is for our *ego* to take note of what our *self* may be saying to us through a dream, and for this to influence who and how we are. This way, we 'individuate' and become more fully ourselves through a fuller integration of conscious and unconscious elements.

Formative influences: childhood and adolescence

Jung portrayed the period when he was growing up as one when he often felt isolated and misunderstood by his peers, not to mention bored by some of the dry lessons he experienced at school. Although he clearly had friendships, there was an intensely introspective side to his personality that urged him to look inwards for meaning rather than finding it in contact with others.

This tendency showed itself in his dreams such as the one described above, but also in how he seemed to create ways of expressing his personality in symbolic ways. One way was via a manikin, a figure Carl carved from the end of his wooden ruler 'with frock coat, top hat and shiny boots' (Jung, 1963, p. 36), then sawed off and kept in his pencil case. The manikin acquired great significance for him because it was a secret – and he kept it hidden in the attic to reinforce this.

The importance of 'the secret' came to reflect a growing awareness in Jung that he seemed to have 'two personalities': personality number one was his outward-facing presentation or *persona* of who he was in the world, while personality number two related to the deeper, hidden version of who he was. Jung imagined this character as a wise, powerful older man from a previous era in history who represented the aspect of Jung that was open to dreams, deep rumination, connection with the natural world, and the spontaneous creativity which produced the manikin. This notion of there being more than one version of himself was a precursor to key elements of his model of the psyche.

Key idea: Do we all have a 'personality number two'?

Jung came to the view that we all have a *personality number two*: a 'deeper, timeless' version of ourselves within us, linked to the collective layer of the unconscious. However, Smith (1996) has criticized this idea as a big assumption for Jung to make, based only on his own experiences. This criticism is sometimes deployed more fully – i.e. are Jung's theories *too* reliant on his subjective insights?

Did Jung suffer from schizophrenia?

Donald Winnicott (1964), the highly influential British psychoanalyst and paediatrician, has suggested that Jung had 'childhood schizophrenia', as revealed by his immersion in vivid imagery from the unconscious, aged three (see above). He speculated that 'maternal failure' was at the root of the problem (Sedgwick, 2008) and that the dual personalities ('number 1 and number 2') Jung describes from childhood point towards this possibility, as well as how overwhelmed Jung could be by the contents of his unconscious.

Anthony Storr also concluded that Jung's so-called 'creative illness' (1907–13) after he split from Freud had the hallmarks of an episode of schizophrenia (Storr, 1973). Additionally, could Jung's professional interest in the presentation of schizophrenia – treating numerous patients suffering with what was then called 'dementia praecox' at the Burgholzi and his efforts to understand it in his writing (Jung, 1966) – represent an unconscious wish to 'cure' himself?

Spotlight: Dementia praecox

'Dementia praecox' was the generic term applied to all disorders of a psychotic nature that were degenerative and could be terminal. Jung seemed to concur with the director of the Burgholzi hospital, Dr Eugen Bleuler, that certain patients needed to be categorized differently from this. These were patients whose symptoms (e.g. delusions) would only develop so far before remaining static, or even fading. A few such patients, he maintained (Bleuler, 1911), could even get better and be discharged.

Considering the key criteria now used to diagnose schizophrenia (from the *Diagnostic and Statistical Manual of Mental Disorders V*), can we effectively conclude that Jung suffered in this way? The three key criteria (APA, 2013) are:

▶ bizarre delusions

▶ Schneiderian first-rank auditory hallucinations (e.g. two or more voices conversing)

▶ disorganized speech.

It is possible to argue that Jung did present with at least two of these in some form. He had vivid fantasies of characters, places and events that often had a 'grand' underlying quality (e.g. in *The Red Book* narrative, he describes having met Elijah and Salome). He seemed to 'hear' voices at times (e.g. in 1916 Jung reported the invasion of his house by a crowd of restless spirits who 'spoke' to him). While disorganized speech may not have featured as far as we know, delusional and hallucinatory aspects do suggest themselves.

While others have speculated that these could also be seen as a presentation of 'manic depressive' version of psychosis (Brome, 1978, p. 168) – what we would now term 'bipolar disorder' – the question is hard to answer definitively. While having such experiences, Jung was able to continue working in a high-level professional role and maintain satisfactory family relationships. He had grown up in a setting where religion, and the occult, were vividly present, culturally and psychologically, furnishing his strong imagination with a larger context in which to expand and explore. So the jury remains out on this one, although the suspicion that Jung was vulnerable to psychotic 'invasion' remains strong.

As Jung moved through puberty, he reported an experience which felt like a key transition for him. He was walking to school, at the age of 11, and, 'suddenly for a single moment I had the overwhelming impression of having just emerged from a dense cloud. I knew all at once: now I am myself! It was as if a wall of mist were at my back, and behind that wall there was not yet an "I". But at this moment... I happened to myself' (Jung, 1963, p. 49).

Jung reports having felt a strong sense of inner authority arising from this experience, one that also followed a period where he had fainted regularly and forgotten about his treasured manikin in the attic. Frankel (1998, p. 72) observes that, in adolescence 'the dialectical interplay between separateness and connectedness... expresses... (itself in)... moments of rich psychological experience.' It seems that Carl experienced such a moment here, signifying a transitional period between childhood and adolescence, which had culminated in this sudden breakthrough of self-awareness.

Spotlight: Jung's difficult moment at school

Jung reported how a teacher had not believed that a composition he had written was his, because it was 'too good'. Instead he was quizzed: 'Where did you copy it from? Confess the truth!' (Jung, 1963, p. 83). Jung was furious but this incident was salutary in helping Jung listen to, and trust in, himself rather than overreact to outer provocation.

JUNG, HIS FATHER AND HIS FATHER'S RELIGION

The transition described above also needs to be seen in the light of young Carl's reaction to the faith of his father. Here, it seems that (on the one hand) he wanted to be loyal to his father but, on the other hand, he was finding it increasingly difficult to stomach the tenets of a Christian view of the world which had changed little since the Middle Ages. It was as if the Enlightenment, and the scientific and technical progress that had followed it, had never happened. The Age of Enlightenment (Berlin, 1984) had consisted of a cultural movement of European intellectuals in the seventeenth and eighteenth centuries who emphasized the primacy of scientific knowledge, reason and the value of the individual over conventional religious beliefs and cultural practices. The religion of his priestly father did not seem to show any cognisance of these developments which had radically changed the way people across the continent viewed the world, and themselves.

Instead, the premise on which his father held to the established theological 'truths' revealed in the Bible, and which promised salvation to all who subscribed to them, was, according to one biographer of Jung: 'You have to believe, not think' (Bair, 2003, p. 35). That is not to say that father and son could not joust intellectually over the philosophical ideas Carl was beginning to immerse himself in. However, the demarcation between the traditional Christian theology of his father and the rigorous application of scientific and philosophical principles to religious ideas was, Jung realized, becoming a line in the sand between them.

A recurring daydream seemed to confront him with this problem. In it, Carl is walking past Basle cathedral, looking up at the magnificent building silhouetted against a deep blue sky and bright sunshine. He imagines God sitting on his throne up in the sky. God is in his heaven, and all seems right with the world. But then, although he keeps repeating to himself, 'Don't think of it, just don't think of it!' (Jung, 1963, p. 53), eventually he allows himself to experience the conclusion of the daydream: 'God sits on his golden throne, high above the world – and from under his throne an enormous turd falls upon the sparkling new roof, shatters it, and breaks the walls of the cathedral asunder' (Ibid, 1963, p. 56).

As the shock of seeing God shitting on the cathedral, built in praise of Him, passed, Carl's initial self-reproach for having dared imagine such a thing was replaced by relief at the acknowledgement God had been revealed as less than perfect. There was a sense, for Carl, of God wanting him to 'sin' by thinking such thoughts. This not only tested the lad's courage to break convention, but also provided a fuller picture of the relationship between the divine and the human.

This was a picture the older psychiatrist, analyst and writer would fill in further, principally through his theories on shadow, which will be explored in more detail in Chapter 6. A key part of what makes us human is our darker, messier aspects – the drives, desires, resentments and avarices that we all possess. Jung would suggest that the religious convention of trying to rid ourselves of these and 'be pure' for God (a convention which was particularly strong in the Protestantism of his father's church), was counter-productive. Like Freud's notion of repression, Jung's thinking on shadow held to this principle:

the more we push away shadow influences, the more likely they are to come back and undermine us (Samuels et al., 1986). You may have already gathered the relevance of this to the religious question. For Jung, God has a shadow, too. We will come back to this in Chapter 16.

Key idea

Jung's dualistic approach to scientific and psychological study, modelled in his doctoral study on occult phenomena, mentioned above, reflected a lifelong project to maintain balance between objectivity and subjectivity. This in turn reflected a keen awareness of tensions inherent in archetypal dualities: between arts and sciences, what is known and not known, and what can be measured and what cannot. This can be traced back to Carl's childhood when he began to wrestle with the stark contrast between the beliefs of his father and the scientific principles he was learning about at school, as well as the influence of the mysterious world revealed in his dreams.

Key terms

Collective unconscious: According to Jung, the layer of the unconscious beneath the individual's personal unconscious. In the collective unconscious, archetypally shared instincts, memories and symbols gathered from across human history across the world, can appear – or 'constellate' – in the psyche of the individual dreamer.

Creative illness: The term sometimes used to describe what Jung fell into after his break from Freud. This describes how Jung apparently 'used' his breakdown in a creative way, drawing important ideas and images from his forays into his unconscious.

Dementia praecox: The general term applied in the late nineteenth and early twentieth century for patients suffering from delusional and disordered states of mind that we would now term 'schizophrenia'.

Ego: The centre of our conscious mind, which mediates between this and the unconscious.

Persona: Jung's term for the 'mask' at the front of the ego. This mask will vary according to situation we are in, and we will use this consciously or unconsciously, to adapt to the context. Over-identifying with the persona can lead to 'a loss of self'.

Schizophrenia: The established current term to describe people who suffer from acute delusional psychoses and other distorted mental states where ego awareness of these states becomes unavailable.

Self: The underlying centre of each human psyche, which also encompasses the whole psyche. Guides the ego, if the latter is able to listen to it.

Dig deeper

American Psychiatric Association, *Diagnostic and Statistical Manual of Mental Disorders V* (Arlington, VA: APA, 2013)

Bair, D. *Jung: A Biography* (Boston: Little, Brown and Company, 2003)

Berlin, I. (ed.), *The Age of Enlightenment: The 18th-century Philosophers* (New York: Plume Books, 1984)

Bleuler, E., *Dementia Praecox: Or the Group of Schizophrenias* (New York: International Universities Press, 1911)

Brome, V., *Jung: Man and Myth* (London: Macmillan, 1978)

Frankel, R., *The Adolescent Psyche: Jungian and Winnicottian Perspectives* (Hove: Routledge, 1998)

Freud, S. (1896), 'The Aetiology of Hysteria' in Gay, P. (ed.), *The Freud Reader* (London: Vintage, 1995), pp. 96–111

Jung, C. G. (1902), 'On the Psychology of So-called Occult Phenomena' in Jung, C. G., *Psychology and the Occult* (London: Routledge, 1982), pp. 5–106

Jung, C. G. (1963), *Memories, Dreams, Reflections* (Glasgow: Fontana, 1995)

Jung, C. G., *Man and His Symbols* (New York: Dell,1964)

Jung, C. G., *Symbols of Transformation* (trans. 2nd ed. Hull, R. and Adler, G.) (London: Routledge, 1966)

Samuels, A., Shorter, B. and Plaut, F. (eds.), *A Critical Dictionary of Jungian Analysis* (London: Routledge, 1986)

Sedgwick, D., 'Winnicott's Dream: Some Reflections on D. W. Winnicott and C. G. Jung', *Journal of Analytical Psychology*, 53, 543–60 (2008)

Smith, R., *The Wounded Jung: Effects of Jung's Relationships on His Life and Work* (Evanston, ILL: Northwestern University Press, 1996), p. 25

Storr, A., *Jung (Modern Masters)* (London: Routledge, 1973)

Winnicott, D., 'Memories, Dreams, Reflections: By C. G. Jung', *International Journal of Psycho-Analysis*, 45, 450–55 (1964)

Fact-check (answers at the back)

1 What was the Swiss social milieu Jung was born into known for?
   a   Its neutrality
   b   Its conservatism
   c   Its architecture
   d   Its chocolate

2 What did Jung later see the dream he had, aged three, as representing?
   a   The problem of the Church
   b   King Phallus
   c   The problem of cannibalism
   d   His life's work in exploring crucial archetypal polarities

3 What is the 'Great Mother'?
   a   A giant mother
   b   An archetype of severe weather
   c   The collective archetype of the mother
   d   The symbol of the perfect mother

4 What were Jung's number one and number two personalities?
   a   His persona in the world and his secret inner self
   b   His favourite and second-favourite personalities in fairy tales
   c   Two imaginary figures inside him
   d   How he described the shift between feeling whole and feeling split

5 On what did the young Carl Jung disagree with his father?
   a   That God exists
   b   That God is purely good
   c   That God is the Father of Jesus Christ
   d   That God is omniscient

6 When Jung said 'I happened to myself', what did he mean?
   a   He saw a mirror image of himself
   b   He started talking to himself all the time
   c   He suddenly became aware he was a separate human being
   d   His second personality dialogued with his first

7 What, respectively, are the ego and the self?
   a The underlying centre of the psyche and the centre of the conscious mind
   b The persona and the 'deep ego'
   c The personal unconscious and the collective unconscious
   d The centre of the conscious mind and the underlying centre of the psyche

8 Why did Jung agree with Bleuler's use of the term 'schizophrenia'?
   a He thought 'dementia praecox' an outdated phrase
   b He agreed that some patients could experience limited or full remission
   c He fell out with Freud who preferred the old term
   d He hoped this would help him gain Bleuler's approval

9 What was Jung's interest in the occult stimulated by, at least in part?
   a Some unexplained experiences at home and his cousin's spiritualism
   b A wish to prove something contrary to his father's religious beliefs
   c A ghost in the attic
   d A teacher who was enthusiastic about the occult

10 Why do some people think Jung may have suffered from schizophrenia?
   a Because he talked to himself
   b Because he had two personalities and became overwhelmed by his unconscious
   c Because he was preoccupied with his schizophrenic patients
   d Because he had hallucinations and thought these were absolutely real

3

Jung's early career and key influences

How was Carl Jung drawn towards psychiatry? How did his innovative word-association experiments help him formulate his ideas on complexes and the unconscious (which would later draw Freud's interest towards his work)? These questions will help us explore key aspects of Jung's approach to understanding the workings of the unconscious and the development of his analytical approach in therapy. This practical side of his explorations was complemented by an extensive reading of philosophy, which had begun as he became more dissatisfied with what he felt were the outdated Christian strictures of his father. We will consider how key philosophers such as Kant, Schopenhauer and Nietzsche influenced his thinking.

Jung's turn towards psychiatry

We have already observed how Jung noticed, from quite early on in his life, the tension between two different kinds of knowledge. On the one hand, there was what could be established through the scientific study of concrete information via empirical research; and, on the other, there were personal encounters with and subjective reflections on lived experience that could not be so easily measured or explained. Some philosophers, such as Kant, spoke to this distinction, and Jung would draw on their ideas to help develop a philosophical framework for his thinking.

More pressing for Jung, while he was a medical student at the University of Basle (1895–1900), was the question of how to reconcile these competing influences and find a successful career at the same time. As he came nearer to completing his studies, he had to make a choice, and for a time it appeared that the best option was to remain firmly encamped in orthodox medicine. He had the opportunity to accompany Friedrich Von Muller, the director of the medical clinic, to Munich. Had he taken up this option, he would almost certainly have devoted himself to the field of internal medicine (i.e. the workings and surgical treatment of the body).

Spotlight: The world in 1895–1900

While Jung studied in Basle, events in the wider world included the Boer Wars in South Africa, the opening of the first underground railway in the US, the publication of *Studies in Hysteria* by Sigmund Freud and Josef Breuer, and the invention of the paperclip.

Instead, he had recently come across a book by Richard von Krafft-Ebing (1880), *Text-Book of Insanity, Based on Clinical Observations*. In this book, Krafft-Ebing posed the question of whether it is truly possible for psychiatry to be an objective science, considering the inescapable element of subjectivity involved in trying to assess patient symptoms and personality. This question struck a chord with Jung, as he struggled to reconcile the tensions between empirical science and phenomenological experience.

It also reflected his efforts to identify powerful influences in his own psyche, and those affecting the behaviour of others. These influences often seemed to have a life of their own. This question about objectivity and subjectivity remained a live one for Jung throughout his career. As Shamdasani (2003, p. 45) notes: 'When Jung came to designate his work as psychology, it was this question that he repeatedly posed...' This helps to explain Jung's career choice as a psychiatrist and why Jung found himself looking beyond the *intellectual* or *cognitive* to understand what guided the behaviour of patients in the Burgholzi. When he began working there in 1900, he followed the trend of the time to rely on hypnotism to try to 'cure' symptoms of mental ill health, for example low mood or physical symptoms of this, such as recurring headaches.

This approach paled for Jung after a while. Hypnotism can be used to diminish or remove symptoms via, for example, auto-suggestion (where the patient under hypnosis is given a prompt to forget the symptom when they come out of the hypnotized state). However, it does not in itself explain the meaning of a symptom – why it was there in the first place. Like Freud, Jung thought it crucial to understand what might be the causes of, or influences on, a disturbance in the psychological health of an individual, in order to get to the root of the problem.

Key idea: Neuroses and complexes

Freud's term for a psychological disturbance, which may manifest itself through physical or other symptoms, was 'neurosis' (Freud, 1920). Jung would later pick up this term and expand its meaning beyond Freud's identification of it as indicative of a deep unconscious problem, which the patient needed to identify and recognize before the symptom disappeared ('the talking cure'). Jung went further and came to describe neurosis as: 'the avoidance of legitimate suffering' (Jung, 1969). This perspective on neurosis reflected Jung's ideas about the individuation process; in his view, psychological disturbance can reflect our psyche trying to point out something in ourselves that we are avoiding or refusing to address, such as relying too much on others to solve our problems, or addictive behaviours.

Jung argues that neuroses can be effectively tackled and dissolved if we face and take ownership of them, bearing the pain of what the underlying difficulty is rather than avoiding it. This necessitates some suffering as the problem is finally acknowledged, with the discomfort, work and required adjustments to one's way of life involved.

Word association and Jung's 'complex' theory

As we have seen, Jung was influenced by Bleuler's innovative approach to what we would now term schizophrenia (*Dementia praecox*). Bleuler thought he had discovered an important aspect of what made schizophrenia treatable. He noted how those suffering from schizophrenia lacked insight into what was happening to them, and instead concretize delusional states they believe are real – for example, seeming to completely identify with a belief they are Jesus Christ. This is a **psychotic** tendency as distinct from a **neurotic** one, and it describes a state of mind over which the ego has little or no influence. Unconscious contents (as manifested, for example, by delusions, florid language and ideas or hallucinatory voices) flood the mind, pouring over the lowered perimeter of ego–consciousness, like water crashing through a dam wall and flooding the valley below.

Bleuler speculated that, if the association between an ego state and a delusional belief or thought could be loosened, there might be some room for manoeuvre in helping the affected individual gain insight. They could be helped in this sense to distinguish between what was 'me' and what was 'not me'. On the basis of this idea, Bleuler asked Jung to experiment with word-association tests to see whether these could be used to identify patterns of 'over-association' that might feed psychotic influences in the psyche.

Word-association tests were not new: Francis Galton (1822–1911) came up with the original model in psychology and others refined this, although the fundamental procedure remained the same. The experimenter reads out a series of words, and the subject of the experiment provides a word in response to each word given. These are all recorded in sequence. Then the experimenter looks at any patterns arising, related, for example, to similarities, opposites, or sequences in time and space. This approach was used to build up a picture of how mental contents are linked, as part of attempts to understand the workings of the brain, rather than as a tool for trying to penetrate into unconscious influences on the subject of the experiment.

THE POWER OF ASSOCIATION

In getting to grips with the psychology of word association, it can help to think about how advertisements work. Think of how catchphrases and jingles for supermarkets, fizzy drinks and cars stay in your head, uninvited. The idea is to get us to automatically see the product in our mind's eye when we hear the jingle or see the words on the screen. In the same way, unconscious links to emotion and memory can be activated by the presentation of a word or a list of words.

Spotlight: Word-association test

Here is a simplified version of a word-association test for you to try. Don't look at the words before you begin – place a piece of paper over them now!

Here is how to do the test:

1 Pull the piece of paper down until you can see the first word. **What is the first association that springs to mind when you see it?** (Do not think about it, just allow an association, image or word, to come to mind.)
2 Write on the left side of the paper the first word from the list, and then a word that represents what you associated with it, next to it on the right.
3 Do the same thing with each of the other nine words remaining.

SEA

HEART

WINDOW

PARENT

WAIT

ANGER

DRIVE

BIRD

UNDER

CHILD

Now spend a bit of time with each of the associative words you have come up with, based on the following questions:

1 What are your reactions to each pair of words as you look at them now?
2 Are the associations you made expected, or were any a surprise?
3 Is there any kind of connection on the list between individual words you came up with?
4 Is there any kind of pattern or connection between all, or most, of the words you came up with?*
5 What reflections are you left with (if at all) about any possible meanings behind the words spontaneously recorded?
6 What do you make of the value of such a test?

Note: This test is just a 'taster', not a formal word-association test. (For an overview of how these tests have evolved alongside new models of testing, see Flanagan and Harris, *Contemporary Intellectual Assessment: Theories, Tests, and Issues* (New York: Guilford Press, 2012)

(*If you wish, try this: Draw a circle on a piece of paper and write the words you came up with (in no particular order) around the perimeter. Then try making links between the words, e.g. by drawing lines between them with a word that expresses the link on that line. You may end up with a portrayal of some useful themes in the circle.)

When Jung took up Bleuler's directive, he soon realized the potential of this approach, recognizing that it was not just the words patients responded with during the test that was important. After repeated use of the test (often made up of 100 words in order to enable fuller patterns to emerge), Jung came to the view that it could make useful and legitimate hypotheses about important unspoken factors at work underneath the surface. One of the most valuable indicators of the influence of these factors was the length of time taken by the individual to come up with an association to a given word. The longer they took, the more likely was the presence of a disturbance in feeling activated by that word. Jung also listed other types of factor, such as slips in the reproduction of words, reactions to the directions given by the experimenter, and exaggerated facial and bodily responses.

Jung (1976, para. 101) asserted that 'All these reactions are beyond the control of the will.' Instead, he proposed that such responses indicated a **complex** at work, exerting powerful unconscious influence on the psyche of the person. This became a key tenet of Jungian theory and analytic practice: revealing the emotionally charged complex (or complexes) at work in a person's psyche with their combination of individual, environmental and archetypal influences – as a baseline for identifying the analytic approach to be taken. Jung's work with word-association tests enabled him to properly uncover *complexes*, developing the ideas of Janet (1859–1947) and Ziehen (1862–1950), who had first proposed this important idea.

Uncovering a complex

A 65-year-old woman at the Burgholzi reported hearing voices and had vivid delusions (e.g. of having inherited untold wealth). Jung conducted experiments with her to check her responses to the words proffered (Brome, 1978). Alongside relatively quick responses (e.g. 3.4 seconds for 'butter' in response to 'bread'), came some that took longer (e.g. 11.4 seconds for 'thread' in response to 'needle' and 14.8 for 'yes, irreplaceable' to 'head') and one (12.4 seconds) for 'Socrates', in response to 'pupil'. This latter response appeared to Jung to be incongruous, thus indicating a complex (not to mention the length of time it took her to respond).

As Jung continued with these tests, he also encouraged the patient to free-associate. This was a method borrowed from Freud (1895) which encourages the patient to allow whatever thoughts, feelings or images they have to express themselves. Between these two approaches, he uncovered what he thought were a number of complexes that seemed to indicate wish fulfilments generated to compensate for this woman's tough working life as a dressmaker. Her frustrated dreams and drives he clustered under three headings:

1 'Dreams of Happiness'
2 'Complaints of suffering injustices'
3 'Sexual complexes' (Ellenberger, 1970)

Jung found that identifying these complexes did not necessarily enable the individual to break free of them. In this case, the patient, who suffered from severe *Dementia praecox*, remained, as Ellenberger notes; 'imprisoned in her delusions' (op. cit., p. 693). However, the approach used with this patient and others at the Burgholzi helped lay the foundation for Jung's analytic method for exploring the human psyche.

Searching for inspiration: Jung's philosophical framework

As Jung moved towards defining the direction his career would go, immersing himself in scientific and medical thinking, he was also exploring philosophical thinking. As described in the previous chapter, his relationship with his father was charged with profound differences about religion and the philosophical basis for knowledge and belief. From his mid-teens, and partly to keep away from the continual arguments which seemed to be a feature of his parents' relationship, Jung spent significant time in his father's study, reading books. These were predominantly theological in their focus, but also included general philosophical thinking. This helped to open Jung's perspective on life, feeding his hungry mind in a way the creeds beloved of his father could not.

His mother did provide him with some openings into important areas that he would come to develop within his later theorizing about the psyche. As well as her interest in spiritualism, mentioned above, she pointed him towards the philosopher Johann Wolfgang von Goethe (1749–1832).

THE INFLUENCE OF GOETHE

Probably the most famous of Goethe's literary works, *Faust*, portrays the struggle between good and evil. Mephistopheles makes a bet with God that he can tempt Faust away from doing good. Developments then ensue that allow Goethe to play with various philosophical and religious ideas, including the idea that the ultimate 'good' also has a flipside that is dark and malignant. This idea and others seem to have influenced Jung (Bishop, 2014), who explored the idea of God having a shadow, and humanity having a key role in helping to tackle this, in his *Answer to Job* (see Chapter 17).

THE INFLUENCE OF PLATO

Jung was also influenced by Platonic thinking. Plato (427 BCE–347 BCE) established a **theory of forms**, which proposed that the imperfections of reality and its constantly changing nature stemmed from the fact that all objects are transient and imperfect versions of ideal forms (Howard, 2000). He likewise proposed that the lived principles we wrestle to attain and sustain, such as truth and love, also emanate from ideal forms. These forms are unknowable and cannot be experienced or 'seen' in their pure form, but they are pivotal in defining the reality we experience.

Some of these principles can be found in the nineteenth-century flowering of Romanticism (Ferber, 2010), which also influenced Jung. Likewise, Jung proposed that archetypes were a ubiquitous and fundamental feature of human experience and of nature. As with 'forms', so with archetypes: 'one can only infer their existence from the manifestation of archetypal images' (Casement, 2001, p. 40). Jung himself acknowledged the influence of Plato's forms on his concept of archetypes (Jung, 1959), so it is clear that, in this respect, Plato's thinking had an important influence on Jung's theoretical framework.

THE INFLUENCE OF SCHOPENHAUER

One philosopher that Jung discovered via his father's books was Arthur Schopenhauer (1788–1860). Schopenhauer's *weltanschauung* ('world view') was rather bleak but it offered an insight into the powerful forces at work beneath the surface of human life. In this respect, he seemed to Jung to be naming something familiar, something we might broadly describe today as **unconscious process**. Schopenhauer proposed, in his most famous book *The World as Will and Idea* (1883), that there is at work in each of us a **will** that supersedes all our attempts to define our own path through life. The most obvious way this operates is through the will to procreate, in order for the human race to survive and evolve. This can manifest itself irrespective of our rational, individual plans, and change the course of a life in an instant.

As Schopenhauer put it, 'we can often give no account of the origins of our deepest thoughts' (1883, p. 328). In this regard, the tone of Schopenhauer's more pessimistic perspective on what drives the human psyche comes through more in the writings of Freud than Jung. Schopenhauer proposed that there is a deeper layer of mind we are not conscious of (using the metaphor of the surface of the earth to illustrate this, suggesting we are not conscious of what lies beneath it). This way of looking at things strongly influenced Jung in establishing his theories, based on a principle that what leads us to operate consciously has a deep, unconscious, origin, although Jung's model of the unconscious was more nuanced by creativity and spirituality.

THE INFLUENCE OF KANT

Another key philosophical influence was Immanuel Kant (1724–1824). One of his most important ideas was to identify two types of knowledge: the **phenomenal**, which is what we experience and then understand through cognitive processes; and the **noumenal**, which describes what we cannot grasp in this way, 'the thing in itself'. Jung's notion of the archetypes as ephemeral essences, which nevertheless provide the template in the unconscious for human behaviours and experiences, reflects this idea of there being 'essences' which we cannot know through ordinary experience, but which profoundly influence it.

In turn, this general formula is a modern reflector of an ancient way of looking at reality, initiated by Plato. For Jung, Kant's emphasis on *a priori* knowledge supported his view that we do not enter the world, nor engage with it, as a *tabula rasa* (or 'empty slate'). Rather, there are things we innately 'know' prior to experiencing them, such as the law of causality, which we seem to instinctively know as part of our evolved survival mechanisms (e.g. 'If I don't eat, I will be hungry'), as well as our need to understand what causes, or underlies, what we experience. The direct influence of this idea of Kant's can be seen in Jung's words here:

> 'The need to satisfy the law of causality accompanies us everywhere like a faithful shepherd..., does it not step into our path... (and)... challenge us to halt on the path and, overcome by doubt, to say 'What was I yesterday, what am I today, what will I be tomorrow?... What is the purpose of the starry sky with its countless worlds which whirl and swirl on their paths for millions of years?'
>
> Jung, 1898, para. 187

THE INFLUENCE OF NIETZSCHE

The works and ideas of Friedrich Nietzsche (1844–1900) had a powerful effect on Jung. Nietzsche emphasized the centrality of the individual who wrestles with themselves, in a constant state of inner conflict and open to the vagaries of life and fate, without the formerly assumed presence of God. His term for the individual who takes on the task of overcoming the challenges of all aspects of their nature, and goes against the rationalist and materialist tendencies of the age, is *Ubermensch* (which can be translated into English as either 'Overman' or 'Superman'). There is a clear imprint of Jung's notion of individuation here and Jung took inspiration from Nietzsche in its formulation.

Jung thought Nietzsche must have been in the grip of an archetype – Dionysus, the Greek god of wine (representative of instincts, pleasure and the human impulse to satisfy its urges). Nietzsche juxtaposed Dionysus with Apollo – often associated with clear thinking and civilized values – in his writing, seeing these influences pulling against one another as part of the flux of human experience. For him, nothing was fixed. Instead: 'According to Nietzsche, we must not seek knowledge of life that is *a priori*, rather, we must seek experience of life and our own interpretation of the world' (Huskinson, 2004, p. 23).

This stance resonated with Jung as he approached the challenges presented by the psyches of his patients, not to mention the mysteries of his own. In a sense, this emphasis from Nietzsche on the primacy of individual experience over shared social, scientific and linguistic conventions, complemented the other key influences described. Plato's *forms*, Schopenhauer's unconscious *will*, and Kant's separation of the *noumenal* and *phenomenal* helped Jung, along with the power of Nietzsche's ideas, to establish the philosophical and theoretical foundations of his approach.

Although there were other thinkers who helped shape Jung's view of the human psyche, plus wider cultural, intellectual and spiritual ideas, the impact of the philosophers described in this chapter on his approach should not be underestimated.

Spotlight: Is Jung the original 'New Age' thinker?

Jung and his ideas have often been associated with so-called 'New Age' thinking. This term is catch-all for a whole range of alternative spiritual, psychological and social/political ideas that have been around since the 1960s. Some of Jung's ideas on dreams, the imagination, archetypes and spirituality crop up in the writings and activities associated with 'the New Age', e.g. his view that we are entering 'the age of Aquarius' (see Chapter 17 where this question is scrutinized in more detail).

Key terms

Complex: A coming together or 'constellation' of powerful influences in the unconscious of the individual, which forms an autonomous psychic entity. This is made up of formative personal influences, current events which bring these back into play, and personality features; all given a powerful archetypal charge. A classic example would be a mother or father complex. A complex has enormous power in the psyche, and its dissolution is a key task of analysis.

Neurosis: Freud used this term to describe the underlying problem that lay behind a patient's presenting symptom (e.g. recurring headaches, high anxiety). This had a psychosexual root and needed to be identified and recognized by the patient, before the symptom would disappear ('the talking cure'). For Jung, neurosis had a broader aetiology ('cause'). Avoidance of legitimate suffering – needed to face and overcome underlying psychological or spiritual problems – perpetuates the neurosis.

Noumenal: An unknowable essence we experience but cannot grasp cognitively.

Phenomenal: What we experience and then understand through cognitive processes (Kant's ideas, which influenced Jung).

Platonism: Based on Plato's emphasis on reality being an imperfect version of a perfected set of 'forms'; influenced Jung's ideas on archetypes.

Superman (or *Ubermensch*): Nietzsche's term for the stance needed by someone who is trying to confront and overcome their own nature/weaknesses. Influenced Jung's ideas on individuation.

Dig deeper

Bishop, P., *Carl Jung* (London: Reaktion, 2014)

Brome, V., *Jung: Man and Myth* (London: Macmillan, 1978)

Casement, A., *Carl Gustav Jung* (London: Sage, 2001)

Ellenberger, H., *The Discovery of the Unconscious: The History and Evolution of Dynamic Psychiatry* (London: Basic Books, 1970)

Ferber, M., *Romanticism: A Very Short Introduction* (Oxford: Oxford University Press, 2010)

Flanagan, D. P. and Harris, P. L., *Contemporary Intellectual Assessment: Theories, Tests, and Issues* (New York: Guilford Press, 2012)

Freud, S. (1895) and Breuer, J., *Studies in Hysteria* (London: Penguin, 2004)

Freud, S., *A General Introduction to Psychoanalysis, Part Three: General Theory of the Neuroses* (London: Penguin, 1920)

Howard, A., *Philosophy for Counselling and Psychotherapy: From Pythagorus to Postmodernism* (London: Macmillan, 2000)

Huskinson, L., *Nietzsche and Jung: The Whole Self in the Union of Opposites* (Hove: Brunner-Routledge, 2004)

Jung, C. G. (1898), 'Thoughts on the nature and value of speculative inquiry' in Jung, C. G., *The Zofinga Lectures* (Princeton, NJ: Routledge and Kegan Paul, 1983)

Jung, C. G., *Psychology and Religion: West and East,* CW11, 2nd ed. (Princeton: Princeton University Press, 1969)

Jung, C. G., *The Archetypes and the Collective Unconscious*, CW9i (London: Routledge and Kegan Paul, 1959)

Jung, C.G., *The Tavistock Lectures*, Lecture 2, CW18 (London: Routledge, 1976)

Schopenhauer, A., *The World as Will and Idea* (London: Routledge, 1883)

Shamdasani, S., *Jung and the Making of Modern Psychology: The Dream of a Science* (Cambridge: Cambridge University Press, 2003)

Fact-check (answers at the back)

1 Why was Jung influenced by reading Krafft-Ebing's *Text-Book of Insanity, Based on Clinical Observations*?

  a The book provided a guide to different psychiatric diagnoses

  b The author described exciting stories of his work as a psychiatrist

  c The author acknowledged how subjective psychiatric diagnosis could be

  d The book linked psychiatry to Kantian philosophy

2 What important principle about schizophrenia did Bleuler identify?

  a Delusions of grandeur can be diminished through hypnosis

  b A person suffering from schizophrenia cannot word associate

  c If the delusional state is exaggerated by suggesting relevant words, the person with schizophrenia will gain insight and can get better

  d If the identification with the delusional state can be loosened, the person with schizophrenia will gain insight and can get better

3 What can word association form the basis for identifying?

  a Complexes

  b Ego states

  c Archetypes

  d Shadow

4 What makes association to a word more significant?

  a Speaking it very slowly

  b Making it immediately

  c Taking an unusually long time to produce

  d Speaking it in a low voice

5 Whose work did Jung's mother point him towards?

  a Nietzsche's

  b Goethe's

  c Kant's

  d Socrates'

6 How does Schopenhauer's unconscious 'will' most clearly operate?
   a Through falling asleep
   b Through the drive to procreate
   c Through the drive to develop self-awareness
   d Through automatic writing

7 What template did Jung derive from Plato?
   a Individuation
   b Shadow projection
   c Ego and self
   d Archetypes

8 What does Kant's phenomenal and noumenal distinction refer most closely to?
   a The familiar and the unfamiliar
   b What we can understand and what we cannot
   c The personal and the collective unconscious
   d The old and the new

9 What did Kant's critique of the *tabula rasa* idea influence Jung to assert?
   a We need to clear our minds to do 'active imagination'
   b We are born as a 'clean slate' wholly shaped by the environment
   c We are not born as a 'clean slate' but bring our personality into life with us
   d We need to make sure the table is clean when writing clinical notes

10 How did Nietzsche's *Ubermensch* inform Jung's 'individuation'?
   a He suggested we should all try to be like 'Superman'
   b He argued that our task is to fully embrace life as well as who we are
   c He proposed that we need to get over the fact that we cannot control anything
   d He argued that we should follow all our drives and desires all the time

Freud and Jung: a meeting of minds?

Jung first met Freud, the founder of psychoanalysis, in February 1907, after a period of correspondence between them, stimulated initially by Freud's appreciation of Jung's short book *Diagnostic Association Studies* (1906). Freud was pleased that Jung – on the basis of his word-association work – had seemingly come to similar conclusions as him about the roots of neuroses and the nature of repression.

This chapter describes the key features of their work together and considers Jung's debt to Freud's ideas, as well as the ways in which Jung took analytical psychology off in directions which were very different from Freud's model. The discussion will also trace the build-up to the rupture between them.

Common insights and ideas

Jung had, after an initially cool response to Freud's seminal *The Interpretation of Dreams* (1900), increasingly come to see the importance of the insights Freud came up with in this book. In particular, Freud's notions about how unconscious influences operate in the human psyche had been informing Jung's work at the Burgholzi for at least three years before they met.

Freud was also pleased that Jung, in his 1906 paper: *Freud's Theory of Hysteria: A Reply to Aschaffenburg*, had explicitly supported Freud's ideas in the face of attacks in the academic world, despite the professional risks involved. Tellingly, however, the developing correspondence which followed Freud's initial letter commending Jung on his book included an acknowledgement from Freud of Jung's differing view, that the roots of hysteria were not exclusively sexual. Freud expressed the hope that Jung's views would move more fully alongside his, and said there was a risk that people would use this difference between them to undermine the psychoanalytic project in the future (Donn, 1988).

Spotlight: Freud and Jung's first meeting

When they met in Vienna for the first time, Freud and Jung talked non-stop for 13 hours. There was clearly much to talk about... but this outpouring of thoughts and views may also reflect how isolated and misunderstood both men felt about their attempts to understand the workings of the unconscious. Each now seemed to have found a kindred spirit, and the two pioneers made the most of the time, though Freud had to politely but firmly intervene after his younger colleague talked almost exclusively for the first three hours. Freud 'interrupted him with the suggestion that they conduct their discussion more systematically... and proceeded to group the contents of the harangue under several precise headings...' (Jones, 1955, p. 36). As Jones also reports, this systematic ordering of the areas Jung had been describing relentlessly to Freud greatly impressed Jung, as did all else about Freud.

There is a clear sense in the accounts of their initial meeting and friendship of Jung idealizing Freud, who was 21 years older than him. One might speculate that this was Jung's father complex at work: here was a man a generation older than him, who had a razor-sharp brain and was at the cutting edge of contemporary thinking about the nature of human consciousness and the search for curative methods.

Inevitably, it would have been difficult for Jung not to compare this impressive figure with his own father, and with his exasperation with his father's identification with traditional religion, as the source of the 'truth' about the human condition. Kerr (1994) has even suggested that this first meeting with Freud fulfilled Jung's search for a replacement 'religion'; the connection between Freud's Jewishness and the powerful new ideas to be found in psychoanalysis provided this.

Likewise, Freud was struck by how intelligent and insightful the younger man was, and would come to the view that it was Jung who was best placed to take up the mantle of chief advocate of psychoanalytic ideas and practices when he (Freud) would eventually step aside. Jung acceded to Freud's offer, in 1910, to become president of the International Psychoanalytic Association and edit the first psychoanalytic journal. However, while an undoubtedly strong bond existed between the two men, the seeds for their eventually acrimonious split were perhaps sown in the shadow dynamics (to use a relevant Jungian term) of their initial coming together, and the differing expectations each of them had.

The honeymoon period of the first few years of their friendship and professional collaboration meant that the cracks did not show significantly (other than in the distinction around the exclusivity of psychosexual causation, noted above). However, what they each wanted from the other did not match sufficiently for them to remain comfortable, in the longer term, with the other's personality and views. Storr (1994) expresses it in terms of what we could describe as 'father–son' and 'son–father' transferences. Jung wanted a version of father he had never had, and Freud the idealized son he was unconsciously looking for:

> *'the kind of son Freud wanted was one who would be willing to defer unconditionally to his authority, and to perpetuate, without modification, the doctrines and principles of his rule... Jung needed a father figure through whose influence he could overcome his adolescent misgivings and discover his own masculine authority.'*
>
> Storr, 1994, pp. 21–2

This *shadow* behind the initially convivial and enthusiastic partnership of Freud and Jung gradually worked its divisive power over the situation, as each of them became more disappointed and frustrated with the other. The differences in opinion over key tenets of psychoanalytic theory, unconsciously charged with the unspoken and unfulfilled needs the one had of the other, became too great to sustain within a workable professional relationship and personal friendship. So what were those key differences?

Sticking points between Freud and Jung

The differences between the ideas and theories of Freud and Jung can be divided into four main categories: the influences of libido, of the collective versus the personal, of science versus religion, and the nature and purpose of dreams.

THE NATURE OF LIBIDO: DETERMINISTIC VS PROSPECTIVE

As already indicated, the place of sexuality in influencing the human psyche, and the behaviours and relational patterns arising from this, had been a source of differing views between the two men, as early as 1906. Jung consistently found it hard to stomach Freud's notion that *libido* – the energy which flows around the human organism and which generates sexualized (and aggressive) drives and behaviours, was as thoroughly dominated by the sexual imperative. For Freud, this famously converted into his developmental schema whereby, for him, all human infants pass through 'psychosexual stages' (Freud, 1962) – oral, anal, phallic, latent and genital. All adult neuroses could be traced back to where something faulty had crept in during one or more of these. Freud often believed he was encountering individuals 'stuck' unconsciously at one of these stages in his consulting room.

As mentioned in Chapter 3, Jung – like Freud – was influenced by Schopenhauer's (1966) ideas on the presence of the unconscious, and the primacy of the procreative drive in the human species; a biological impetus that overruled individual human intentions. However, he felt there was more to libido than this. Jung noticed from his work with patients, as well as from his own personal experiences, how powerful energy from within the human psyche could be channelled into activity, and areas for gratification that may not have a predominantly sexualized root. This includes the development and sustaining of relationships, creative and artistic endeavours, and more contemplative activities which some might term 'spiritual' (or possibly 'religious').

While Freudians might argue these are all, at root, influenced by sexual impulses – either directly gratified (intimate relationships), sublimated (through artistic expression of otherwise repressed drives), or denied (spirituality as an avoidance of full expression of one's sexuality) – Jungian perspective sees these having a key place in the human psyche in their own right. This is not to leave sexuality out of these influences; rather, Jung tended to see all archetypal, instinctual and intuitive influences such as these as a reflection of where the human psyche is able to marshal together all needed inner resources, including the psychosexual, in order to enable an individuation 'task' to be addressed, and maybe fulfilled.

Jung linked this idea to his thoughts on individuation and the journey through life. He felt that differing kinds of libido were suited to different life stages. The more playful, formatively creative and imaginal libido suits childhood, while sexual and relational (possibly also 'vocational'-oriented) libido suits adolescence and early adulthood. Creative libido also has its place in later adulthood, especially for those who have not expressed some aspects of themselves while being busy making their mark on the world.

Likewise, more spiritually oriented libido usually comes to the fore in mid to later life. This can be expressed in religious form, or in less formal expressions of meaning making (including humanistic and existential reflections not based on religious or spiritual beliefs). Jung saw these influences, noticed and incorporated as fully as can be, as part of the individuation process, where unconscious energies are directed into helping us become 'more fully who we are'.

This developing perspective of Jung's, which applied a wider lens on what drives and influences the human being, contributed to his gradual distancing from Freud's position. The latter was convinced of the veracity of a wholly deterministic stance: all we are in the 'here and now' being determined by what happened *back then*, when profoundly powerful, biologically led impulses laid down the road we are now on. In contrast, for Jung, the route we take through life is not just determined by the 'road building' at the beginning. For him, there is a forward-looking, *prospective*, aspect to our being and becoming. Where we are heading is therefore strongly influenced by how we embrace present and future possibilities, as well as the past.

Key idea: The unconscious and the libido

Jung prioritized the need to listen to the unconscious, working with it to draw on different types of libido to bring into life aspects of ourselves that have not found proper expression as yet, then integrate these into the totality of who we are. A perspective on unconscious libido arose for Jung, perhaps as much from his encounters with his own unconscious as from his clinical practice and theorizing.

COLLECTIVE VS PERSONAL INFLUENCES

However, in the period leading up to his break with Freud, Jung had not yet immersed himself in these encounters, in the way he would do from 1913 onwards, when he had his 'creative illness'. Rather, the underlying tension between the two men's standpoints would show up more in theoretical debate. For Jung, his work on what would become *Symbols of Transformation*

(Jung, 1967) was moving him towards exploring archetypal psychological influences on the individual psyche.

Freud had a keen interest in anthropology and other cultures, as testified by his impressive collection of artefacts from a swathe of old and exotic cultures from around the world (on display at the Freud Museum in London). However, this was more oriented towards illustrating the ways in which sublimation of psychosexual impulses and drives showed itself through cultural expression. Here, civilization's channelling of otherwise uncontainable *id* drives could be expressed, often with great artistic skill.

Jung, meanwhile, became more and more convinced of the underlying power of collective influences on individual psychological development. Listening to the dreams of his patients, for example, he noticed where archetypal images came in, even where there did not seem to be a relevant link to the current or past experience of the dreamer. Jung also reckoned he had *evidence* of the autonomous activity of the collective unconscious, as demonstrated (he thought) by a case of a man with schizophrenia who seemed to experience features of an old Mithraic myth in his delusions, despite having no knowledge of this (see Chapter 5).

Spotlight: Sabina Spielrein and Jung

The influence of Spielrein (1885–1942) – whose alleged affair with Jung was portrayed in the film *A Dangerous Method* – on the early development of depth psychology is often overlooked. Covington and Wharton (2006) describe how she played an influential part in helping Freud in his thinking about the **death instinct,** but also Jung's work on the anima. Yet her place is rarely recognized as significant in the history of depth psychology. Is this a reflection of the male-dominated, patriarchal nature of early psychoanalysis? If you are interested in this question, then do have a look at Covington and Wharton's book!

POSITIVISTIC SCIENCE VS RELIGION AND THE SPIRITUAL

The implications of Jung's developing perspective stretched further. Freud was adamant about how problematic and distracting religious belief was for getting to the root of neuroses and helping people to accept the 'reality principle'. This means a capacity to be able to get 'instinctual gratification by accommodation to the facts of, and the objects existing within, the external world' (Rycroft, 1995, p. 152). For Freud, it was most unhelpful for patients to remain in thrall to delusions about God, religious faith or the existence of further layers of reality.

He saw it as the task of the psychoanalyst to help the individual come to terms with the **common unhappiness** (Freud, 1974, p. 393) of their existence, rather than indulge what to Freud would be fantasies, which only enabled them to avoid the psychosexual basis of their suffering. For Freud, religion represented a historical overhang from previous eras where irrational beliefs were a source of succour, prior to scientific discoveries of the nature of reality. Irrational beliefs had had an evolutionary role in helping people deal with the childlike helplessness of human beings in the face of all-powerful nature, and of death. 'God' was an illusion, created to meet this need, and to help hold society together. Freud's faith in scientific materialism, with its positivist emphasis on the reliability of what can be *proved*, thoroughly superseded his Jewish religious heritage.

From Jung's perspective, he could see where religious belief enabled some of his patients to find meaning in life and to orient themselves in an otherwise empty, and at times frightening, universe. He did not see how this, or the longstanding traditions of genuine religious and spiritual experiences (however ossified he thought the Christian church had become in its rituals and dogmas), could be discounted so easily. The spiritual for Jung, where defined and lived by in an individual way (even when within a broader religious tradition), was a part of who we are as human beings, as well as an aspect of the individuation process. Therefore, it was something that should be afforded its place within a framework for understanding the psyche, and working with it in the therapeutic context.

Jung's studies of cultural and religious myths and ideas from across the world and throughout human history were also feeding his curiosity about the deeper strata of the unconscious.

He wondered how this might be influenced by the apparent commonalities of religious and cultural themes he noticed emerging from different patients. Though he broadly concurred with his older colleague regarding the reality and nature of the personal unconscious, the impact of internal and environmental factors on the present, and the ways in which human suffering could be understood as products of powerful internal and relational influences, his perspective was shifting towards an emphasis on the importance of collective, archetypal and spiritual influences on the human psyche.

THE NATURE AND PURPOSE OF DREAMS

For Freud (1900), dreams were famously 'the royal road to the unconscious'. They enable us to see what is happening within the unconscious process of the dreamer. This is framed for him in psychosexual terms, whereby the *manifest* content of a dream – that is, what imagery can be remembered by the dreamer – indicates the *latent* significance. This significance will have a psychosexual or deeply libidinal root, and for Freud, the purpose of dreaming is to discharge the libidinal energy previously repressed into the id as unsafe to express in a conscious way. So, images of, say, a rocket would be seen as a manifest expression of unfulfilled desire for the phallus, or a box might be seen likewise in relation to the vagina.

Jung also thought dreams provide a snapshot of what is happening in the unconscious of the dreamer, and recognized psychosexual influences in them. In contrast, however (see Chapter 11 for further details), dreams for Jung are one of the most potent vehicles the unconscious has to alert the conscious mind to what is going on 'down there'. They often have a compensatory function, indicating where we might need to adjust our attitude or behaviours in order to find or restore balance in the psyche. This principle of **compensation** is also reflected in how the *self* communicates deeper insights to the *ego*, which cannot see the whole picture surrounding a situation or theme. Dreams also sometimes suggest collective themes, which make them pertinent to more than just the individual having the dream.

Jung's 'House' dream

While in the USA with Freud on a lecture tour, Jung had a dream in which he found himself in an unfamiliar house – although he knew it was, somehow, his house (Jung, 1961). Beginning on the upper storey (which had furniture from the eighteenth century), he descended to the ground floor (sixteenth century), then the cellar, which had Roman features. Finally, he discovered a passageway down into a cave where he saw scattered bones and pottery, and in the midst of them, two very old human skulls.

He told Freud about this dream, as Jung had become used to sharing dreams with him (although this was not reciprocated – a bone of contention, seemingly, for Jung). Freud was most struck by the closing scene of the dream, and came to see the two skulls as representative of what he thought was Jung's 'death wish', in the sense that for Freud (1913) 'killing the father' is an common unconscious fantasy within the activation of the Oedipal complex, and Freud was much older than his colleague, reflecting the 'father–son' transferences suggested above. This interpretation is classically Freudian, in the sense that Freud would be looking for what of the manifest content pointed to more viscerally based latent themes. He might also have considered some connection between mother/vagina with the house/room 'enclosed-space' imagery in the dream. However, the potential destructive fantasy, suggested by the skulls, clearly held more interest for him.

Jung instead connected the 'two-ness' to his wife and sister-in-law, though he was not primarily interested in this aspect of the dream. Instead, he saw this dream as a representation of the human psyche. The first floor was the conscious mind, the ground floor and the floors beneath it symbolizing layers of the unconscious, from personal to collective, with the cave scene representing the primitive beginnings of the human psyche. For Jung this was a powerfully archetypal, not personal, dream, through which the collective unconscious was revealing itself to him.

Points of agreement between Freud and Jung

It is important to remember that, alongside these deeper divides in perspective, there were a number of clinically related approaches and principles upon which the two men broadly agreed. These all initially stemmed from the pivotal pioneering work of Freud, and they included:

▶ the use of free association

▶ the value of dream analysis

▶ the transference and projective processes

▶ the importance of sticking to the boundaries of the therapeutic hour.

They also concurred on the use of the couch, although, as with other aspects of theory and practice, this later evolved for Jung. He came to see the value of sitting face to face with the patient, where the interaction of the human encounter was called for. He would then use the couch where a deeper engagement with the unconscious was likewise suggested. This would depend on the stage of the analysis: for example, the couch might be utilized more as the analysand went further and deeper into their unconscious influences and processes.

To that degree, as indicated, Jung owed much to Freud for the 'tools of his trade'. They also both shared a passionate belief in the importance of what they were uncovering, and of the need to develop and make available psychoanalytically based treatment. However, in the years while they worked together in this enterprise, the *shadow* of the underlying differences between them – philosophical, theoretical and clinical – mixed in with personality factors, were quietly drawing the fault lines which would irrevocably drive the two men apart.

Spotlight: A weighty correspondence

Freud and Jung wrote 360 letters between them in their period of correspondence, from April 1906 to January 1913.

The end of the friendship

As Jung continued to develop his thinking, Freud remained certain of the veracity of the psychoanalytic principles he had established. Tensions between the two men grew, and Jung set out distinctions in his thinking from Freud's in a lecture at Fordham University, New York, in 1912. These included his belief that libido and sources of pleasure did not just emanate from sexual roots, as well as the possibility that neurosis could be strongly influenced by the present as well as the past. Freud attempted to convince Jung to realign his thinking with his. However, Jung began to think in terms of an updated 'analytical psychology' and the publication of *Symbols of Transformation* in 1912 laid the foundations for a new theoretical basis for this.

Correspondence between the two became increasingly fraught. Also in 1912, Jung told Freud he was behaving in an overbearingly parental manner towards him and his other followers, while Freud responded by suggesting Jung's behaviours were 'abnormal'. In January 1913 they finally agreed on something amid all the discord – they would cease to send letters to, or have any contact with, one another (McGuire, 1974).

It was a moment that created a schism in the field of depth psychology, the effects of which are still being felt today. However, it was a split which, though painful, generated a burst of creativity in Jung without which the generation of the Jungian model would probably not have been possible.

Key terms

Compensation: In dream work, as well as analytic work generally, Jung identified the compensatory nature of how unconscious processes work to maintain balance or homeostasis in the psyche, including the body, in the face of life's pressures and potential ill health.

Libido: A term to describe mental energy which originates in bodily based id drives of a fundamentally sexual nature, according to Freud. Jung saw libido, like pleasure, as having more than just a sexual root. He proposed creative, relational and spiritual versions, as influences that could act as a resource for the individuation process.

Repression: 'The process by which an unacceptable impulse or idea is rendered unconscious' (Rycroft, 1995, p. 157). A defence mechanism whereby id-driven sexual and aggressive desires and drives are pushed into the unconscious to enable the ego to maintain its stability in daily life. Influenced Jung's concept of shadow.

Sublimation: The channelling of powerful sexual and aggressive id drives into activity that enables their healthy expression, e.g. playing a sport or painting a picture.

Transference: The unconscious 'transfer' of a key parental relationship on to another person. Freud coined the term in relation to where a psychoanalyst can 'become mother or father' for the patient, and argued how influential this is in terms of how the projection of strong feelings from the earlier relationship on to the psychoanalyst allows important roots of the patient's neurosis to be identified and worked through.

Dig deeper

Covington, C. and Wharton, B., *Sabina Spielrein: Forgotten Pioneer of Psychoanalysis* (London: Brunner-Routledge, 2006)

Donn, L., *Freud and Jung; Years of Friendship, Years of Loss* (New York: Collier Books, 1988)

Freud, S., *Three Essays on the Theory of Sexuality,* trans. James Strachey (New York: Basic Books, 1962)

Freud, S. (1895), in Breuer, J. and Freud, S., *Studies in Hysteria* (London: Pelican, 1974)

Freud, S., (1900) *The Interpretation of Dreams*, Illustrated Edition (New York: Sterling, 2010).

Freud, S. (1913), *Totem and Taboo* (London: WW Norton, 1989)

Jones, E., *The Life and Work of Sigmund Freud. Vol. 2. Years of Maturity*, 1901–19 (Oxford: Basic Books, 1955)

Jung, C. G. (1906), *Diagnostic Association Studies* (Leipzig: J. A. Barth) (Chapters in this book can be found in C. G. Jung, *Experimental Researches*, CW2 (London: Brunner-Routledge, 1957)

Jung, C. G. (1912), *Symbols of Transformation*, CW5 (London: Brunner-Routledge, 1967)

Jung, C. G., *Freud's Theory of Hysteria: A Reply to Aschaffenburg* (1961)

Kerr, J., *A Most Dangerous Method: The Story of Jung, Freud and Sabina Spielrein* (London: Sinclair-Stevenson, 1994) Film partly based on this is Cronenberg, D., *A Dangerous Method* (Canada: Sony Pictures, 2011)

McGuire, W. (ed.), *The Freud /Jung Letters* (London: The Hogarth Press, 1974)

Rycroft, C., *Critical Dictionary of Psychoanalysis* (London: Penguin, 1995)

Schopenhauer, A., *The World as Will and Representation*, Vol. 2 (Dover Edition, 1966)

Storr A., *Jung: A Very Short Introduction* (Oxford: Oxford University Press, 1994)

Fact-check (answers at the back)

1 What was Jung's view of Freud's *Interpretation of Dreams*?
   a Initially he thought it lacked significance, but he came to see its importance
   b He thought Freud should have stuck to writing about neuroses
   c Initially he thought it was very important but later felt it was insignificant
   d He thought Freud should only ever write about dreams from then on

2 What was Freud's view of Jung's work on word association?
   a Less significant than his
   b Too fixated on the idea of 'complexes'
   c Confused
   d Valuable in shedding light on unconscious processes

3 After they began working together, how did Freud see Jung?
   a As a rival
   b As more knowledgeable about the human psyche than him
   c As his 'heir apparent' as future leader of the psychoanalytic movement
   d As unable to grasp the key principles of psychoanalysis

4 What were Freud's and Jung's differences on sexual influences due to?
   a Freud's insistence on sexual libido as the dominant influence on the psyche
   b Jung's insistence on the dominance of the spiritual in the psyche
   c Freud's need to prove dominant psychosexual influences scientifically
   d Jung's need to disprove dominant psychosexual influences spiritually

5 What are deterministic versus prospective influences about?

    a Remembering your past in therapy versus avoiding the future in it

    b Early psychosexual influences versus how the psyche unfolds into the future

    c Freud had more determination versus Jung being distracted by his prospects

    d Early prospective influences versus future psychosexual influences

6 How did Freud and Jung disagree about the structure of the unconscious?

    a Freud thought the unconscious was formed purely by the environment

    b Jung thought the unconscious was made only of archetypes

    c Freud thought the personal unconscious was collective, too

    d Jung thought there was a collective layer of the unconscious

7 Why did they disagree about the place of religion?

    a Freud had a Jewish background and Jung a Christian one

    b Jung thought the whole unconscious was spiritually based

    c Freud thought religion was an illusion and Jung thought it served a purpose

    d Jung thought science was an illusion and Freud thought it served a purpose

8 Why did Freud and Jung come to different views on the role of dreams?

    a Jung thought dreams are all collective and Freud did not

    b Freud thought they were all about sex and Jung thought they were all about religion

    c Jung saw dreams as all about the future and Freud saw them as all about the past

    d Freud saw dreams as wish fulfilments, Jung as compensatory and archetypal

9 Which of Freud's clinical tools did Jung take and use?
  a Therapeutic hour, neuroses, manifest and latent dream content
  b Transference, archetypal processes, free association
  c Therapeutic hour, transference, working with shadow
  d Transference, free association, therapeutic hour

10 What did Freud and Jung do when they split?
  a They still kept writing letters to each other
  b They agreed to stop writing letters to each other
  c Jung threw all Freud's letters into Lake Zurich
  d Freud burned Jung's letters to light his pipe

Section 2

The world within: Jung's model of the human psyche

5

Self and ego: listening to the inner voice

The nature of ego and self, and the relationship – or 'axis' – between them, was a key element of Jung's 'map' of the psyche, located within the context of Jung's notions of the collective, the archetypal and the personal. In this chapter we will explore the tasks of ego, and the compensatory capacity of the unconscious to express what self is trying to convey. There will be examples of how this can play out in ordinary life, including the case study of a man who kept locking himself out of his car... Finally, the 'bigger picture' around the self will be explored.

As well as a driver of individuation, we will look at how the self can act as archetype of the numinous (or divine), and what this can mean – in both destabilizing and enriching ways.

A new formula for ego?

We have seen how the painful split between Freud and Jung played out, and how this was about more than just personality or the politics of the psychoanalytic world. The theoretical and philosophical tensions between the two men reflected Jung's move away from the purely deterministic and psychosexual emphasis of Freud's model. Although their 'divorce' was traumatic, once the two went their separate ways, the silver lining for Jung was that he could foster a model of psyche and its workings, free from the pressure to stay aligned to Freud's. He could build a conceptual structure in the spirit of the more expansive view of the human condition that informed his growing emphasis on the realization of hidden potential in the psyche.

Spotlight: Does psyche look forwards as well as backwards?

Jung thought the human psyche had a 'prospective function'. In other words, he thought the unconscious has the capacity to sense, or intuit, what may lie ahead, or is yet to unfold in our journey through life. This does not usually refer to 'prophetic' phenomena such as dreams, which we think might 'tell the future' (though, on occasion, they may provide such hints). More, it refers to the nature of the individuation process and how the self (which we shall explore in more detail in this chapter) carries some sense of where we may be heading, although the ego still holds the power to change course in life. This clearly differs from Freud's emphasis on how, almost exclusively, past (psychosexual) influences are the determining influences on psyche.

Although Jung retained parts of the essential profile of Freud's model, he made some subtle but profound adjustments to it. What remained was Freud's identification of ego as the centre of the conscious mind, managing the many pressures and possibilities of daily life, as well as governing the tensions between powerful internal forces. Freud's proposition that – given the right conditions – ego was able to notice and retrieve previously unavailable information from the unconscious also remained an important principle for Jung in his analytic approach, although the emphasis shifted.

Why was this shift in the place of the ego in Jung's model significant, and why did it contribute to the deepening of the divide between Freudian and Jungian perspectives on the human condition? To answer this, we need to explore what Jung meant by 'self' – a construct that lay outside the classical psychoanalytic framework and radically redesignated the place and role of ego in the human psyche.

Self: the missing piece for Jung

If the idea of the collective unconscious was to be appended to the notion of a personal unconscious, there was a risk that this might be seen as having only a tangential influence on the day-to-day life of the individual, unless it was represented within the personality structure of the psyche. The 'self' provides this by representing deeper wisdom associated with who we most deeply *are,* and by representing archetypally numinous ('mysterious' or spiritual) possibilities of human experience. Jung argued that *self* can guide us aright in our individuation process – a wisdom we do not find readily available most of the time. Jung wanted to find a place in his structure of our inner world for this voice that emanated from something beyond the day-to-day life of ego.

Jung's formative experiences of life – his contact with organized religion, and the many flaws, and qualities, he saw in it, and the numerous encounters he had with unconscious influences via his imagination and dreams, led him to a fresh conclusion. Leaving out something deeply personal and yet also connected to the evolution of the numinous in the collective psyche would be like leaving out the centrepiece of a jigsaw puzzle. So, before considering the significant implications of the presence of the self for ego, we need to elucidate the notion of *self* and explore the way, according to Jung, it operates.

Self and its place in the psyche

How can we envisage the place of *self* in the human psyche? Jung provides a helpful guide by referring to what happens if we acknowledge the influence of the unconscious on our lives:

> 'if we can live in such a way that conscious and unconscious demands are taken into account as far as possible, then the centre of gravity of the total personality shifts its position. It is then no longer in the ego, which is merely the centre of consciousness, but in the hypothetical point between conscious and unconscious. The new centre might be called the self.'
>
> Jung, 1966a, para. 67

Jung is describing a centre of who we are that is able to connect us to the depths of the unconscious and archetypal processes; but also to contact, and influence, our conscious mind.

Taking this specific quote of Jung's and comparing it to Freud's model of the psyche, *self* may perform one function of his model of *ego*: i.e. the latter is able to relate to unconscious *id* and *superego* influences which Freud would posit are close to the surface of conscious awareness (in the *preconscious*). However, the *self* is not, for Jung, just able to tune into images, words, thoughts, feelings and sensations with a psychosexual provenance. In line with the observations about his way of thinking about libido in the previous chapter, *self* enables contact with a broad range of energies in the unconscious, including creative and relational ones that are conducive to the stage of life, and of the individuation process, the person is in.

In a sense, then, *ego* and *self* both mediate. *Ego* mediates between day-to-day reality and the guidance of the self. In turn, *self* mediates between resources which the unconscious can provide, and the demands of the *ego* to be guided and contained (as it wrestles with the demands of life). An implication of this, which we will come back to, is when we do *not*, as Jung recommended we do in the quote above, take unconscious demands into account alongside conscious ones; then the guiding and containing functions of the *self* may become unavailable, and the relationship between ego and self gets thrown out of kilter.

Staying with the theme of location, we need to say more about what Jung means by *self* being the true centre of who we are:

'The symbols of the process of individuation that appear in dreams are images of an archetypal nature which depict the centralizing process or the production of a new centre of personality... The self is not only the centre, but also the whole circumference which embraces both conscious and unconscious; it is the centre of this totality, just as the ego is the centre of the conscious mind.'

Jung, 1953, para. 44

Here Jung is proposing that the *self* is doing two things at once – it is being both the central point of psyche and the boundary around all of the conscious and unconscious contents of it. Rather than seeing this as a contradiction, this idea works if one bears in mind the idea of archetypes as *bipolar,* as described in Chapter 1 (see Key terms). In this instance, the topography of the archetype of the self has two poles: '*self* as centre' and '*self* as totality'. Jung contended that reality is full of paradoxes, and that what he is describing here speaks to our lived experience. On the one hand, we feel a sense of our unique identity as encompassing all of who and what we are: mind and body (for some also something about 'soul', perhaps?). But we can also have a sense of there being some elemental sense of 'I' at the core of our being.

Jung thought of self's operation as 'core', in the sense where we experience a 'call' from deep within us to attend to something crucial, say something we have overlooked in our lives up to now. He also referred to it in the 'encompassing' sense, where we notice a sense of all elements of our being working together – say in working on a project that demands a blend of physical, mental and creative energies, drawing fluidly on conscious and unconscious resources.

Key idea: A single self?

In line with contemporary thinking on the complexity of being human, Andrew Samuels (1989), a post-Jungian thinker, writes about plural versions of self. He argues that Jung's model does not take into account the ways in which we can feel and be quite different in how we are with others, and ourselves, at different times. He argues that this is more than just different personas we wear to adapt to different contexts and demands; it is, rather, deeper identities of self that seek to find expression across our experience of life. An example would be how different versions of our sexuality may reveal themselves at different times.

Jung's Liverpool dream of the self

Jung refers above to dream images portraying the workings of the self. He had a dream in 1927 that illustrates this point. In this dream he found himself in Liverpool, and walking towards the centre of the city. He noticed the way the layout of the city in the dream seemed to converge on to a central square around which the four quarters of the city were arranged (for Jung the number four represented 'totality' or completeness). As he comes to the centre of the square, he sees a pool, at the centre of which lies a small island with a magnolia tree on it. He tells himself he would like to live in this city (Jung, 1963). This is a dream about the development of the self, in Jung's view, as it portrays a movement towards the centre, where there is a 'tree of life', in a city with the name 'Liver – pool', which means 'pool of life'. The city represents the totality and circumference of his conscious and unconscious, and the tree on the island represents the centre where both meet.

This, then, is a dream that portrays what Jung means by self. It is something that works quietly within us, behind the hubbub of daily life, to integrate all aspects of us. It also holds together the totality of who we are, as the centralizing influence promotes wholeness and takes us to the centre of who we are. Of course, for such a process to work well enough across our lifespan, our ego has to listen and respond to the demands of this process, so as not to wander too far off track, or in extreme cases suffer a loss of soul, where neurosis haunts the individual with the very values they need (Jung, 1966b). An example of this could be where an addiction reflects the very thing a person is seeking out but cannot find – e.g. seeking spiritual meaning but this being drowned out by the consumption of alcoholic 'spirits'.

Through the *self*, archetypal polarities are presented to us to test our capacity to deal with the paradoxes and tensions of life, e.g. the archetypes of *good* and *evil*. It is for us to make the *ego* choice around which direction to take things when confronted with an ethical dilemma, e.g. where we may get gratification from a choice that then harms another person rather than upholding the priority to protect their well-being. At times we may need to make a decisive choice while we still have the chance, but often *self* seems to challenge our capacity to hold both possibilities when confronted with a choice, e.g. over the future of a relationship we are in, rather than jump in one direction too hastily. All of this is relative to external circumstances, life stage, personality and formative influences.

The other key archetypal dynamic, held by self, concerns the relationship between the human and the divine. Jung came to the view that the self is the source and container of all symbols of the numinous. As Samuels et al. (1986, p. 136) put it: 'Symbols of the self often possess a numinosity and convey a sense of necessity which gives them transcendent priority in psychic life. They carry the authority of a God image...' As implied, this means key religious, or mythological, images representing God or Gods, such as Christ, Rama and Sita or Aphrodite, are actually symbols of the *self*, when it is charged with divine, or numinous, energy. The self can also be seen as a complex of opposites where archetypal good and evil reside (Casement, 2010). Jung was also keen on the symbol of the mandala as being one that represents *self* : it has a 'whole' quality with a clear central point, like the imagery found in the 'Liverpool' dream.

Spotlight: A mandala a day...

In *Memories, Dreams, Reflections* (1963), Jung reported how he would spontaneously draw a mandala every day, as a kind of 'snapshot' of what was happening in his psyche. As he put it: 'With the help of these drawings I could observe my psychic transformation from day to day' (Jung, 1963, p. 220). Some of these changing mandalas can be observed in *The Red Book*.

The ego–self axis

How does *self* enable access to deeper archetypal influences, and transmit its messages to *ego*, to help psyche stay on its individuation path? Jung's model of psyche stressed how important each was to the other – *self* needs *ego* to represent and actualize it as much as *ego* needs *self* to help it navigate through this challenge. Jung proposed a dynamic of relations between the two, bridged by conduits of communication, for example where dreams serve to convey from *self* to *ego* what is going on at a deeper level (as described in the example below), or where *ego* then responds to this by adjusting conscious attitude or making an ethical choice. He did not give this bridge a name, but a Jungian thinker later did – Edward Edinger, who termed this the 'ego–self axis' in 1972 (Edinger, 1991).

This axis has two main functions: first, it enables the kind of access to depth experience as described in this chapter, as well as acting as a channel through which that depth can be manifested in the real lives of people. Second, it allows for the relationship between ego and self to be regulated, so that an organic balance can be sustained between the 'mover' (*self*) and the 'moved' *(ego)*. There is a parallel here with the primary carer / infant interaction. Both need each other to provide the reciprocal role in order for the child to receive the care and guidance of the primary carer, while the latter needs the baby to fulfil and represent some vital aspects of themselves in the world.

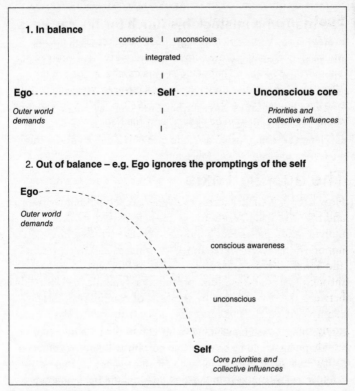

1. In balance

conscious | unconscious

integrated

|

Ego ---------------------- **Self** -------------- **Unconscious core**

Outer world
demands
|
Priorities and
collective influences
|

2. Out of balance – e.g. Ego ignores the promptings of the self

Ego

Outer world
demands

conscious awareness

unconscious

Self
Core priorities and
collective influences

The ego–self axis

When the balance between *ego* and *self* is not present, there is a risk that the *ego* might forget its place and over-identify with *self,* thus becoming over-inflated and assuming it 'knows best' or even has powers that do not belong to it (this can be seen where political leaders become self-aggrandised and tyrannical). Or, where the *ego* is brittle, contents of the unconscious can flood it and psychosis and delusion can result. One other possibility, which is illustrated in the diagram above, is where *ego* ignores *self,* as it is too consumed with day-to-day concerns and the need to uphold the *persona* in professional and other domains of life. The following case study is an example of what can happen in this situation.

The man who mistook his lunch for his car keys

A busy professional man who had ambition and drive in spades, but struggled to really listen to himself, lived with his partner, but they only saw each other in passing during the week. At weekends she had to try hard to get him to stop working and spend some quality time with her. At times, after a typical working day of 12 hours or more, he would fall asleep soon after arriving home, and he had developed a habit of using drugs to give him a quick escape from the frantic lifestyle he was following.

He had a sense of being pulled in two directions at once. On the one hand, he remained as driven as ever in wanting to get as far as he could, as quickly as he could, in his career. On the other hand, he could feel something in him starting to come loose, as if what he was doing was splitting his sense of self into many parts. He had a recurring image in his head of someone pulling furiously at a gate to try and get it open, and all it seemed to be doing was wrecking it (and the gatepost). It also exhausted and exasperated the person pulling the gate.

He had also locked himself out of his car twice in the past month. Each time he would be so preoccupied with speaking to someone on his mobile, or anxious not to be late for a meeting, that he would leave his car keys in the ignition, grab the thing nearest to him – a plastic bag with his lunch in it – and, forgetting that the automatic locking system was on, leap from the car. The first time this happened, he did not realize his keys were inside the car until he returned to it later. The second time the realization hit him as soon as the alarm blipped after he got out of the car.

He knew things were not right but it took a couple of weeks for him to decide to speak to a therapist about what was going on. This was prompted by a dream in which he was rolling very fast down a bowling alley towards some skittles, over and over again. Each time, he careered into the skittles and someone shouted 'strike!', and he could see the points clocking up and up on the screen above him. But he just wanted it to stop...

When thinking about this dream, he did not need much help to realize he needed to pay heed to the part of him that wanted to slow down, a part he had ignored for some time. The image of the man trying to wrench the gate open also gave him pause for thought around what it was he was trying to achieve by being an *uber-businessman*. It turned out that his heroic efforts were, in part at least, a wish to 'break free' from something. While what this was from his past would take time in therapy to explore and address, it was at least clear that there was something more important for him to be able to express than his drive to become the CEO of a large company in record time. In a way, leaving keys locked in the car could be seen as a metaphor for what was 'key' in him being locked inside an uncontained 'drive' to fulfil a persona image of himself, which was certainly not the full picture of who he was or could be.

Through the 'bowling' dream, the 'gate' image and the unconscious placing of his keys in the car, the self had found three different, but allied, ways to finally wake the ego up to what was going on. He was then able to notice the problem and, with difficulty, make adjustments to moderate the impact his attitude to work was having on his health and relationships (e.g. spending an hour or two less at work, and having designated drug-free evenings, focused on his family, whenever he could).

Ego and its place in the psyche

As will be clear from the discussion in this chapter, Jung's notion of *ego,* though sharing some characteristics with Freud's version, has a different flavour. In his developmental framework, Jung, like Freud, saw *ego* as forming in the third or fourth year of life but his emphasis was different because of the presence of *self.* For Jung, *ego* arose from, and needed to differentiate itself from, *self.* Most contemporary practitioners and thinkers in the field would now disagree with both theories, as the consensus now is that ego forms within the first year of life, and one Jungian thinker, Michael Fordham, developed a new schema for understanding the *ego–self* relationship which took this into account (see Chapter 14).

Irrespective of the debate over its development, what we are left with is a notion of *ego* that is strongly tied in with Jung's view of the relationship between the conscious and unconscious mind. While *ego* can influence *self,* the influence of the deeper intelligence of *self* on ego is a pivotal principle for Jung. The *self* needs to be listened to and interacted with – and sometimes challenged – in order for individuation and healthy psychic growth to be facilitated, both in the therapeutic encounter and in life more generally.

Key terms

Ego: Centre of the conscious mind.

Ego–self axis: A psychic 'pole' or continuum that links ego and self and enables them to communicate and influence each other.

Numinous: This refers to experiences where we encounter phenomena that are mysterious or awesome. Religious or spiritual experiences can be seen as numinous.

Self: The centre of psyche, located where conscious and unconscious meet, as well as the whole of, and circumference around, our psychic, physical and spiritual totality.

Dig deeper

Casement, A., 'Self', in Leeming, D., Madden, K. and Stanton, M. (eds.),*The Encyclopedia of Psychology and Religion* (New York: Springer, 2010)

Edinger, E., *Ego and Archetype: Individuation and the Religious Function of the Psyche* (Boston, MA: Shambhala, 1991)

Jung, C. G., *Memories, Dreams, Reflections* (Glasgow: Fontana, 1963)

Jung, C. G., *Alchemical Studies*, CW13 (London: Routledge, 1966a)

Jung, C. G., *Two Essays on Analytical Psychology*, CW7 (London: Routledge, 1966b)

Jung C. G. (1953), 'Individual Dream Symbolism in Relation to Alchemy' in *Psychology and Alchemy,* 2nd ed., CW12 (London: Routledge, 1968)

Samuels, A., Shorter, B. and Plaut, F. (eds.), *A Critical Dictionary of Jungian Analysis* (London: Routledge, 1986)

Samuels, A. *The Plural Psyche: Personality, Morality and the Father* (London: Routledge, 1989)

Fact-check (answers at the back)

1 How did Jung's model of ego differ from Freud's?
  a Jung thought the ego repressed instinctual material in the unconscious; Freud did not
  b Freud, unlike Jung, thought ego strength was an important aspect for patients to work on
  c Freud thought the ego mediated between conscious and unconscious; Jung did not
  d Jung thought the ego could draw on differing forms of libido, not just psychosexual

2 Where did Jung describe the self as being located?
  a In the collective unconscious
  b At the intersection of the conscious and unconscious
  c Behind the ego in the personal conscious
  d Between the ego and the numinous

3 How does the ego 'mediate' with the self?
  a Ego mediates between self and superego, while self does so between id and ego
  b Ego mediates between collective and personal, self between ego and personal unconscious
  c Ego mediates between external reality and self, self between ego and the collective unconscious
  d Ego mediates between self and the numinous

4 In what way could the place of the self be seen as 'bipolar'?
  a Self is both the centre and the circumference of the psyche
  b Self is both solid and fluid
  c Self is the opposite of ego
  d When the self fragments, people develop bipolar disorder

5 Why did Jung think the self carried the numinous?
  a Because it was big enough to carry God around
  b Because it couldn't stop archetypal influences flooding it
  c Because symbols of the numinous, like gods, were really representations of the self
  d Because symbols of gods belonged only in the collective unconscious

6 Why did Jung see the self as crucial to the individuation path?
   a It was the centre of the psyche
   b It could help the ego stay on course
   c It provided symbols of the numinous
   d It stopped people getting lost when walking

7 The ego-self axis is a way of describing what?
   a How ego and self relate and communicate
   b How self provides the axis of the 'vehicle' of the psyche for the ego
   c The direction the ego needs to take on the individuation path
   d The vague relationship between conscious and unconscious material

8 What is 'compensation'?
   a Where the ego recompenses the self for ignoring its directions
   b Where the self tries to point out to the ego what it is not taking into account
   c Where the ego–self axis rewards both self and ego
   d Where the analysand still pays the analyst when they miss a session

9 What does it mean where ego 'over-identifies with the self'?
   a The ego leaves all the work to the self
   b The ego thinks the self is crushing its identity
   c The ego becomes deflated and feels inferior to the self
   d The ego thinks it is the self, and becomes inflated, possibly deluded

10 Why does the ego have a crucial active role to play in the individuation process?
   a The self needs the ego to respond to it autonomously, and realize it actively in the world
   b The ego has more energy in it than the self, and provides the libido for individuation
   c The self is too inward-looking to be able to make anything happen by itself
   d The ego helps the self to find its path and then follows it down the individuation path

6

Ego's face and back: persona and shadow

Having described the place of ego in relation to self, we will now look at how ego operates in other ways: how it is represented via the often numerous personas we show to the world; and how the dark, hidden side of ego operates. This second aspect is shadow – the hidden, messier and less pleasant parts of ourselves we would rather other people did not see. We will consider its significant implications for the individuation process. We will also acknowledge where it might hold aspects of our hidden potential, and the implications of working with this area in therapy. To help you grasp both concepts, the chapter includes a couple of case studies and prompt questions for personal reflection.

Ego: outward looking and inward facing

As was made plain in the previous chapter, ego is a key player in the psyche. Where it is healthy, ego actively engages with daily life, and manages the many interactions and challenges thrown up by it. Where this is less so – say, where depression and anxiety dominate a person's world – ego can become very uncertain of its role, and either retreat into an avoidant state or become over-reactive or hyper-sensitive. These defences can then become default ways of engaging with life.

The quality of ego engagement with self, others and the world will also reflect how the inner dynamics of a person's psyche are working. In other words, if different aspects at work in the psyche are interacting in an alive and complementary way, then ego will likewise be able to operate in the external environment effectively and comfortably (and it will not if things are unhelpfully conflicted or stuck within). If ego is listening to self, for example, there is more prospect of healthy engagement with the outer world; but if not (maybe because a complex is gripping the psyche), then the ego will probably act this out in their relations to others, say by becoming angry and defensive, or anxious and overly deferential.

How can we better understand the ways ego responds to the dynamics it experiences from within psyche, as well as from influences arising in its outer relationships and circumstances? Jung's way of making sense of this was to propose that ego had both an outward-facing aspect and an inward-looking one. It is not difficult to see the possible link between this idea and Jung's childhood experience of having two versions of himself: his personality's number one and number two (as described in Chapter 2), one the outwardly directed (or 'extraverted' as he would come to term it) version, and the other inwardly directed (or 'introverted').

Jung used the term 'shadow' as something of a catch-all term to describe how the darker, hidden side of the ego collects together difficult, under-developed and unpleasant aspects of ourselves and seems to bracket them out of view (most of the time). It is like us, standing on the earth and staring into the night sky, not being able to see the dark side of the moon, and wondering what is hidden there; except, where shadow is concerned, we may not even realize there is anything there to wonder *about*.

> **Spotlight:** Shadow and persona in books and films
>
> There are many examples of this such as Robert Louis Stevenson's characters of Dr Jekyll (persona) and Mr Hyde (shadow) (Stevenson, 1886). In the film *Star Wars* (Lucas, 1977), Luke Skywalker represents the heroic, good persona, while Darth Vader symbolizes shadow. Can you think of any other examples of where this split between persona and shadow is portrayed in books and films?

On the other hand, **persona** refers to what we can clearly see of a person's presentation and character, like being able to stare at the full moon through a pair of binoculars. We can see many craters and bumps, lit up by the light of the sun reflecting on its surface. It is how the moon presents itself to us on earth, sometimes as a crescent, sometimes as a half moon, sometimes full (so it has at least three personas, one could say). The following diagram shows how persona and shadow represent outer- and inner-facing aspects of the ego.

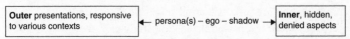

Persona and shadow as key features of ego

Persona: a version of ourselves

While 'persona' is a relatively straightforward concept to describe, it is important not to oversimplify things by saying that what we can see or experience of another person – in a social, work or other context – tells us the whole story. In the same way, and going back to the image above, what we can see of the moon from a distance does not tell us what it is really like to be on its surface or close up. We might meet one version of a person we know at work or college, for example – where they seem shy and courteous – but we do not know what they might be like with their close family. They might be gregarious and sometimes even rude to those they are more familiar with. As Jung (1953, para. 305) put it:

> 'The persona is a complicated system of relations between individual consciousness and society, fittingly enough a kind of mask, designed on the one hand to make a definite impression on others, and, on the other, to conceal the true nature of the individual.'

Fundamentally, the goal of a persona is to present a version of ourselves that fits the situation we are in; it is like having different sets of clothes for different occasions, varying between the casual to the explicitly formal. At times there is something heroic about this capacity (it is 'I' alone who manages to do all this), and the persona is seen as having an archetypal connection to 'hero/heroine'. Where this works well, such as in obvious ways where a public figure or business leader is able to utilize their persona to garner support, the benefits can be clear and measurable. It is also usually possible for us to foster a flexible capacity to switch between personas comfortably as we move between work, family and other responsibilities and activities.

What are the possible risks that might be associated with persona? Here is a fictionalized case study exploring aspects of this, followed by a reflective activity for you to do.

Persona as default

Lisa had been a school teacher for around 20 years. Although the job was demanding, sometimes all-consuming, she loved it and was passionate about providing her pupils with the best teaching and care she could offer. Over time she had developed a style of communication with her pupils that was warm but firm, and which they usually responded to well. She noticed, though, that, on occasion, the 'warm' aspect of this could attract an irritated, even angry, response, not only from a pupil but from a colleague she might have a difference of opinion with. She had been told she could be 'patronizing' more than once. Lisa worried about this a bit and wondered whether she had got too caught up in her role as teacher, but thought it not something worth getting too concerned about, since she could see how much most people appreciated what she offered them and the school.

She carried on working hard and putting her 'all' into her teaching and involvement in the school community. She did not have much else in her life (she lived alone and her original family lived a few hundred miles away, so she only saw them three or four times a year). She did not mind, though. School life provided a sense of belonging and purpose; there was always something going on after school and trips to help organize. She had belonged to a choir elsewhere in the town but had dropped that when asked to run the school choir.

Then she met up with an old friend who said she remembered Lisa playing the guitar and 'singing her head off' when they were both about ten years old. Lisa said she couldn't remember 'being that wild', and gave her friend her 'warmest teacher smile'. Her friend had seemed to wince, and Lisa felt sadness flow around her body. She could not seem to find the natural warmth and excitement her friend had described.

As this case study illustrates, if our persona seems particularly reliable or successful to us, it can become our default way of being in life. This poses a risk that is thrown into stark relief when the role is no longer available (for example, when we retire from a job), and we can feel lost or even become ill without it. Another risk is that 'worlds can collide'; for example, we can be at a party and, if two people are there who recognize us as different personas from the context they know us in, which persona do we adopt? Do we choose, say, the 'serious student' one or the 'wacky friend' one?

Spotlight: Reflection on this case study

1 What does Lisa's story suggest to you? Does it bring up any thoughts or feelings? If so, jot these down.

2 What do you think it might be like for Lisa when she retires?

3 Have you ever become over-identified with a job or a role you have performed at work, college, school, etc.? What happened and how did you realize this was happening?

4 How many personas do you have and in what contexts do they appear?

5 Have you ever been in a situation with people you know from *different* contexts who know you as *differing* personas ('where worlds collide')? What was that like?

Overall, the persona performs an important function in enabling us to operate effectively in the world. Sometimes there is a danger that a persona we adopt might actually inhibit our development or even undermine the cohesiveness of our identity, an idea which parallels Donald Winnicott's 'false self' (Jacobs, 1995). His concept suggests the presence of a deep psychological wound from early life, whereby the infant is not unconditionally accepted for who they really are and learns to behave and present themselves in ways which are 'acceptable' to others, but at great cost to themselves.

The idea of persona also has some echoes in Carl Rogers' person-centred concept of conditions of worth (Wilkins, 2003) – imposed expectations of how we need to behave as children in order to gain our parents' or carers' love. Jung had picked up on the importance of personality adaptation in order to be able to survive, and even flourish, among the challenges and uncertainties of the world we live in. The ego needs to be able to rely on its personas to be credible, but not too rigid to enable this.

Shadow: a moral problem

In Jung's view, shadow carries weaker, hidden and less pleasant aspects of our personality, which have the capacity to undermine us if we do not face, and own up, to them. In relation to ego, *shadow* therefore has the capacity to destabilize its healthy functioning (Casement, 2006). One example of this, linked to the discussion in the previous chapter on how ego and self relate to one another, is where an aspect of ourselves which is strongly charged instinctually or emotionally keeps impacting on our relationships – for example, in the form of inappropriately aggressive responses. Here, the ego has a problem because *shadow* aspects are literally currently outside its control, even if ego has some awareness of them (for example, remembering the last time they suddenly found themselves swearing repeatedly at someone they were annoyed with). These aspects can therefore be difficult to stop from bubbling up again at the next provocation.

You may have noticed some similarity here with Freud's concept of repression – the defence designed to stop powerful instincts and drives from overwhelming us. Where this cannot hold, sexual or aggressive instincts burst through in ordinary life in ways that can be disturbing, even dangerous. Clearly, Jung's way of describing these processes owes something to Freud's original formulation. A key distinction comes in, however, when we consider more fully what Jung regards as the nature and function of *shadow*. This quote from Jung sets out his position well:

'The shadow is a moral problem that challenges the whole ego personality, for no one can become conscious of the shadow without considerable moral effort. To become conscious of it involves recognizing the dark aspects of the personality as present and real. This act is the essential condition for any kind of self-knowledge, and it therefore, as a rule, meets with considerable resistance. Indeed, self-knowledge as a psychotherapeutic measure frequently requires much painstaking work extended over a long period.'

Jung, 1968, para. 14

Substantial knowledge of who we really are (what makes me 'me') involves a big struggle to face aspects of ourselves we would rather not look at, let alone acknowledge being part of us. Hence the image of *shadow* as what is 'behind us', or 'at our back' (sometimes portrayed as a bag full of stuff we carry over our shoulder) and which is therefore hard to see without considerable effort (symbolically, being prepared to turn right round to see, or using a mirror). *Shadow* is generally not a comfortable thing to engage with, and therefore the default position we may often adopt is one of avoidance. In turn, this can give *shadow* enormous power, turning it into a **shadow complex** that unconsciously dominates our psyche. This can be seen in the following case study.

Case study

Jerome was a student who found it difficult to face reality beyond his studies. He tended to get very good marks for his assignments and was confident in his ability to talk and write about his subject. He had a number of good friends and was active in student life, having done a stint as the president of the students' union. However, as he came closer to the completion of his degree course, he took a different approach to the future compared to most of his friends. He decided that, rather than thinking about, and planning for, life after university, he would deliberately not look for a job or further studies. He told his friends he would rather not think about it 'until I have to'. It was not so much that he wanted to have a 'gap year' where he could perhaps travel or take time out because he needed to (he had done this already before he started his degree). It seemed to be more a kind of 'head-in-the-sand' approach to things.

Then he had a dream which made a strong impression on him. In this dream he was walking down a long road which seemed to go off into the distance, with no end in sight. Jerome thought he was on his own, but then he heard footsteps behind him. He wanted to turn around but he could not turn his head, nor stop himself walking forward. The footsteps got closer and closer and he was getting anxious, panicky even. The last moment in the dream came when he could feel the breath of the person on the back of his neck, and then felt a tap on his shoulder which jolted him awake. He woke up sweating with anxiety.

Although Jerome was not sure what the dream was about, he knew it related to the current situation and his choice to ignore the fast-approaching end of his time at university. Jerome recognized that time, like the hidden walker in the dream, was catching up with him and he needed to face the situation: the road (university) he was on would not last for ever. He needed to turn and deal with the harsh reality of its end and the need to prepare properly for the next stage in his life.

What he had avoided – his need to take responsibility for his future – had become bottled up in his psyche, and a *shadow* complex had taken hold, which related to previous difficulties in taking responsibility. With this dream, his unconscious (through a mobilization of the *self,* alerting the *ego* to the problem) had woken him up to the urgency of the situation and the need to confront, and work with, this *shadow* aspect of himself. He began to start thinking about 'what next'. It was not an easy thing, as part of him seemed to go to any lengths to get him to avoid doing so; but little by little he began to plan.

The case study above demonstrates how working with *shadow* is often literally just that, hard work. There is often a strong magnetic pull dragging us back to the path of least resistance where it is easiest for us to remain stuck, avoidant, addicted or whatever other strategy we have established to not have to face our *shadow*. Another such strategy, principally unconscious but one which can still plague us even when we are conscious of it, is *shadow projection*.

SHADOW PROJECTION

Jung realized, through his work with patients, that it is a common human tendency to see in other people our faults and unhealthy ways of relating to self and others, when really they belong to us. As he put it:

> 'While some traits peculiar to the shadow can be recognized without too much difficulty as one's own personal qualities, in this case both insight and good will are unavailing because the cause of the emotion appears to lie, beyond all possible doubt, in the other person. No matter how obvious it may be to the neutral observer that it is a matter of projection, there is little hope that the subject will perceive this himself. He must be convinced that he throws a very long shadow before he is willing to withdraw his emotionally toned projections from their object.'
>
> Jung, 1968, para. 16

A useful way of noticing when we are projecting our *shadow* is to notice the strength of feeling (or 'emotional tone', as Jung puts it here) we experience when we find ourselves criticizing someone else. For example, when someone we work with has made a mistake, if we notice that we feel a little irritated with them because it creates more work for us, but otherwise accept that we are all human and make mistakes, that is not projection. If, on the other hand, we find ourselves filled with self-righteous anger because we 'would never make such a mistake – what is the matter with them?', then we are clearly investing a lot of energy in that response, and it suggests we are projecting our own *shadow* fear of getting things wrong on to them.

Spotlight: Your shadow checklist

Have you ever done any of the following, and if so what does this tell you about your *shadow*?

* Found yourself avoiding a pressing issue or task (like Jerome in the case study above)?
* Been intensely critical of another person, whether to their face, or to others or yourself?
* Gone to considerable lengths to cover up an activity you feel guilty about?
* Found yourself getting very angry or dismissive of a fictional character in a story, play or film?

✱ Convinced yourself that a trait you don't like in yourself does not really matter, or has somehow been eradicated?

Make some notes about times and situations where these might have cropped up and then reflect on what you might be able to do to own these *shadow* aspects of yourself. A book that gives further help on working with this area is *Was that Really Me? How Everyday Stress Brings Out Our Hidden Personality* by Naomi Quenk (2002), who also links our hidden characteristics to Jung's work on personality types (see Chapter 9).

Shadow as a resource

Despite the ways itemized in which shadow can be seen as a problem, its presence also provides us with opportunities to face aspects of who we are which may be under-developed and flawed. This often becomes a key part of Jungian analysis, because shadow inevitably shows itself as the client comes to trust the therapist and lets their mask (persona) slip. The analyst's role is to respectfully notice and challenge the analysand's presentation of shadow and help them to notice, acknowledge and eventually own this.

In this respect, working with shadow can be a good way to help deflate ego when it becomes over-inflated and identifies with the self, as described in Chapter 5. Where ego gets to see itself as 'knowing everything', then shadow will intrude somehow, through some obvious mistake or indiscretion the person finds themselves falling into which embarrasses them. Jung goes further than this and argues that our shadow gives us substance. In other words, without a shadow, we would all be fairly one-dimensional, boring, people. In analysis, helping someone to recognize what they are missing by being too 'pure' or 'spiritual', and so helping them accept their bodily and instinctual desires in healthy ways, is one example of the value of embracing shadow, while not denying its potentially undermining and destructive aspects. Also, by facing up to a trait, a person can discover something of value hiding behind it.

Spotlight: The golden shadow

Robert Johnson (1991) describes the challenge presented by the so-called 'golden shadow'. He says this is where aspects of ourselves exist but have not come into our conscious awareness yet (and may never do so). If we can uncover these aspects while confronting the more difficult aspects of our *shadow*, we have a chance of finding strengths and creative capacities that we can, after all, live out before it is too late. The *golden shadow* is therefore often associated with the second half of life, once our earlier *personas* have fallen away.

Key terms

Extraverted: The way we relate outwards to the world and the people around us.

Introverted: The way we relate inwards to ourselves and our inner world.

Persona: The way we present ourselves to the world; the masks we wear to represent our identity in differing contexts; the outward face of ego.

Shadow: What we would rather not be, but are; the hidden, repressed and under-developed aspects of ourselves; the hidden, inward-facing aspect of ego.

Dig deeper

Casement, A., 'The Shadow', in Papadopoulos, R. (ed.), *The Handbook of Jungian Psychology: Theory, Practice and Applications* (Hove: Routledge, 2006), Ch. 4.

Jacobs, M., *Winnicott* (London: Sage,1995)

Johnson, R., *Transformation: Understanding the Three Levels of Masculine Consciousness* (San Francisco: Harper, 1991)

Jung, C. G., *Two Essays on Analytical Psychology*, CW7 (London: Routledge, 1953)

Jung, C. G., 'The Shadow' in *Aion*, CW9ii (London: Routledge, 1968)

Lucas, G. (director), *Star Wars* (film: Los Angeles, CA: 20th Century Fox, 1977)

Quenk, N., *Was That Really Me? How Everyday Stress Brings Out Our Hidden Personality* (Mountain View, CA: Davies-Black, 2002)

Stevenson, R. L. (1886), *The Strange Case of Dr Jekyll and Mr Hyde* (Ware: Clays Ltd, Wordsworth Classics,1999)

Wilkins, P., *Person-centred therapy in focus* (London: Sage, 2003)

Fact-check (answers at the back)

1 How may Jung's distinction of persona as outward facing and shadow as inward (and hidden) relate to his childhood?
  a He was very introverted and did not want to face the world
  b He thought, when he stepped 'out of a mist' to be himself, this mist was his shadow
  c He thought he had two personalities, one outward facing and the other inward
  d He identified his persona with his mother and his shadow with his father

2 What is the main purpose of the persona?
  a To give a person a sense of identity
  b To enable a person to adapt the way they present themselves to different contexts
  c To help people develop role-playing skills
  d To allow us to be who we want to be in different contexts

3 What happens to shadow when we are actively in a persona way of relating?
  a It becomes hidden
  b It goes to sleep
  c It disappears
  d It retreats behind the self

4 What is the risk involved in being too reliant on a persona?
  a If we forget to use it, it can be embarrassing
  b We might impose it on other people
  c We might get over-identified with it and forget who we really are
  d We might borrow a persona from someone else which does not fit

5 According to Jung, what is contained in our shadow?
  a Potential personas and ego states
  b Dark matter from behind the moon
  c Aspects of the self that have got lost in childhood
  d Aspects that are unpleasant, weak or that we don't like

6 How is Jung's shadow similar to Freud's concept of 'repression'?

  a Both involve pushing powerful or difficult aspects of ourselves out of conscious awareness

  b Both involve us not relating to others healthily

  c Both require us to withdraw from social contact

  d Both involve staying in the dark so we don't cause harm to anyone else

7 What does Jung mean when he says shadow is 'a moral problem'?

  a Others will make moral judgements about our shadow if we cannot hide it

  b We will make moral judgements about other people's shadow if they cannot hide it

  c It takes considerable moral effort to face our shadow and acknowledge it

  d It takes considerable moral effort to keep our darker side within shadow

8 What is shadow projection?

  a We project into our shadow to avoid exposing our weaknesses

  b We project our shadow aspects on to others and think they belong to them, not us

  c Where we are walking with a light behind us and our shadow projects in front of us

  d Where our shadow projects into the future and creates confusion about it

9 What is our 'golden shadow'?

  a Where our shadow has a fringe of sunlight around it

  b Where we reveal our shadow side to someone and, surprisingly, they like it

  c Aspects of our personality that are effective at dealing with shadow

  d Aspects of our potential we have not lived out, as they are trapped in shadow

10 When can shadow and persona work together to support individuation?

    a   When persona uses shadow elements to trick others

    b   When shadow hides behind persona to protect itself

    c   When a worn-out persona falls away and an authentic one emerges, drawing on shadow

    d   When shadow dissolves and turns into a number of personas

7

Anima and *animus*: inner partners or adversaries?

This chapter gives an overview of Jung's ideas on the presence of feminine and masculine influences in the human psyche. His notions of *anima* as the feminine in men and *animus* as the masculine in women are explained and applied via case studies and reflective exercises. There is an initial consideration of whether these are relevant or otherwise to current analytic practice and to personal development. This includes an investigation into the question: was Jung sexist?

Contra-sexuality: personal and collective

There has been long-standing criticism of the way Jung characterized the differences between the feminine and the masculine, especially how he portrayed this in terms of essential distinctions between men and women (e.g. Goldenberg, 1976). We will look at these criticisms more closely in this chapter, as they can help to explain why Jungian thinking is swiftly discounted in some quarters. Here, Jung's name can become shorthand for retrograde attitudes, towards women in particular. However, there is much more to Jung's work in this area and real value to his attempts to draw on gender to provide insight into psyche's workings.

As Susan Rowland (2002, p. 93), who writes about the value of Jungian approaches for feminist perspectives, puts it, Jung is now perceived by some to: '...connect to progressive debates on gender'. How has this broadening of perspectives on the value of Jungian theory regarding the influence of gender come about? We address this question in this chapter and in Chapter 20, where we will consider the relevance of post-Jungian ideas on 'gendered otherness' for contemporary thinking on culture, politics and society.

We start with some crucial terms and definitions in this area of Jungian thinking. The term **contra-sexuality** literally means 'opposite' sex/gender and suggests that, within the binary (where 'binary' refers to the duality or 'two-ness' of a relationship) of the male–female relationship, each carries the opposite within them. Put more simply, for Jung, each man carries an image and influence of the feminine within them, and each woman likewise carries an image and influence of the masculine. In saying that this applies to all of us, Jung is again referring to something *archetypal*. He took names from Latin to represent these archetypal dynamics. For the feminine in men Jung applied the term **anima**, and used **animus** for the masculine in women.

Anima and *animus*

Jung's upbringing in the conservative atmosphere of early twentieth-century Switzerland (see Chapter 2) meant that his approach was inevitably influenced by the monolithic thinking of that time and place, heavily seasoned by the mores of the Christian church. This was a purely heterosexual lens on relationships and gender identity (the idea, let alone the expression, of variances in sexuality, was not permissible). This came with a fixed notion of where man and woman each 'belonged' – he out in the world, making, achieving and protecting (in the worlds of business, government and the military); she firmly ensconced in the home (tending to the domestic environment, family and motherhood). This historical and cultural ambience permeates Jung's thinking on *anima* and *animus* but does not obscure the creative intelligence of their utility, in making sense of the complexity of being human.

Both terms in Latin allude to notions of the 'soul', but with feminine and masculine inflections, respectively. As Samuels et al. (1986, pp. 23–4) point out, Jung was trying to say something important about what these opposites represent and how this plays out in women and men. More than just soul images, Jung came to see *anima* and *animus* as each:

> 'the not-I. Being not-I for a man probably corresponds to something feminine, and because it is not-I, it is outside himself, belonging to his soul or spirit. The anima (or animus, as the case may be), is a factor which happens to one, an a priori element of moods, reactions, impulses in man; of commitments, beliefs, inspirations in a woman – and for both something that prompts one to take cognisance of whatever is spontaneous and meaningful in psychic life.'

We will explore Jung's distinctions hinted at here, between *anima* and *animus*. An important theme arising from Jung's ideas, which has enabled Jungian thinkers to work creatively with gender, is of *anima and animus* representing – as a further step beyond the discarded and unseen aspects of self in the *shadow* – the presence of the genuinely 'other' in the human psyche. *Anima* in man and *animus* in woman are unconscious opposites, but they can nonetheless be made more consciously available if we notice and work with them. From a post-Jungian perspective, it is often thought more helpful to see both *anima and animus* as present in both men and women, for example where a woman has unexpressed aspects of her identity, e.g. sexuality *(anima),* or a man likewise *(animus)* (Gordon, 1993).

Whichever formulation is used, the notion of 'inner-partner' or 'inner-partnership' (e.g. Sanford, 1980) provides much material to work with in terms of therapy and personal development. Jung formed the view that the two *contra-sexual others (anima and animus)* could be observed at work in their differentiated ways in the women and men he encountered in the hospital and private-practice spheres of his professional life, as well as in the general issue and flow of human activity and relations to be found in day-to-day life. He also linked these concepts to the crucial influence of *mother* and *father*. How a son experienced *mother* would reflect and inform the presence of the feminine *(anima)* within him. Likewise this formula pertained to a daughter's relation to father and the masculine *(animus)* within her. In turn, this would inform how the *anima* or *animus* got projected on to the later partner chosen for a long-term heterosexual relationship. Descriptions of how *anima and animus* (according to Jung) operate in practice will be given.

From his personal and professional insights, Jung came to view *anima* and *animus* as the gatekeepers to the collective unconscious, which enable us to access its archetypal processes and imagery. In terms of location in the human psyche, they sit between the area occupied by the more active players in the human psyche (persona/ego/shadow) and the territory of the collective, as shown in the following diagram. The *self* straddles all aspects of psyche, as well as being its centre.

Through interior 'voyages' into his own unconscious, Jung was struck by the prominence of feminine and masculine figures he met on his travels. This comes across in *The Red Book* (Jung, 2009), where the appearances of Elijah are counterbalanced by those of Salome, each seeming to point to archetypal polarities in the human psyche around different versions of wisdom: truth-seeking higher religiosity in Elijah's masculine manifestation; and the bringing of Eros and bodily based feminine spirituality in the shape of Salome. Certainly, Salome could be seen as a manifestation of Jung's *anima*, and if one applies a post-Jungian lens to Elijah, he may represent unexpressed *animus* aspects of Jung's identity.

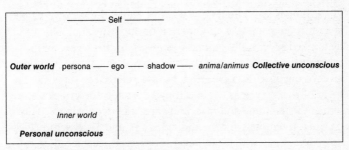

Anima, animus and the human psyche

In some ways, *anima and animus* are elusive, like the *self*. We experience encounters with these where ego needs to redirect its focus, or when the numinous unexpectedly breaks into our lived experience. To get in touch with *anima and/or animus*, we have to work hard on our self-knowledge. Jung posited that, analytically, we cannot properly get to 'meet' our contra-sexual opposite within until we have worked sufficiently on our personal *shadow*. This has to be sufficiently acknowledged and integrated first, otherwise we will not be able to 'see' through our own darkness. By gatekeepers to the collective unconscious, it is implied that *anima* and *animus* are archetypes of the feminine and masculine, which enable us to experience an awareness of the depth and scale of this archetypal layer. Jung puts it thus:

> 'They evidently live and function in the deeper layers of the unconscious, especially in that phylogenetic substratum which I have called the collective unconscious. This localization explains a good deal of their strangeness: they bring into our ephemeral consciousness an unknown psychic life belonging to a remote past. It is the mind of our unknown ancestors, their way of thinking and feeling, their way of experiencing life and the world, gods and men.'
>
> Jung, 1968, para. 518

Here, Jung is also alluding to what he called the **syzygy**, which is a term referring to a conjunction of opposites, but which he applied specifically to *anima–animus*. In this sense, the relationship itself between the two is also archetypal. At a deep level of unconscious operation, he also referred to the ideal form of this syzygy as the 'androgyne' – which describes a state where the feminine and masculine are in perfect balance. This provides a template for the individuation and analytic processes, though it is one which can never be 'perfectly' achieved, in this imperfect world.

When we are able to notice and work with our 'inner partner' (*anima* for a man and *animus* for a woman) – say, via work with images of the masculine or feminine in our dreams – then we have a powerful resource available to facilitate our personal growth and individuation. However, when we are not conscious of their influence on us, this might spark unconscious activity that is challenging and at times disruptive to our most intimate personal relationships. Here, the *anima and animus* of each partner (in Jung's formulation heterosexual, but these ideas can equally be applied to same-sex and bisexual relations) can clash in a maelstrom of unconscious energies.

As Jung (1968a, para. 31) powerfully observes: 'The anima/animus relationship is always full of 'animosity', i.e. it is emotional, and hence collective... often the relationship runs its course heedless of its human performers, who afterwards do not know what happened to them.'

Discussion about gender is charged with the risk of stereotyping and over-generalization about possible distinctions between men and women. The key here is to hold on to the importance of *archetypal* process with regard to the continuum between the feminine and the masculine and how that can present in a myriad and mixture of forms. The richness this can offer can sometimes be lost in our reactions to assertions about gender, and the fear of falling into essentialist stereotyping. As we go on to explore Jung's formulations of *anima and animus,* I invite you to notice your reactions and responses to these, and allow for all possibilities in thinking about 'inner' and 'outer' gender, plus influences on your own life experience in this area. This should help you make sense of at least some of the complex and at times contentious ideas in this area of the Jungian framework.

ANIMA

As mentioned already, *anima* refers in Jung's original formulation to the presence of the feminine in a man. This 'otherness' can show itself through his ways of relating to himself and how he *behaves* in personal relationships and wider social activity. 'She' also reveals herself in images of women, or creatures or objects associated with the feminine – to be found in dreams or in the imagination – for example, the idealized lover, a heroine such as a famous female political leader (positive), or an unreliable or rejected lover or helpless girl (negative).

Negative *anima* at work

Jung reported a young male patient who spontaneously produced drawings depicting his mother, first as superhuman and then as a mutilated and distressed figure (Jung, 1968b). This seemed to reflect the man's process of first idealizing the mother, and life in general, and then coming down to earth with a bump, as he grew up. He then struggled to come to terms with the mundane reality of life. Here, *anima* is strongly wrapped up with a mother complex, and is showing herself in polarized (idealized vs degraded) imagery. But this insight into the man's *anima* problem gave Jung the basis of a crucial understanding into this patient's situation and therefore helped the analytic process. What Jung would term *negative anima* is at work here. We will now look at what Jung believed we could observe where either positive or negative *anima* present.

▶ Positive *anima*: life-giving, feminine 'soul'

Anima, where it constellates in a positive way, enables what Jung saw as the traits readily available to women to likewise become available to a man. Qualities such as tenderness, patience, care, consideration, kindness and compassion may be activated in the man. Again, it is worth bearing in mind the time in which Jung was formulating these ideas, because to us it may be obvious that men should be as capable of offering these qualities as women anyway. However, early twentieth-century Europe was much more reliant on attitudes towards gender which split capacities and qualities in a 'black-and-white' way between women and men. This informs Jung's approach and is seen most baldly in the way he allocated the domain of 'thinking' to men and that of 'feeling' to women, something which got his approach into difficulty, as we shall see. However, in relation to positive *anima*, this explains why the positive attributes he associates with it are connected to feeling and relating, as his perception was that, in general, men were more disconnected from these areas than women.

For Jung, a man who is able to contact his capacity for feeling and empathy (though he did not use the latter word) would be healthily in touch with his *anima* and able to draw on her presence to resource his offer of care and consideration towards others. This means that the *anima* is the 'inner partner' who provides the complementary qualities to the man's (so-called) natural capacity for logical and useful thinking. More profoundly than this, however, is the notion of *anima* as 'soul'. This relates to the point made about the contra-sexual 'other' as gatekeeper to the collective unconscious. For Jung, *anima* brings life to the psyche of a man (literally represented by his passage into life via his mother). In his thinking, 'she' made it possible for a man to get in contact with his spiritual maturation, particularly in midlife as he begins to turn inwards and work on the deeper soul demands and possibilities.

Spotlight: James Hillman on *anima*

A key thinker heavily influenced by Jung's ideas about archetypal influences, James Hillman (1979) applied the influence of *anima* to both genders, but concurred with Jung's premise that *anima* provides access to the work of the soul, and was therefore a crucial player in the psyche. There is more on Hillman's ideas, rooted in archetypal psychology, in Chapter 19.

▶ Negative *anima*: self-sabotage through feeling?

If positive *anima* draws on the best attributes of how Jung characterized the feminine, then the negative version pulled on the opposite, and manifested itself in a man's way of relating to himself and others. This is where Jung got himself into more awkward territory, which he then followed to a logical but unhelpful conclusion in his framing of negative *animus* (see below). He perceived the negative feminine, in what now seems a big generalization (not to mention an uncomfortable one), as relating to characteristics such as: vanity, moodiness, promiscuity, bitchiness and over-sentimentality. He described negative *anima* within this frame of reference:

'When the anima is strongly constellated she softens the man's character and makes him touchy, irritable, moody, jealous, vain, and unadjusted. He is then in a state of "discontent" and spreads this discontent all around him.'
Jung, 1968b, para. 144

The negative *anima* therefore sabotages a man's capacity to think straight and to engage at a feeling level. Instead, he is flooded by exaggerated and over-sensitive emotions, which affect his relationships. Here, *anima projection* can creep in, in unhelpful ways:

▶ If he is in a close relationship with a woman, she may catch the projections of his moodiness or irritability, through him blaming her for these very traits which he is unable to notice in himself and deal with.

▶ He may become jealous for no good reason as a projection on to her of *his* tendency towards promiscuous activity or fantasies. This correlates with the idea that we may fall in love with someone who personifies our *anima* (negative or positive); and the same applies to *animus*.

ANIMUS

Animus operates generally to the same principles in women as *anima* does in men, according to Jung. That is, it provides a presence of the 'opposite' to a woman's characteristics and interacts with other features of psyche such as ego, self and shadow, to generate ways of operating in the world, and responding to others. *Animus* likewise presents himself in image form – in women's dreams and imagination in the shape of male figures and masculine imagery: for example, the idealized lover or a hero such as famous male political leader (positive), or an unreliable or rejected lover or helpless boy (negative).

Like *anima*, *animus* can therefore act as a resource to reveal aspects of unconscious activity and meaning for a woman, highlighting what her masculine attributes have to offer, as well as where they may be undermining her.

Spotlight: Was Jung sexist?

In developing the concept of *animus*, Jung found himself making generalizations about women and their attributes and behaviours that at times are thoroughly out of tune with contemporary Western and feminist perspectives. He was convinced women were dominated by the eros principle (i.e. feelings), while men were strongly influenced by thinking (logos). Following the 'logic' of this line of thinking, combined with the traditionalist beliefs about gender and gender roles which dominated the society in which Jung had grown up in, led him to make assertions that to us might seem at the very least awkward, and possibly shocking in places. For example, he asserted that men had to do women's thinking for them. He thought clear thinking was generally beyond women's capacity – as it would be infused with feeling and therefore would be skewed by emotions and uninformed conclusions.

Here again, one can see where 'essentialist' social perspectives on gender roles (where there are seen to be fixed 'essences' to being a man or a woman) affected Jung's thinking. The presumption was that women were, in the main, one step removed from the intellectual and vocational streams of thought 'out there' in the world, while they tended to domestic responsibilities inside the home. But where he asserts that a woman's 'Logos is often a regrettable accident' (Jung, 1982, p. 171), it appears dismissive, if not insulting.

However, as Susan Rowland (2002, p. 41) points out, Jung makes such misogynist distortion(s) about women and negative *animus* through his own subjective viewpoint, which in turn is strongly coloured by *his* negative *anima*. As she also points out, he makes it clear in his writings that he is aware of this problem. These are views which, using his own formula, are tinged with oversensitivity and charged with unhelpful emotional energy. (The influence of his mother complex is also suggested.) That does not excuse sloppy – and what we may now see as sexist – thinking about women, but it does help to explain why Jung got himself into difficulty alongside his innovations about contra-sexual influences.

▶ **Positive *animus*: spirit and mind**

As Jung explains, in its positive form, *animus* 'gives to women's consciousness a capacity for reflection, deliberation and self-knowledge.' (Jung, 1966, para. 33). He uses the symbol of father as representative of this, where a father is able to (he says) distinguish between conventional wisdom and his own ideas, based on informed knowledge of philosophy and culture.

This *positive animus* quality, for Jung, provides a counterbalance to what he saw as a tendency in women to follow collective ideas from society (e.g. through newspapers) and not form a distinct view of their own (!). Again, in the face of this awkward perspective (to put it politely), hold in mind the historical and social context in which he took this view. This capacity to be self-informed also arises for Jung from the notion of *animus* as 'spirit', not unlike *anima* as 'soul', except that, for women, the unconscious offers the capacity for using one's mind more fully and skilfully through the presence of *positive animus*.

This also reflects an observation Jung made about women's dreams; he thought *animus* tended to appear in a collective form – a group of men, or male animals, and so on. So, the presence of 'spirit' could support the efforts of a woman to distinguish herself from the collective by pointing out in dreams where she might need to become more individual (or individuated), so becoming more self-informed in her dealings with the world. As you may have noticed, the awkward tinge of presumption about women's capacity to think independently is evident, even where Jung is writing about *positive animus*.

▶ **Negative *animus*: opinions and emotions**

We have already got a sense of the difficulty around this side of *animus*, where Jung applied it to women's ways of thinking and relating. For example, he thought: 'in women it expresses itself in the form of opinionated views, interpretations, insinuations and misconstructions, which all have the purpose (sometimes attained) of severing the relations between two human beings' (Jung, 1966, para. 32). It is important to mention here that Jung felt that both negative *anima* and negative *animus* have this capacity to damage relationships. However, in the case of negative *animus*, the emphasis is more on faulty thinking, rather than feeling, doing the damage – although it is the infusion of thinking with strong emotions that Jung felt lent it the potentially destructive flavour. Although his wife Emma Jung (1957) wrote well about *animus*, including the negative side, the sense of this being an idea tarnished with traditional misogynistic views has never left it.

Negative *animus* at work

A woman who ran a small voluntary organization helping children from low-income families and unsettled backgrounds had a reputation for being very efficient, as well as being a passionate defender of the rights of the children she helped to look after. She also got into confrontations with local politicians and policy-makers. When she criticized a well-respected politician for 'not caring one iota for children' when a funding bid was turned down (despite that politician having previously helped acquire funding for the organization), this created a storm in the local paper.

In Jung's formulation, she had spoken from her *negative animus*.

Anima and *animus* – still relevant?

It is important to note that either of the case studies could have been describing a man or a woman; we can all be over-sentimental, or unhelpfully opinionated. However, what Jung was trying to do was make sense of possible, subtle, distinctions in how men and women experience themselves and their relationships. His thinking on this can appear outdated and unacceptable.

However, this framework has provided the basis for innovative approaches in psychotherapy and personal development, as well as valuable contemporary thinking on the internal and external impacts of gendered and sexed identity.

Key idea: Jung and the gender debate

Jungian writers continue to debate the way Jung thought about gender. A possible developmental schema (Goss, 2010) highlights how anima and animus may influence subtle areas of difference in the life path of females and males. A critique by Barone-Chapman (2014, p. 17) of how both Freud and Jung approached thinking about gender offers this interesting thought about Jung: 'he read into the reproduction of gender performance and culture *as if* his identification of its contents was fact, confusing fears and fantasies with real women.' Such ideas reflect the problematic place of gender in Jung's thinking, but also the potential that Jungian and post-Jungian ideas have to offer to contemporary debates in this area.

Key terms

Androgyne: Archetypal blending of feminine and masculine, in perfect balance; an idealized state that cannot be attained but which acts as a model for individuation and analysis.

Anima: The feminine in men; also the 'soul'.

Animus: The masculine in women; also 'spirit/mind'.

Contra-sexuality: Literally, 'opposite' sex/gender, and in Jung's model the notion that within the psyches of women and men lies the opposite to their, bodily sexed, gender identity.

Syzygy: The conjunction, or 'yoking together' of archetypal opposites, applied to *anima and animus* by Jung, to denote their complementary as well as oppositional relationship.

Dig deeper

Barone-Chapman, M., 'Gender Legacies of Jung and Freud as Epistemology in Emergent Feminist Research on Late Motherhood', *Behavioural Sciences*, 4, 14–30 (2014)

Goldenberg, N., 'A feminist critique of Jung', *Signs, Journal of Women in Culture and Society*, 2:2, 443–9 (1976)

Gordon, R., 'Look! He has come through!', in *Bridges: Metaphor for Psychic Processes*, Ch. 23 (London: Karnac, 1993)

Goss, P., *Men, Women and Relationships, a Post-Jungian Approach: Gender Electrics and Magic Beans* (London: Routledge, 2010)

Hillman, J., *Anima* (New York: Spring,1979)

Jung, C. G., 'The Syzygy: Anima and Animus' in *Aion*, CW9ii, 2nd ed. (London: Routledge, 1966)

Jung, C. G., 'Conscious, Unconscious, and Individuation' in *The Archetypes of the Collective Unconscious*, CW9i, 2nd ed. (London: Routledge, 1968)

Jung, C. G., *Aspects of the Feminine*, ed. J. Beebe (London: Routledge Ark, 1982)

Jung, C. G., *Aspects of the Masculine*, ed. J. Beebe (London: Routledge Ark, 1989)

Jung, C. G., *The Red Book: The Reader's Edition* (London: Norton, 2009)

Rowland, S., *Jung: A Feminist Revision* (Cambridge: Polity Press, 2002)

Samuels, A., 'Gender, sex, marriage', in Samuels, A. (ed.), *Jung and the Post-Jungians*, Ch. 6 (London: Routledge, 1985)

Samuels, A., Shorter, B. and Plaut, F. (eds.), *A Critical Dictionary of Jungian Analysis* (London: Routledge, 1986)

Sanford, J., *The Invisible Partners: How the male and female in each of us affects our relationships* (Mawhah, NJ: Paulist Press, 1980)

Fact-check (answers at the back)

1 What does Jung's use of the term 'contra-sexuality' refer to?
- **a** The contradictions between masculine and feminine
- **b** The opposition between feminine and masculine archetypes
- **c** The presence of sexual contradiction in the female and male psyche
- **d** The presence of the feminine in men and the masculine in women

2 How did Jung define anima and animus?
- **a** Animus is the masculine 'soul' of women and anima the feminine 'spirit' in men
- **b** Anima is the feminine 'soul' in men and animus the masculine 'spirit' in women
- **c** Animus is the masculine 'soul' of men and anima the feminine 'spirit' in women
- **d** Anima is the feminine 'spirit' in women and animus the masculine 'soul' in men

3 Why are anima and animus the gatekeepers of the collective unconscious?
- **a** They are like passport control between the personal and collective unconscious
- **b** They don't let anything through from the collective unconscious
- **c** They can open up collective and archetypal imagery and processes to us
- **d** There are only two gateways so they each look after one of them

4 What did Jung say we must do before we can engage with our anima or animus?
- **a** Confront our shadow, work on it and integrate our awareness of it into consciousness
- **b** Let go of our ego completely, however dangerous that could be
- **c** Circumvent our shadow so that it does not get in the way of anima or animus
- **d** Bring together ego and self to create a route to anima or animus

5 What did Jung describe positive anima as offering a man?
   a Contact with his ability to think straight
   b Connection with his spirit and body
   c Connection with his feelings and soul
   d Contact between his ego and self

6 Jung described negative anima as leading a man to be overtaken by what?
   a Big ideas which could never be fulfilled
   b Moodiness and oversensitivity
   c Sexual instincts and desires
   d Sadness and depression

7 What idea were Jung's views on the capacities of women and men based on?
   a Men were dominated by 'logos' (thinking) and women by 'eros' (feeling)
   b Women regretted their thoughts and men regretted their feelings
   c Men were dominated by 'eros' (feeling) and women by 'logos'
   d Women regretted their feelings and men regretted their thoughts

8 What did Jung describe positive animus as offering a woman?
   a Contact with her capacity to feel
   b Connection with her soul and feelings
   c Connection between persona and the collective
   d Connection with her independent thoughts and spirit

9 Jung described negative animus as leading a woman to be overtaken by what?
   a Hopelessness and lethargy
   b Uncontained feelings
   c Irrational thoughts and judgements
   d A mother complex

10 What has been the positive legacy of Jung's work in this area?
   a It makes people more aware of their strengths and faults
   b It provides a model for 'otherness' in analysis, and opens up debate on self and gender
   c It offers a 'logical' challenge to feminism
   d It provides a way of narrowing ideas about identity so it's much clearer

8

From archetype to complex

We have already discussed the concepts of archetype and complex, since they are central to Jung's model of the psyche and inevitably arise in discussion of other key themes. However, in order to have a fuller understanding of how unconscious influences affect us, we need to explore them in more detail. In this chapter we will look more closely at the notion of the archetype, and how complexes are formed and charged with archetypal energy, as well as how they can affect individuals and relationships. The discussion is supported with a case study portraying how complexes operate, as a scene setter for looking at how we can work with them therapeutically. There is a preliminary link to Jung's ideas on personality types, as well as a reflective exercise for applying these ideas to ourselves.

Jung, archetype and complex

The development of Jung's approach to archetypal process and the notion of the complex have their roots in key personal and professional experiences, which have already been highlighted. In Chapter 2, we learned how his childhood and later experiences strongly informed his conviction that there are different layers to the unconscious, and that within the collective layer there are instincts, images and experiences rooted in the history of human development (which have a ubiquitous quality across all human cultures). His own dreams, from the 'giant phallus' dream aged three, through to the 'house' dream of 1907, threw up symbols which had their roots in depths beyond common personal experience, and which drew on the inheritance of hundreds of thousands of years of human development.

As we also saw in Chapter 3, Jung's work at the Burgholzi, and elsewhere, brought him closer to the firm view that such phenomena were present in the psyches of all people. This was vividly revealed in the psychotic presentations of patients who reported delusions, florid imagery and hallucinations; but it was also evident in the dreams and imaginations of his private patients (and those who populated Jung's life away from his clinical work). The link to *complexes* arose as he noticed archetypal patterns and other influences in how his patients' mental health problems presented, for example via word-association tests.

Through detailed recording of factors like words used, time taken to respond and excitability in motor and sensory nerves, he gradually established a way of revealing the combination of powerful archetypal and personal influences that could hold a person in a grip of strong, volatile or stuck emotions. This is where the notion of a *complex* arose: it was a way of depicting the mix of suffering, defences and fantasies that could stand in the way of a person's well-being. This crucial concept in Jungian psychology will be elucidated further after we have taken a closer look at how archetypes provide the collective root for the complex.

Archetypes: the collective and the personal

Jung did not come to use the term 'archetypes' until 1919. Before this, he had referred to notions such as 'dominants' in the collective unconscious (meaning elements in psychic life that seem to attract energy and then influence the individual). Earlier, he had described these as 'primordial images' (images that crop up everywhere in dreams, art, etc.). In both cases, Jung was striving to find terminology that captured the underlying power of influences which went beyond personal experience. He moved further away from Freud's emphasis on the libidinal (psychosexual) factors as exclusively determining a person's state of mind. Instead, he came to the view that it was the innate nature and structure of *archetypes* which held the power to deeply influence this.

Key idea: What is an archetype?

The crucial thing to state first is that an archetype is an *unknowable essence* that profoundly influences our experiences, but *not* the form this essence takes that we then become aware of – an instinct, image or experience. As he put it: 'The archetype is essentially an unconscious content that is altered by becoming conscious and by being perceived, and it takes its colour from the individual consciousness in which it happens to appear' (Jung, 1968, para. 6). The term 'archetype' is now a well-used term to describe familiar behaviours and phenomena, for example in popular films such as *Star Wars*, where polarities of light and dark, hero and villain are portrayed to dramatic effect, capturing our attention because of their archetypal resonance.

An archetype, then, is not, for example, the image of a house in Jung's dream described in Chapter 4 – rather, there is some kind of 'essence' to the dream image (which in itself is not knowable), which is archetypal about home/self/psyche. We can call this an 'archetypal image' but it is not the archetype itself. This has connections across collective experience, which would make an almost unlimited number of interpretations possible except for one important point. That is, the dream image has been generated through the psyche of one particular human being, in this case Jung, and so the constellation of the archetype in this case will be germane to the personal experience, nature and unconscious process of this dreamer. It then becomes possible to read in meanings relevant to the dreamer. In this case, it seemed to relate to a time in Jung's life when the possibilities of working with collective unconscious phenomena were opening up, and the contents of the different floors in the house were pointing to this.

This is what can make the presence of archetypal images in dreams so powerful, and we will return to this in Chapter 11. However, it is again important to emphasize that images are generated by the individual psyche and provide the 'clothes' by which the archetype's presence might be detected. They are not the archetype themselves. This point corresponds to Plato's *forms* and Kant's *noumenal* (see Chapter 3), which are unknowable in themselves but nonetheless *present*, and significantly influence the structuring of our experiences. Jung emphasized this distinction, but it can sometimes cause confusion.

Archetypal phenomena are not 'inherited', therefore, in the sense of an image, idea or experience being passed down from our forebears. Rather, the *potential* for each of us to experience something archetypal *is* inherited, because the innate archetypal structures lie in us, waiting to find their form in our lived experience. When they do so, they link across body and mind, as well as instinct and image, affecting us at every level. This can be described as '...an inherited mode of psychic functioning, corresponding to the inborn way in which the chick emerges from the egg... and the eels find their way to the Bermudas, in other words it is a "pattern of behaviour"' (Jung, 1976, para. 1,228).

Spotlight: The roots of the word

The etymology of the word 'archetype' can help us get hold of the significance of the word: 'arche' from the Greek meaning original and 'type' meaning to copy or stamp. The 'original' form lies in wait within us, and we can get 'stamped' by the original archetype where experience, instinct or image brings it to life. So, when we fall in love, for example, the potential for this to happen lies within us, but it needs a person and the event of meeting them for this 'original' potential to be realized.

These patterns of behaviour most obviously translate in human terms to stages of development, which we all either pass through or have the potential to. Birth, childhood, adolescence, adulthood, old age and death are the obvious examples. Some archetypal life experiences, such as parenthood, will not be experienced by all, but are nevertheless archetypal templates which humanity shares with the natural world.

Other ways in which archetypes can be brought into life include manifestations via *role,* for example, in domestic terms, roles such as mother, father, sister, brother; or, in more generic and cultural terms, roles such as hero, victim, wise old man/woman, scapegoat, and so on. Archetypes come to life inside us, too. Jung identified the archetypal figures of psyche, as we have been finding out about in the previous chapters: *ego, self, persona, shadow, anima, animus*. One could also describe an array of feeling states as archetypal, as we can all experience them: love, hate, happiness, sadness, anger, boredom, etc. Bodily states likewise: sleep, alertness, tension, relaxation, illness, health. More conceptually and imaginatively, there are also archetypal realizations in religious and magical forms (as found in the myths, stories and fairy tales of different cultures and religions): gods, goddesses, demons, fairies, monsters. Other kinds of archetypal manifestation are to be found in the world of nature: the four seasons, the solar and lunar cycles, and so on. Archetypal influences can therefore be found all around, and within, us.

Spotlight: Peter Pan as *Puer aeturnus*

An archetype Jung saw as an important influence on some people is the 'eternal child' (*Puer aeturnus* in its male form, and *Puella aeturna in the* female). This is the archetype of the child who always wants to stay that way and never grow up. Some adults, Jung believed, get caught like Peter Pan, in a kind of psychological 'Neverland', where they want to stay for ever and avoid the responsibilities and challenges of adulthood. The positive side of the archetype is the availability of playfulness and creativity.

The notion of archetypes can also be mapped across to scientific studies, as we shall see in Chapter 16. The key point in terms of understanding how influential, though unseen, archetypes are in our lives is conveyed here:

> '*archetypes are not only disseminated by tradition, language, and migration, but... they can re-arise spontaneously, at any time, at any place and without any outside influence.*'
>
> (Jung, 2003, p. 12)

Spotlight: Reflective exercise

To help you grasp and apply the notion of 'archetypes', try the following:

1 Find a quiet space and sit comfortably with your eyes closed, taking slow, deep breaths.
2 Allow your mind to clear.
3 Hold in mind the idea of finding a fictional character you are drawn to or react strongly to (from a film, TV, a book or a play).
4 Once you have found this figure, slowly open your eyes.
5 When you are ready, draw or write something on paper which reflects this character.
6 Be spontaneous about it (it does not matter about 'being artistic or not'; it is the process of revealing something on the edge of your conscious awareness that matters).
7 Spend a few minutes reflecting on why this character has the impact on you they do.
8 What features, attributes, values and failings do they have? Notice if any of these show through in your personality,

relationships and ways of experiencing life. Play with the idea that these may be archetypal influences which structure at least some aspects of you.

9   If you need a tool to help you end the activity and come back into the 'day-to-day', write two lists – first, 'How am I similar to this figure?' and second, 'How am I different from them?' The second should help remind you that the chosen figure is *not* you.

This activity, and the examples given above, should have shown you the ubiquity of archetypal influences in our lives. Where they become more insidious and powerful within the psyche, they are very difficult to contend with because they are drawing on elemental energy which, through its very elusiveness, can present us with the illusion that we are in control of our feelings, thoughts and behaviours, when in fact we are not master of our own house. This latter description accurately applies to the situation where we are in the grip of a *complex*, charged with archetypal energy. This link between archetype and complex will emerge more clearly as we explore the nature and influence of complexes, below.

'The Wounded Healer'

Jung applied the archetypal notion of 'The Wounded Healer' to psychotherapists. He drew on the Greek myth of Chiron, who sustained an incurable injury after Hercules fired an arrow at him and, to overcome the pain he suffered, he decided to provide healing to others. Jung saw this as a very important archetypal principle, which therapists need to stick with in two respects:

✻   Firstly, this is important from the point of view of not denying or avoiding their own wounds when they are activated by interaction with an analysand.

✻   Secondly, Jung pointed out the risk of an analyst becoming inflated by their capacity to heal and overvaluing themselves in a potentially dangerous way. The wound, which reminds the therapist of their weakness and vulnerabilities, provides a good antidote to this and so helps them stay grounded and

balanced in their view of themselves and
their work.

Research (Barr, 2006) has demonstrated Jung's belief that people train to be psychotherapists principally because of the psychological wounds they sustained earlier in their lives, which then generates a compensatory wish to tend to the wounds of others. Barr found that 79 per cent of therapists she asked via a questionnaire had experienced a wound (e.g. abuse, bereavement) earlier in their lives.

This archetypal term utilized by Jung is now in common parlance across professions that have a healing function, not just counselling and psychotherapy. The term has even been adopted in another way by Jungian thinker Robert Romanyshyn (2007), who has written about *the wounded researcher*, as being relevant to the explorations of unconscious influences arising from psychological wounds sustained during our lives. He argues these provide a valuable resource to open up the deeper influences on us as we research areas of study which we find ourselves drawn to. In this sense, the unconscious plays a key role in choices researchers make, not just psychotherapists.

Complex and its influence on the psyche

As we have seen, Jung's work on the word-association tests he carried out at the Burgholzi moved his thinking towards trying to find a way of describing what happens when strong emotions grip the psyche, sometimes tipping people into states of disorientation or despair. The use of the tests strongly suggested the presence of unconscious processes which have great power over the human mind, as these processes seemed to be able to block access to thoughts and memories as well as overwhelm with feelings. He would come to the view that, whatever we called it, something powerful was able to take charge of our psyches and determine how we responded to life and its various challenges. Somehow a kind of autonomous 'other' is able to set up shop in us and expose us to emotional influences leading us into irrational and sometimes self-destructive patterns of behaviour.

Jung plumped for the term 'complex' to describe this somewhat mysterious influence, as it captured its literal *complexity* and influence. So how might we try to describe what a complex is and how it links to the archetypal? Samuels et al. (1986, p. 34) provide us with a clear definition as a starting point:

'A complex is a collection of images and ideas, clustered around a core derived from one or more archetypes, and characterized by a common emotional tone. When they come into play (become constellated), complexes contribute to behaviour and are marked by affect, whether a person is conscious of them or not. They are particularly useful in the analysis of neurotic symptoms.'

This helps to establish the picture of a complex as containing a mix of influences and factors, underpinned by archetypal influences that provide its deeply rooted core in the psyche. One way to envisage how pervasive a complex is is to use the metaphor of the moon again. As it orbits the earth, we can imagine the moon as the *ego* and the earth as *self*. When 'all is right with the world', the ego is in a balanced relationship to the self, literally 'in its orbit', taking heed of its place in relation to the 'bigger' celestial body of the self. If you then imagine a rogue planet, moon or asteroid coming in close to this balanced dyad, the gravitational pull of the 'space invader' is going to throw this balanced set-up out of kilter, pulling the 'moon' ego towards it (see the diagram below). This is how a complex interrupts the natural rhythm of the ego–self dynamic, pulling

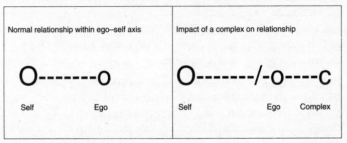

The impact of a complex on ego and self

the ego as well as the link to self (the 'ego–self axis') out of synch and allowing the psyche to become strongly influenced, if not dominated, by the complex. This is a way of envisaging how 'other', and autonomous, a complex is.

We will look at some examples shortly, but to further enunciate the model described in the quote above we can identify the following key factors at work to create the conditions for the formation of a complex:

1 Current influences and situation

2 Environmental and historical influences

3 Predominant personality traits

4 Archetypal energy, which constellates problematically when 1–3 come together

The good doctor

A middle-aged man was devoted to his work as a doctor, partly because he genuinely felt 'called' to provide a healing role to others, but also because it seemed to fulfil a need in him to be valued and praised by people. At times there seemed something a little narcissistic (or self-promoting) about this. He would enjoy coming home from work and recounting to his partner what everyone he had helped that day had said about him. She got a little fed up with this and told him to 'get over himself'. This provoked a huge outburst of anger and hurt from him. His over-sensitive *anima* problem was linked to a *mother complex*. He had been born and raised in India and his mother had doted on him as a growing boy, while his father had been barely present, serving in the military so away a lot of the time. When he was eight his sister was born and his mother shifted the focus of her attention more on to her baby, although she was still affectionate and admiring towards him whenever she could be.

For him, though, this change had been significant and difficult. Although he knew his mother still loved him, he was no longer the only apple of her eye. He developed strategies to get her adoring look and approving words whenever he could, and if she was being particularly attentive to his sister, he would do things like pick flowers or vegetables in the garden and bring them in, unbidden, to his mother. Or he would offer to look after his sister so his mother could have a rest. There was almost a sense of him trying to fill his father's shoes, and his love for his mother ran very deep, something which his partner now found difficult at times, especially when he would compare his mother's care for him to hers. He would do this sometimes when he slipped into *negative anima* and felt she was not appreciating the importance of the work he did for his patients. Here, one could see the environmental and developmental impact of his childhood around both the real and the internalized relationship he'd had with his mother. This was a key influence on his *mother complex.*

Another influence in a complex is **personality type**, an area we will look at in detail in the next chapter. Jung came to the view people were dominated by certain registers of functioning. In this case study we are considering a man who seemed dominated by his **feeling function**. He tended to experience the world, and especially relationships, through this function. When situations became highly charged, his thinking and perceptions of others became dominated by feelings. This explains his seeking out of a feeling of being valued or prized as 'special', as well as his over-reaction to not getting such responses.

There are also factors in the present which activate the complex. In this case study, whenever his need to be praised was not assuaged, this man seemed to be taken over by very sensitive, touchy, reactions; a kind of regressed protest against the unavailability of the delicious feeling of being adored by mother.

Finally, underneath these three factors is the archetypal core of the complex: 'mother' as a kind of goddess whose love this man must have. Jung wrote about this version of 'the great mother' in terms of how important it is, for a man in particular, to be 'delivered' from her, something which the doctor described in the case study was apparently far from achieving. Remember again, though: we are not describing archetype as 'thing in itself', more as something *archetypal* which structures experience of life via the complex and generates the emotional tone of the complex, which in this case was an over-sensitive response to hurt.

Archetypes, complexes, analysis

Jung initially called his overall approach 'complex psychology' because he saw his discovery of the workings of the complex as fundamental to the way in which analysis operates to address the underlying unconscious dynamics in it. Dissolving the analysand's dominating complex or complexes is a key task of analysis. Although he later shifted his stance and decided upon 'analytical psychology' to give it a more general title and reflect the breadth and depth involved in working with psyche, it is fundamentally the unveiling and analysis of the complex that characterizes the focus of therapy.

Spotlight: Cultural complexes?

Post-Jungian thinkers have built on Jung's interest in the *collective* and his observations about how whole communities and nations can find themselves in the grip of a complex (which then leads to all kinds of problems). An obvious example would be those movements of the twentieth century dominated by an overpowering set of principles and/or a powerful leader who embodied these. Fascist and communist ideology, as embodied for instance in the Nazi movement and Hitler in Germany, or the Cultural Revolution of Mao in China, are obvious examples. Joseph Henderson (1903–2007) posited such phenomena as 'cultural complexes', which are formed in a layer of the collective unconscious and able to activate chain reactions in how people respond to political and social influences. Singer and Kimbles (2004) and others have built on Henderson's concept, to apply this to a range of current political, economic, social and cultural phenomena.

Key terms

Archetypes: Undefinable and ubiquitous 'essences', which nevertheless structure human experience, such as via life stages or roles.

Complex: A powerful, autonomous influence that forms in the human psyche from current and past influences, personality factors and an archetypal core. This also has a common emotional tone, which strongly influences how a person responds to circumstances and relationships.

Personality type: A constitutionally generated influence that influences a person's way of experiencing, and relating to, themselves, others and the world (see Chapter 9).

Dig deeper

Barr, A. (2006), 'An investigation into the extent to which psychological wounds inspire counsellors and psychotherapists to become wounded healers', University of Strathclyde, accessed at http://www.thegreenrooms.net/wounded-healer/

Jung, C. G., 'Archetypes of the Collective Unconscious' in *The Archetypes and the Collective Unconscious*, CW9i (London: Routledge, 1968)

Jung. C. G., *The Symbolic Life*, CW18 (London: Routledge, 1976)

Jung, C. G., 'On the Concept of the Archetype' in *Four Archetypes* (London: Routledge Classics, 2003)

Romanyshyn, R., *The Wounded Researcher: Research with Soul in Mind* (New Orleans: Spring Books, 2007)

Samuels, A., Shorter, B. and Plaut, F. (eds.), *A Critical Dictionary of Jungian Analysis* (London: Routledge, 1986)

Singer, T. and Kimbles, S., *The Cultural Complex: Contemporary Jungian Perspectives on Psyche and Society* (Hove: Brunner-Routledge, 2004)

Fact-check (answers at the back)

1 What are archetypes?

  a The ubiquitously shared human images, instincts or behaviours themselves

  b The unknowable essence of patterns which get structured in image, instinct or behaviour

  c The knowable essence of our instinctive and behavioural reactions to images

  d The unknowable, random, pattern of our images, instincts or behaviours

2 What are two key philosophical influences on Jung's use of 'archetypes'?

  a Hegel's *dialectics* and Kant's *phenomenal*

  b Nietzsche's *eternal return* and Socratic *questioning*

  c Kant's *noumenal* and Plato's *forms*

  d *Neo-Platonism* and Nietzsche's *Uberman*

3 In what ways can archetypes influence our experience of life?

  a Through life stages, roles and cultural and religious manifestations

  b Through our beliefs, attitudes and achievements

  c Through types of personality

  d Through images of different types of arcs

4 Why did Jung identify the archetype of 'The Wounded Healer'?

  a His most challenging analysand was a spiritual healer

  b People who go for psychotherapy take their psychological wounds to be healed

  c When he fell out with Freud, they were both wounded

  d People choose to be psychotherapists because they have been wounded earlier in life

5 What factors come together to create a complex?

  a Shadow and the contra-sexual 'other'

  b Ego forms the core and that is surrounded by persona problems

  c Personality and past factors, the present situation and an archetypal core

  d Personality type, past factors and the ego-self axis archetype.

6 What other factor binds a complex together?
  a A common archetype
  b A common emotional tone
  c An axis between ego and complex
  d Archetypal personality influences

7 Why does a complex have particular power?
  a It is autonomous and unconscious
  b It is full of psychosexual energy
  c It has at least three archetypes inside it
  d It consciously controls us

8 What is the difficult link sometimes seen in mother or father complexes?
  a Activation of shadow
  b Activation of ego
  c Activation of self
  d Activation of negative anima and/or animus

9 What is a personality type?
  a A person with a strong personality
  b An inner influence on personality
  c An outer influence on personality
  d A kind of complex

10 Why did Jung initially call his approach 'complex psychology'?
  a Because of the significance of complexes to his theory and practice
  b Because he thought Freud's theories were too simplistic
  c Because that was the only thing he thought analysis is about
  d Because of his own complexes

9

Jung's typological model

Jung observed differences in how people behaved and interacted, suggestive of differing types of personality. His model features an *introversion–extraversion* dynamic and a hierarchy of functions. This chapter explains how Jung's work on word association and complexes led him to create his typological model, which is a framework for describing how personality types impact on human motivation, behaviour and pathology. We will explore Jung's notions of *introversion* and *extraversion* and then relate these to his theory of four functions of personality: *thinking, feeling, intuition and sensation.* The framework on psychological types is explained in detail, with a case study and reflective activity.

Personality: *tabula rasa* or constitutional factors?

Jung's work at the Burgholzi did not just alert him to the ways in which the unconscious operated to keep emotionally charged material at arm's length from conscious awareness. His work on complexes highlighted distinctions between individuals, which he thought must be more than purely the result of environmental factors. His answer to the much-debated question of whether we are born as a 'blank slate' (*tabula rasa* in the Latin), or if there are already established constitutional factors, was a clear one. For Jung, fundamental personality characteristics are already established when we are born.

Whether or not you agree with Jung's point of view, the idea that certain personality factors may play a key role in making us 'who we are' is one worth exploring, as it can provide us with a fresh lens through which to consider aspects of our own being and behaviour that may intrigue or challenge us.

Spotlight: The introversion–extraversion dynamic

As you may remember, Jung became convinced in his childhood that his being housed not just one personality, but two. Number one was outward facing, or *extraverted*, and reflected where he was in life: a boy struggling to get to grips with the world's expectations. Number two, on the other hand, was inward looking and psychologically and spiritually mature – so mature, in fact, that Jung experienced him as an 'old man who belonged to the centuries' (Jung, 1963, p. 87) and where his intuitive and feeling life held sway. This introverted personality looked inwards and paved the way for the encounters he would have with his unconscious after the split with Freud.

While Jung would recognize environmental factors as important, he would see both number one and number two personalities as having their roots in something fundamentally *him*. Likewise his emphasis when applying these ideas more generally to all of us: there is something which makes you *you*, alongside all the environmental factors at work.

Jung explained how the influence of the introversion–extraversion dynamic worked in the following way, where the subject is the person and the object whatever they are relating to at a given time (another person, a job, the world in general):

> 'the introverted standpoint is one which sets the ego and the subjective psychological process above the object... This attitude therefore, gives the subject a higher value than the object... The extraverted standpoint, on the contrary, subordinates the subject to the object, so that the object has the higher value.'
>
> Jung, 1971a, para. 6

Jung's emphasis on *value* is important here, because it suggests a kind of magnetic field at work between the wider world and the individual psyche, and which at different points in life, or in different contexts, will draw us either outwards or inwards. He is also suggesting that people are not all affected by the introverted or extraverted 'gravitational pulls' in the same way; some people are more extraverted than introverted overall, in a way that affects definitively their whole life, and others vice versa. Extraverts are naturally drawn to, and motivated by, the external world, while the introvert is likewise influenced by the internal world.

An awareness of these more rooted personality emphases is helpful, according to Jung, because it helps explain why, for example, two siblings in the same family could be so different – one the gregarious and overtly ambitious extrovert, the other a shy and reflective introvert. Not only are such differences due to formative experiences, how they were parented, or whether they were older or younger than their sibling: it is because of *who they are*.

Jung also applied the principle of **compensation**, since he thought the unconscious of the person would always be striving to compensate for the one-sidedness of the conscious attitude. A strongly *extroverted* person would therefore have an overly *introverted* unconscious attitude: they will suppress subjective thoughts and feelings and this inner directedness of forgotten deeper influences can lead them to become egocentric, and even infantile, in their way of relating to others.

Likewise, a markedly *introverted* person is compensated, in the unconscious, for over-valuing their subjective experience by being exaggeratedly influenced by the very objects the person has consciously stood back from. So, the views of others and practical considerations (such as finance and career) can come to seem oppressive and deeply troubling.

As we explore further, bear in mind that Jung's descriptions can seem rather polarized at first glance. Many Jungian thinkers and practitioners would see the relationship between *introversion* and *extraversion,* for example, better described as a continuum, where a person may have a predominance in one direction or the other, but there will still be features of both *introversion* and *extraversion* present to some degree.

Key idea: Introversion vs extraversion

While Jung makes a case for the importance of our capacity to 'introvert' – to look inwards and foster a reflective, exploratory attitude towards the unconscious – it could be said that such an attitude does not equip us well for the tough realities of a competitive and often stressful world.

There is also the question of whether it is healthy for us to become too self-absorbed and the possibility that we may become withdrawn and isolated. However, writers such as Storr (1988) point out the value of solitude where it enables self-awareness and creativity to arise. Cain (2012) argues that the Western world has made a mistake in making extraversion the cultural ideal, and reminds us of the importance of the contribution introverted people have made to human progress.

Four personality functions

Jung identified four global functions which he thought impacted on how we each engage with life: thinking, feeling, intuition, and sensation. He labelled thinking and feeling as *rational* functions and intuition and sensation as *non-rational*, and visualized these as archetypal polarities on vertical and horizontal axes (see the diagram below). Each of us, for Jung, carries in us our own combination of these four functions, and will be dominated more by some than others. These influences could be positive or negative. Here is a brief description of each function, with applications given where either *introversion* or *extraversion* dominates.

Rational axis

Thinking

Non-rational axis Sensation ———+——— Intuition

Feeling

(**Note:** Functions at each axis end can be juxtaposed – so thinking is not 'higher' than feeling.)

THINKING

> 'Thinking is the psychological function which, following its own laws, brings the contents of ideation into conceptual connection with one another.'
> Jung, 1971b, para. 830

Jung's definition straightforwardly indicates what thinking is for – to know something and be able to link it to other things through ascribing names or associations to each thing involved. As such, this function is one that structures our experience and expectations of the outside world (a notion which could be related to the idea of schemas in cognitive psychology, though the latter tends to apply this to describe problematic psychological states where beliefs about self, others and the world tend to get too fixed (Hofman, 2011)).

▶ Extraverted thinking

Extraverted thinking, as the term implies, involves thoughts that are strongly influenced by what is 'out there': facts, views and ideas which come in from that which is objective to us (that is, not emanating from within our own minds). This is the kind of thinking associated with scientific, empirical investigation, as well as concretized, planned thinking. Jung gave Darwin as an example of an extraverted thinker who formed judgements from intellectual assessments of objective data. Extraverted thinking can also include the adoption of ideas and beliefs coming from outside us. Jung also pointed out the risk of overvaluing objectivity, denying feelings (so they are projected on to one's thoughts whereby their importance gets exaggerated), and overlooking the value of inner ideas and resources.

▶ **Introverted thinking**

In contrast, this type of thinking relies heavily on subjective experience and inner reality. Jung portrayed how this works in terms of an individual who feels a sense of there being something at work inside them which will define their judgement more significantly than outer reality. Here, facts from outside are more likely to be used to substantiate a judgement or theory, rather than the empirical accumulation of facts leading to a firm position being taken on the matter in hand. Jung used Kant, and his subjective critique of the nature of knowledge, as an example of this. The risk here is that an introverted thinker will lose a balanced perspective, because they are preoccupied with their discovered inner 'truths' and may invest their feelings in these, leading to a doctrinaire and self-absorbed way of working with ideas and facts.

FEELING

Jung regarded *feeling* as a function which influenced the *rational* aspects of human motivation and activity. This may seem like a contradictory notion because, in popular discourse, feelings are often regarded as *irrational* in terms of where they overwhelm us and seem to lead us into reactions and behaviours that are disproportionate and uncontained. However, Jung was not describing *emotion* here. His term for the latter – **affect** – helped to describe some of the phenomena presented through his word-association tests, which could indicate the presence and nature of a complex. Where sudden or powerful, bodily based emotion presented itself in response to a word, this gave valuable clues about that emotion. The Jungian application of feeling therefore refers to where we have control over our emotion/affect, and what we do with this: whether our tendency is to use this in an *extraverted* or *introverted* way.

▶ Extraverted feeling

In the same way that *extraverted thinking* refers to a tendency to form thoughts and views in response to what is outside of us, so *extraverted feeling* describes a tendency to feel in response to what happens around rather than within us. Jung gives the example of a person admiring a picture in the home of someone they are visiting, not in order to be acquiescent or even deferential, but rather because there is a genuine *extraverted feeling* impulse to generate or sustain a positive atmosphere with the host. *Extraverted feeling* is about putting feeling 'out there' to meet and connect with the values and perspectives of others. In this sense, collective values tend to be appreciated and accepted. The obvious drawback to this is that the capacity for individual judgement or thinking falls into the background. Jung postulated that the unconscious compensates for this through a build-up of thinking which is 'all or nothing'. In other words, if the person, group or set of ideas to which an *extraverted feeling* type has attached their affiliation in any way shows a flaw, then highly critical thoughts rob those involved of any value, not unlike when a public figure turns from being idealized to vilified by the press.

▶ Introverted feeling

Introverted feeling has an elusive quality to it, as it turns inwards and can 'hide' behind surface behaviours and ways of relating. Here is Jung trying to describe what it 'does':

> 'Its aim is not to adjust itself to the object, but to subordinate it in an unconscious effort to realize the underlying images... It glides unheedingly over all objects that do not fit in with its aim. It strives after inner intensity, for which the objects serve at most as a stimulus.'
>
> Jung, 1971c, para. 638

The emphasis is on seeking confirmation *outside* a feeling state *inside,* which can create the appearance of detachment or coldness in the relational style of the *introverted feeling* type, as they carefully observe those around them and 'take in' their experiences of them. Although Jung did not say as much, an implication is that this can generate the capacity to make contact with what is really happening under the surface, in and around them. He uses the term *sympathy* in relation to this, whereas a positive correlation of *introverted feeling* we could now frame in the capacity to be *empathic*: tuning into underlying feelings in others and experiencing them within. A more negative correlation is where thinking is strongly repressed, and anxieties about 'what others think' get projected outwards, and rather paranoid judgements can be made about them.

Spotlight: Typology and the *DSM*

Ekstrom (1988) has usefully applied Jung's typological framework to aspects of the *Diagnostic and Statistical Manual of Mental Disorders*, which is used to classify and guide treatment in psychiatric, and mental and general health contexts. Ekstrom related elements of Jung's model to presentations of personality disorder in the third version of this manual, *DSM III* (APA, 1980). This provided valuable links between personality traits described by Jung's framework and common traits found in disorders such as narcissistic and borderline personality disorders, demonstrating the relevance of Jung's innovative approach to contemporary psychology and psychiatry.

Further development of these links to later versions of the manual (*DSM IV* (2000) and *DSM V* (2013)) is awaited.

INTUITION

This function refers to the capacity to get a sense (or a 'hunch') about what might be happening under the surface of a person's or situation's presentation and how this could unfold: 'The intuitive function is represented in consciousness by an attitude of expectancy, by vision and penetration...' (Jung, 1971c, para. 610). Jung saw this as a valuable function, not least in support of meaningful therapeutic work, as it supports the therapist's capacity to 'tune in' to what is happening for the analysand, and within the deeper processes of the analysis generally.

▶ Extraverted intuition

The emphasis, as with the other non-rational function, *sensation*, is on an opening out of experience of what is outside us, to get hold of what could be possible. This then can become a guide for action. Jung referred to the way in which, when all options seem closed down in a situation, the *external intuitive* can spot a way through. At its most positive, *external intuition* is thus able to unlock resources, cultural, economic and personal, in the most difficult of circumstances. Inspirational leaders (such as Winston Churchill during the Second World War) seem to be in possession of this capacity, but this ability to intuit and enable positive change to occur (a kind of positive *trickster* quality) can equally be available in less prominent circumstances. The less positive aspects of *extraverted intuition* lie in how easily the 'putting out' of intuition into the wider world risks a perilous overlooking of self and a kind of 'giving away' of what one has, so others reap the benefit of what one has highlighted (for example in helping start up a business venture).

▶ Introverted intuition

The *introverted intuitive* directs their intuition inwards and similarly to their extroverted counterpart, focusing their energy on the possibilities inherent in the inner experiences and objects they encounter rather than on the impact of those experiences on themselves. They are constantly seeking out new discovery and possibility, including at the most archetypal levels of the psyche. It is no surprise to learn that Jung saw *introverted intuition* as a strength, bearing in mind all his interior journeying and encounters with the unconscious. His example suggests where this could evince profound insight and be beneficial in the analytic process, where the analyst can draw on their deeper intuitive responses to the analysand to support this.

On the other hand, *introverted intuition* represses sensation and so contact with reality is a problem. At times this can lead to uncertainty as to how real an experience is; Jung gives the example of vertigo, suggesting this would be recorded as an image of an experience rather than as an experience connected to self. To compensate, sensations can become repeatedly and compulsively experienced within the body, the unconscious somatizing what cannot be contacted meaningfully by generating 'phantom' pains/symptoms.

SENSING

As indicated, this is a non-rational function, which refers to what we experience via our senses, and through our body awareness more generally. This is where contact with physical reality is immediate, although the contact made does not always give us understanding – experiencing a shot of pain or a tickle, for example, does not tell us what it is we have made contact with. However, how well we are able to utilize sensory information and our body awareness to engage with life will vary individually.

▶ **Extraverted sensation**

'No other human type can equal the extraverted sensation type in realism. His sense for objective facts is extraordinarily developed. His life is an accumulation of actual experiences of concrete objects, and the more pronounced his type, the less use does he make of his experience.'

Jung, 1971c, para. 606

As our senses give us information about the objects and phenomena our body and bodily functions come into contact with, the *extraverted sensor* will thoroughly value the contact with any of them, whether this is a wholly pleasurable or excited valuing, or a powerfully negative or uncomfortable one. As Jung's words emphasize, it is the actual experience of these contacts, not their implications or meanings, which matter. Because of this formula, on the positive side, skilful practicality (e.g. making or mending things) and passionate sensuality can be associated with extraverted sensation. On the more negative side, addictions and a focus on gratification (e.g. sexual), as well as phobias about sensory experience (e.g. claustrophobia or arachnophobia) can likewise be associated with it. On a more practical level, effective use of physical skills may be more elusive.

▶ **Introverted sensation**

As may have suggested itself from the above, the *introverted sensor* is more concerned with the subjective processing of the experience of contact with objects rather than the actual phenomenological experience itself. This is fundamentally because of the person's unrelatedness to what is externally present, leading Jung to assert that such individuals might often present as apparently passive and self-controlled. It appears that the experience of, say, an insect bite will not have affected them at all. However, the automatic defence to deflect the impact of the experience away from conscious awareness does not make it disappear. Instead, it further fuels an opposing or compensatory subjective reliance on fantasy and the sustaining of an inner world which is somehow 'more important' than the real, outer one.

This can lead to the putting of intuitive capacities to more negative use in the real world, in some cases generating a compulsively neurotic state which really makes day-to-day life a trial. If the individual concerned can establish some kind of direct relationship with the external influence they have experienced through their senses, then a valuable balance can be struck between, say, noticing the reality of the insect bite's painful impact, and one's processing of the significance of the experience for oneself. Nurturing this capacity can enhance sensory and relational experiences, say those of a sexual nature, for the introverted sensation type.

The hierarchy of typological functions

Jung drew together the combination of functions and *introversion–extraversion* dynamics within a model that could provide a kind of *map* to 'read' the individual's typological functioning. This posited that each of us has the following four functions:

1 **Superior function** – as implied, our 'strongest card'; for Jung *extraverted thinking*

2 **Auxiliary function** – the function that supports superior; for Jung *introverted intuition*

3 **Tertiary function** – a weaker function but with some strengths; for Jung *extraverted sensation*

4 **Inferior function** – the weakest function, opposite to superior; for Jung *introverted feeling*

Jung proposed that on the opposite side of the axis inhabited by the superior function (here, the rational axis) was the inferior position. The inferior function is also linked to *shadow*. Likewise, the auxiliary and tertiary functions represent opposites on the other axis (here, the non-rational one).

Another key principle at play, as conveyed above, is how the *introversion–extraversion* dynamic alternates as one goes up or down the hierarchy. In working with this hierarchy in personal development or therapy, a key principle is to focus on strengthening our weaker functions while also utilizing our stronger ones; this is a support to the individuation process.

Typological functioning

To apply these principles briefly to the character of the doctor referred to in Chapter 8, we could postulate the following hierarchy of typological functioning:

Superior: introverted thinking

He was good at theorizing what was wrong with his patients, then diagnosing effectively.

Auxiliary: extraverted intuition

In support of the above, he would often find his hunches about diagnosis were right.

Tertiary: introverted sensation

Contact with people and objects took him time to process, so his responses could be initially passive.

Inferior: extraverted feeling

His image of himself as 'the healer' who everyone prized was easily shattered by the slightest criticism; and his 'all or nothing' perspective would generate his angry verbal attacks.

Typology in Jungian analysis

Some Jungian analysts draw on Jung's typological framework to make sense of the individual patterns in an analysand's behaviours and experiences. They will try to get a sense of what the typological hierarchy of the analysand might be, so as to note what needs working on (regarding their inferior function in particular). Or they may use it to gauge where their own typology may be similar to or different from that of the analysand; this could help to explain aspects of the dynamics between them (conscious and unconscious). Other analysts may not situate the place of typology so prominently in their work, but just hold it in awareness as the therapeutic process unfolds.

Reflective exercise

Having acquired an initial sense from this chapter of what Jung meant by each of the four functions and how they may present when they are *extraverted* or *introverted*, see whether you can do a 'mini case study' on yourself like the one above and try to generally identify your own typological 'hierarchy'. What might be your superior and inferior functions, and what might these tell you about you and the successes and difficulties you might have faced in your life?

JUNG'S TYPOLOGY IN BUSINESS
In organizational psychology and business, Jung's typological framework has been a strong influence. The collaboration between Katharine Cook-Briggs (1875–1968) and her daughter

Isabel Briggs Myers (1897–1980) took his model and worked it into a detailed system for the self-evaluation of personality strengths and weaknesses, in turn providing tools to aid staff recruitment and deployment strategies. The appeal of this model is wide; it is something which can be of general value in helping make sense of our personality traits, and differences, to other people (Briggs Myers, 1995). This illustrates in turn the originality of Jung's approach (however dated in some respects it can seem) to looking at the nature and significance of personality factors.

Applying typology to famous people

It can be interesting to speculate about the typology of famous people. For example, was Albert Einstein helped by having introverted thinking as his superior function (a great mind...)? Or was Margaret Thatcher, in contrast, able to dominate politics in the UK during the 1980s because of her superior extraverted thinking about politics and her auxiliary introverted intuition, which gave her hunches to help her decision making?

To get you started, many websites consider such questions, as well as providing versions of personality tests. However, information on the original model can be found at the site of the Myers & Briggs Foundation: www.myersbriggs.org/

Key terms

Extraversion–introversion: An archetypal polarity conveying the dynamics between extraversion and introversion.

Extraversion: Where motivations and responses are governed by external objects; a tendency towards outer experience and expression.

Introversion: Where motivations and responses are governed by internal influences; a tendency towards inner experience and expression.

Four functions: The four governing functions of personality (feeling, intuition, sensation and thinking).

Feeling: How we use, with rational awareness, our feeling states to relate outwards or inwards.

Intuition: How we use our sense of how a situation may unfold, related outwards or inwards.

Sensation: How we use our senses and embodied capacities, related outwards or inwards.

Thinking: How we use our cognitive capacities and processes, related outwards or inwards.

Typology: Jung's framework for describing how personality types impact on human motivation, behaviour and pathology.

Dig deeper

American Psychiatric Association, *Diagnostic and Statistical Manual of Mental Disorders III* (Arlington, Va: APA, 1980)

Briggs Myers, I., *Gifts Differing: Understanding Personality Type* (Sunnyvale, CA: Davies-Black, 1995)

Cain, S., *Quiet: The power of introverts in a world that can't stop talking* (London: Penguin, 2012)

Ekstrom, S., 'Jung's typology and DSM-III personality disorders: a comparison of two systems of classification', *Journal of Analytical Psychology,* 33(4), 329–53 (October 1988)

Hofmann, S. G., *An Introduction to Modern CBT: Psychological Solutions to Mental Health Problems* (Chichester: Blackwell, 2011)

Jung, C. G. (1963), *Memories, Dreams, Reflections* (Glasgow: Fontana, 1995)

Jung, C. G., 'Introduction' in *Psychological Types,* CW6 (London: Routledge, 1971a)

Jung, C. G., 'Definitions' in *Psychological Types,* CW6 (London: Routledge, 1971b)

Jung, C. G., 'General Description of the Types' in *Psychological Types,* CW6 (London: Routledge, 1971c)

Storr, A., *Solitude* (New York: Harper Collins, 1988)

Fact-check (answers at the back)

1 What was Jung's view of how our personality develops?
   a It is thoroughly formed by the environment we grow up in
   b It is created by the genetics inherited from our parents
   c It is influenced by characteristics of who we are, which are already there at birth
   d It is a constantly changing phenomenon arising on a blank slate beginning at birth

2 What was Jung's theory of introversion and extraversion influenced by?
   a Parents' opposing personalities
   b Personalities number one and number two
   c The study of Kant about the phenomenal and the noumenal
   d Patients' use of the words 'in', 'extra' and 'version' in word-association tests

3 According to Jung, what happens at midlife?
   a We move from an extraverted to an introverted focus
   b We are no longer a *tabula rasa* and our personality is fixed
   c We move from an introverted to an extraverted focus
   d We have a midlife crisis

4 How does compensation operate with extraverted or introverted tendencies?
   a People compensate for being too extra- or introverted by exaggerating the opposite
   b The unconscious takes on the opposite characteristics to the person's tendency
   c People who are introverted can claim compensation for not being extraverted enough
   d The conscious mind compensates for the missing tendency

5 Which pairs of functions are rational and which non-rational?

   a Rational: Thinking and Sensation; Non-rational: Feeling and Intuition

   b Rational: Feeling and Intuition; Non-rational: Thinking and Sensation

   c Rational: Sensation and Feeling; Non-rational: Feeling and Intuition

   d Rational: Thinking and Feeling; Non-rational: Intuition and Sensation

6 How does extraverted and introverted thinking operate?

   a Extraverted is governed by external facts; introverted seeks facts to prove ideas

   b Extraverted ignores the influence of others; introverted ignores itself

   c Introverted is governed by delusions; extraverted by psychosexual drives

   d Introverted defends against intuition; extraverted defends against sensation

7 For Jung, what is the distinction between feeling and affect?

   a Feeling is what overwhelms us sometimes and affect is what affects us

   b Feeling is real, affect is not – i.e. it is 'affected'

   c Affect is the emotion revealed in responses; feeling is how we use emotions and feelings

   d Affect describes how we effect other people; feeling is how we experience ourselves

8 How is introverted intuition both a resource and a problem?

   a It stops us thinking straight but allows us to visualize the future

   b It means we can better engage with the unconscious, but also get lost in it

   c It helps us to solve problems but it also means we seek problems out

   d It can confuse the analytic process but it can help the therapist bury this confusion

9 How is extraverted sensation both a resource and a problem?

   a It helps us see things more clearly and gets us into trouble because of it

   b It stops us from noticing deeper bodily sensations but is good for surface ones

   c It helps us find things in the dark but makes us clumsy

   d It can make us over-dependent on gratification but it strengthens our sensory awareness

10 What is the typological hierarchy designed to illustrate?

   a The way in which we choose the personality type of partners

   b How our personality is shaped by strengths and weakness across the four functions

   c The best way to structure our responses to other people

   d How our personality changes over time

Section 3

Jungian analytic practice

10

Jungian analysis

This chapter introduces the key elements of Jungian analysis, including the therapeutic relationship and process, boundaries, couch vs chair, duration, and ways of working with the unconscious. We will also look at Jung's 'four stages' of analysis and consider how relevant this still is. Tensions between differing therapeutic stances towards fostering a meaningful, healing, process are also considered.

Making space for psyche

'My aim is to bring about a psychic state in which my patient begins to experiment with his own nature – a state of fluidity, change and growth where nothing is eternally fixed and hopelessly petrified.'

Jung, 1966a, para. 99

The principles and practice of Jungian analysis rest on the premise that psyche is a living, evolving presence in the consulting room. What this means is the work of a Jungian analyst is *not* principally about having the right tools to 'fix' what is out of kilter in the life of the analysand (although there are some key elements to analytic practice which provide the framework for analysis). Nor is it to define, in a precise way, what is happening in the analysis. Rather, it is about following the direction of psyche. In other words, it is about staying alert, and paying heed, to the workings of the unconscious and trying to detect, and work with, what emerges in the organic life of the therapy. Being open to what the analysand brings, as well as who they *are,* is a core principle of the work. This means, as the quote above highlights, helping them to 'experiment' with themselves and challenge their own preconceptions about who they are – a prerequisite for self-knowledge and the loosening of the influence of complexes (as discussed in Chapter 8).

The work of analysis will therefore include descriptions of, and reflections on, current life experiences, and the feelings and thoughts these evoke. It will also include work with dreams and imagination, as well as with what the transference and countertransference between the analysand and the analyst bring to light. Terminology, such as that concerned with the transference (which originates in Freud's thinking and practice), will be explained in more detail as the discussion unfolds.

In Jung's view, the *analyst* should be in the analysis as much as the analysand, and be changed by it. The point he is making is that the analyst and the analysand both need to engage with the unconscious in order for the analysand to experience fresh awareness and capacity for growth and change. This will mean that the analyst, too, will encounter aspects of their own unconscious as well as from that of the analysand. This will lead to new insights for the analyst into themselves, as well as about how psychic life operates in general. More significantly, change will have been effected at an unconscious level. If the analyst notices no change in themselves, this would indicate that the analytic process has not properly happened.

Freud's influence and the analytic frame

As we discussed in Chapter 4, despite their definitive differences in opinion on the theory and principles of a depth psychological approach, Jung owed a debt to Freud with respect to some key features of analytic work. These included:

▶ the use of free association and dream analysis

▶ working with the 'transference'

▶ the therapeutic hour

▶ use of the couch.

Mostly, Jung developed these features in line with the spirit of analytical psychology more than classical psychoanalysis, although the influence of the latter shows through.

Spotlight: Jung's consulting room

Jung saw analysands in his consulting room in his family home in Kushnacht, Zurich. The room was upstairs, adjacent to his extensive library, and featured stained-glass windows showing the passion of Christ.

Ethics and boundaries

To be effective and safe, psychotherapy needs suitable boundaries and principles about how the therapist and client or patient will work together. Legal understanding (Jenkins, 2007) and ethical conduct are crucial in providing the parameters for good practice in the provision of counselling and psychotherapy. They inform the establishment of an appropriate and facilitative therapeutic relationship and process. As Palmer-Barnes and Murdin (2001, p. xv) put it, 'Therapists should not impose their own values on patients, but respect their autonomy and choice. Patients should be safeguarded against sexual, financial or informational (that is, respect for confidentiality) exploitation by therapists...'

These principles are worked on closely during therapeutic trainings and beyond; and this applies most vividly to Jungian analytic training (as with other depth psychological trainings) where trainees are preparing for psychotherapeutic work with analysands, which will often be intensive and lengthy. All Jungian analysts, like their fellow professionals working from differing therapeutic modalities, subscribe to such principles and are bound by the ethical protocols of their professional body, which accredits their right to continue to practise.

Spotlight: Jung's problem with boundaries

Jung infamously had an intimate relationship with Sabina Speilrein (1885–1942), one of his patients at the Burgholzi, as portrayed in the 2011 film *A Dangerous Method*, although the specific details of *how* intimate are open to debate (Covington and Wharton, 2006). This could be looked at in the light of how formative a stage professional psychotherapy was in, or in relation to Jung's *anima problem* being enacted in the therapy room. However, this does not excuse or explain away his alleged activity and this remains something that has tarnished his reputation. However, from his writing it is clear he firmly believed in the importance of a boundaried approach to analysis in order to provide a suitable psychological container to enable a meaningful therapeutic process to take place. In this case, though, rather than his *anima*, perhaps it was his *shadow* that got the better of him?

The boundaries concerned include the importance of an appropriate setting and time frames for analysis. Contracting will also play an important part, although analysts will vary as to how concrete to make this. This can take the form of a written document which is agreed and referred back to. However, in order not to cut across the very important first moments of analysis, where often influential and early dynamics from an analysand's childhood can be played out (e.g. about 'making relationship'), some other analysts may look at questions around timing, confidentiality and money (and so on) as they arise during the first session, and then contract verbally.

In terms of time boundaries, Jung concurred with Freud that a fixed time frame around the work, and regularity of analysis, were both crucial in order to provide the conditions in which effective and meaningful therapeutic work could take place. The 50-minute hour instigated by Freud was also Jung's formula for maximizing the potential for the unconscious to reveal itself.

An example of this is the so-called 'door handle effect', whereby people might reveal something important right at the end of the session: for example a buried memory, triggered by anxieties about endings or abandonment that the strict ending at 50 minutes may prompt. Jung also subscribed to Freud's maxim that analysis needs to be intensive in order to enable defences to begin to weaken, transference to form and repressed material to begin to reveal itself. So, analysis at least three times a week was de rigeur in the establishment of a separate Jungian approach to analytic work.

The analytic setting

Finally, the analyst is expected to provide a suitably furnished and appointed consulting room, which will provide confidentiality as well as a sense of something 'different' compared to the outer world. This will include a couch, though its place in analytic work is not as central as in the Freudian model. In the Jungian approach, the couch is still seen as valuable in enabling the analysand, in their more relaxed, supine state, to be open to the unconscious and to allow associations and images to come into awareness. The analyst and analysand can then work together on any meanings arising. However, the *chair* also has an important role. The analysand sits in a chair across from the analyst, though often not directly so as to allow the analysand to have a choice about whether to make direct eye contact with the analyst, and to have their own sense of space for reflection and reverie. Jung thought it important that there be 'face to face' contact between the two, who are, as has been emphasized, 'in the work together'.

Often, the analysis will begin in this mode, as the two participants begin to establish a relationship and working alliance. Then, as the relationship and process deepens, the analysand might opt to use the couch to work at greater depth with the material arising within them and to further loosen up the border between conscious and unconscious. As with all aspects of the work, this latter development needs to be handled in the light of the analyst's duty of care. The analyst has to consider, carefully, whether the analysand is in a stable enough place psychologically to thus open themselves to the sometimes unexpected insights that can ensue.

The analyst as 'blank screen'?

In Jungian analysis, the therapeutic relationship needs to be one where psyche can be given room to breathe and the unconscious can come more into the foreground. Here, the development of the relationship between neutrality and character come into play. Freud introduced the idea of the 'blank screen', based on the principle that the psychoanalytic process is best evinced via the psychoanalyst showing as little of their personality as possible, so they become like a 'blank screen' on to which the patient projects their key relationships, such as to their mother or father.

This way, the psychoanalyst 'becomes' their mother or father, catching all the repressed psychosexual impulses and strong feelings (love, hate, anger, disappointment and so on) they were carrying. This is what Freud termed the **transference**: the ways in which we unconsciously transfer feelings and impulses outside our awareness on to other people, in particular those we build up significant relations with; for example partners, friends, colleagues and, in this case, therapists. The value of working with the transference and countertransference, including projections, is now well established across the psychotherapy and counselling field (Jacobs, 2010).

The question then arises within the Jungian approach as to how much to adopt the Freudian position of a consistently blank screen. Jung stressed the uniqueness of each analysand and therefore how important it was to adapt one's approach as analyst to meet the person as they were. As we have seen, he also emphasized how both analysand *and* analyst are 'in the work together'. Jung was a strong and original advocate of the importance of analysts having extensive personal analysis themselves before they could practise, in order that they sufficiently know themselves, including their *shadow* tendencies, their early wounds and how their complexes might be activated. This was necessary to protect against their own vulnerabilities undermining the therapeutic process, and to be able to draw on their own psychological resources effectively in support of it.

The stance of the analyst is well summed up by Thomas Kirsch:

> *The analysand and analyst are equally involved in the analytical relationship. The analyst's subjective reactions are an integral part of the therapy and are not seen only as neurotic countertransference. Nor is the Jungian analyst considered a blank screen.*
> Kirsch, 2003, p. 29

Key idea: 'In the work together'

As implied here, the Jungian approach is that both analysand and analyst are 'in the work together', with the analyst using their reactions to the analysand ('countertransference') as a resource to intuit further the latter's process. It is, again, the uniqueness of the analysand and how the work is unfolding which guide how the analyst works.

Analytic principles and process

Working with psyche takes time. Deep unconscious influences and processes, such as the hidden dynamics of complexes or those hinted at in dreams, require regularity of therapeutic sessions, but also a time frame which is traditionally open-ended. This is on the basis that the unconscious works to its own rhythm. Movement and change within the psyche happen at their own pace, and it is not uncommon for people to undertake analyses which last for many months, or years. Having said this, the reality in the fast-moving, and financially constrained, world we live in is that Jungian practitioners have had to adapt their approach. Some may provide versions of therapy that offer shorter-term, less intensive, integrative approaches to analysis: these still enable meaningful therapeutic experience and change to take place.

Spotlight: Syntonic transference

Michael Fordham, whose ideas on childhood and analysis will be introduced in Chapter 14, proposed the idea of the *syntonic transference* (Astor, 1995). This referred to the value of the analyst entering a 'primitive' state where they can more fully sense what is happening for the analysand via their countertransference. This involves a willingness to be sometimes overwhelmed by the analysand's material, and so requires careful supervision.

Jung's four-stage model

Jung identified four stages of analysis, with the recognition that any division into categories of what is such an organic, individual and unpredictable process as analysis is bound to be open to variation. Nevertheless, on the basis of his extensive experience of conducting analysis when he wrote about this (1929), he came up with the following four-stage model.

1 CONFESSION

As implied, there is a comparison here with the Catholic church's use of the confession as a way of acknowledging our 'sin' and receiving absolution for this. Being able to share with a therapist what has been burdening us, or making us worried or depressed, does not make the problem go away; but it can lighten the load and help us get a feel for whether we can work with the therapist.

The therapy cannot get far without some kind of 'opening up'; this act of trust in the analyst allows the work to become established. Here, the analysand begins to face up to their *shadow*. It also gives an initial clue to what deep-seated influences, including complexes, may be at work.

2 ELUCIDATION

This stage involves focusing on further understanding what key unconscious influences may be at work, including those coming up in the transference. The therapist may well be asking: 'Who am I for this person?' (e.g. their mother) because of what the analysand seems to be projecting on to them, which is picked up by the latter in their countertransference. Like the first stage, there is a flavour of *shadow* work here, and while stage one might illustrate what could be *present* in *shadow*, the second stage provides a specific way into making this more *conscious*. Here, Jung drew on Freud's reductive approach to interpreting the transference (i.e. tracing it back to its infantile roots).

However, Jung did not follow Freud down such a precise psycho-sexual avenue, or stick purely with transference phenomena (also working with whatever came up, including dreams). The principle of helping the analysand recognize and take ownership of their *shadow* is important in Jungian analysis.

3 EDUCATION

Jung was influenced more by Alfred Adler (1870–1937) than Freud in formulating this stage. Adler's psychotherapeutic model was focused on enabling people to adapt themselves to the world authentically, for example in resolving imbalances between their *superiority* and *inferiority* complexes (Oberst and Stewart, 2003). Jung recognized how important it was for analysands to take what they have gleaned about their deeper influences (including *shadow*) from analysis and integrate this into their lives. In this respect, individuation has a social and interpersonal function as well as a purely personal one. As Jung put it (1966b, para. 152): 'The patient must be <u>drawn out</u> of himself into other paths, which is the true meaning of "education", and this can only be achieved by an educative will.'

4 TRANSFORMATION

It is important to stress that the previous stage can only go so far: adapting oneself, and the insights gathered from analysis, to the demands of the world can become damaging to one's sense of authenticity if focused on at the expense of the key principle of individuation, which is to become as fully 'oneself' as can be. So the fourth stage of the work involves attending to what is within and still waiting to be revealed and actualized. The ground for this has been laid in the previous three stages.

The container has therefore been created within which the final stage of therapy can happen – a realization of what has been lying quietly beneath the other processes of discovery and change thus far. The specifics of how this unfolding of a transformed psychic state will show up will be particular to the analysand and the analysis. It could be a person granting themselves permission to live out a previously repressed aspect of their sexuality, for example, or someone simply coming to life more and being better able to express their wishes, or their creativity.

This stage requires the analyst to reorient themselves and allow whatever is around in the transference–countertransference as well as what might be picked up in other ways (dialogue about past, present and future; dream material, etc.) to guide the process of transformation. This takes us back to a key point about the analyst being part of the transformation, too (Jung, 1966b, paras. 167–8):

'... be the man through whom you wish to influence others... the fourth stage of analytical psychology requires the counter-application to the doctor of whatever system is believed in...'

The analyst therefore needs to adopt within themselves whatever struggle the analysand is engaged in (e.g. becoming more assertive, or more spontaneous) to help them be that, too.

Jungian analysis in practice

In order best to illustrate how the analytic process works, we will explore its application to one fictionalized analysis, which will be referred to again in the following chapters. The analysand concerned is 'Jolanta' and she is a young woman of 28 who moved to the UK from Poland five years before she first went for analysis, seeking work opportunities and a new life. She had managed this to some degree, establishing herself in a job in retail which was not very well paid but promised better prospects.

Jolanta is gay and has had a couple of relationships with other women prior to the analysis; but these have not worked out well and both seemed to fall apart unexpectedly after about a year or so. This is the main factor that has brought her into analysis – she wants to understand better why her intimate relationships, which she had so wanted to work out well, have collapsed. She also wants to explore certain experiences from her childhood in Poland, where she says of her family situation 'all seemed well on the surface, but there was something fragile about it'. There are dreams she wants to bring, too, and one of her friends suggested Jungian analysis because of this. To briefly set the scene, the initial sessions of the work go as far as the confession and elucidation stages.

Confession: Jolanta reports feeling ashamed at how 'controlling' she has been with both previous partners, as well as describing how 'ruthlessly ambitious' and 'restless' she can be.

Elucidation: The analyst is just beginning to identify key themes arising from the above around, for example, her mistrust of others and 'always having to do tasks herself because other people never do them properly'. The analyst notices impatience and intolerance in her initial countertransference, presumably an echo of what Jolanta describes here. The analysis has not got as far as the *education* or *transformation* stages, nor has she brought any dream material into the sessions yet.

LIMITATIONS OF THE FOUR-STAGE MODEL

The four-stage model provides an outline map for describing the analytic process. It can seem somewhat formulaic and it also does not provide a very detailed description of how the analyst should actually work with the material around during the therapy. Nevertheless, the value of the model could be said to lie in its clarity, and as a guide to making sense of how the analyst approaches the challenge of working with both conscious and unconscious dynamics in the consulting room. This, combined with the professional considerations outlined in the first half of the chapter, provide a good basis for analytical clinical practice.

Key terms

Blank screen: Term derived from psychoanalysis to refer to the stance of the analyst where they deliberately avoid revealing their personality (or sometimes their warmth) in order to evince reactions and projections from the patient relating to key unconscious dynamics.

Four stages of analysis: The four stages, according to Jung, which all analyses go through: confession, elucidation, education and transformation.

Transference–countertransference: The unconscious relationship that builds up between the analyst and the analysand. In the transference, the analysand unconsciously transfers feelings, thoughts and impulses belonging in key early relationships (to mother or father, for example) on to the therapist. The analyst can use their countertransference – feelings, sensations and thoughts within them but that seem to come from the analysand – to better notice and understand what might be happening within the unconscious process between them.

Dig deeper

Astor, J., *Michael Fordham: Innovations in Analytical Psychology* (London: Routledge, 1995)

Covington, C. and Wharton, B., *Sabina Spielrein: Forgotten Pioneer of Psychoanalysis* (London: Brunner-Routledge, 2006)

Jacobs, M., *Psychodynamic Counselling in Action* (London: Sage, 2010)

Jenkins, P., *Counselling, Psychotherapy and the Law* (London: Sage, 2007)

Jung, C. G., 'The Aims of Psychotherapy' in *The Practice of Psychotherapy*, CW16 (London: Routledge, 1966a)

Jung, C. G., 'Problems of Modern Psychotherapy' in *The Practice of Psychotherapy*, CW16 (London: Routledge, 1966b)

Kirsch, T., 'The Role of Personal Therapy in the Formation of a Jungian Analyst' in Oberst, U. E. and Stewart, A. E. (eds.), *Adlerian Psychotherapy: An Advanced Approach to Individual Psychology* (New York: Brunner-Routledge, 2003)

Oberst, U . E. and Stewart, A. E., *Adlerian Psychotherapy: An Advanced Approach to Individual Psychology* (New York: Brunner-Routledge, 2003)

Palmer-Barnes, F. and Murdin, L., *Values and Ethics in the Practice of Psychotherapy and Counselling* (Open University Press, 2001)

Sedgwick, D., *Introduction to Jungian Psychotherapy: The Therapeutic Relationship* (New York: Taylor & Francis, 2001)

Fact-check (answers at the back)

1 What is a key principle of Jungian analysis?
a It involves identifying every problem in the analysand and identifying a tool to fix each
b It does not address personality issues
c It takes a prescriptive approach and applies it to all analysands
d It treats each analysis as unique and promotes experimentation

2 Why should the analyst be 'in the work' as much as the analysand?
a They have to work together repeatedly in the analysis
b The analyst has to work hard to interpret what is happening for the analysand
c The unconscious needs to be engaged with by both to enable meaningful change
d They both have to share the same room when they work together

3 Jung was strongly influenced by Freud in adopting which analytic elements?
a The analytic hour, the transference, use of the chair, free association
b Free association, use of the couch, the transference, the analytic hour
c The analytic hour, very regular analysis, work with shadow, dream analysis
d Free association, use of the couch, the transference, active imagination

4 What are three crucial principles for ethical depth psychological practice?
a Self-reflection, interaction without enactment and attendance to boundaries
b Enactment of what matters to the therapist, strong boundaries and confidentiality
c Being flexible with boundaries, self-reflection and interaction without enactment
d Self-reflection, interaction with enactment and attendance to boundaries

5 Why did Jung advocate use of a chair as well as a couch for the analysand?

  a It was more comfortable than a couch and so helped to relax the analysand

  b It enabled the analyst and analysand to engage more fully where needed

  c It meant the analyst could remain more focused on the analysand as face to face

  d Some of Jung's analysands fell asleep on the couch so he thought a chair would help

6 What did Jung mean by confession?

  a Something needed before the analyst would agree to work with the analysand

  b What the analyst needed to do so the analysand knew what to expect

  c Something which represented the important first cathartic stage of analysis

  d What the analyst needed to do with their supervisor after a mistake

7 In the elucidation stage, what is often the key factor that supports this?

  a The working alliance and transference between the analyst and the analysand

  b How fully the analysand has 'confessed'

  c How well the analyst can apply theory to practice

  d How intelligent the analysand is

8 Why did Jung call the third stage of analysis education?

  a Because therapy automatically leads to learning

  b Because sometimes he recommended his analysands go back to college

  c Because the analysand needed to apply what they had learned to real life

  d Because sometimes an analysand would go on to train as an analyst

9 Why does transformation involve the analyst closely?
  a If the analyst does not adopt the same approach, then the analysand will be held back
  b If the analysand transforms in a misguided way, the analyst has to make them stop
  c If the analyst has a misguided attitude, the analysand will leave the analysis
  d If the analysand believes in religious transformation, the analysis will need to go back to the confession stage

10 Why does the four-stage model have limitations?
  a It does not take into account the possibility of a 'fifth stage'
  b It was established before important therapeutic theory emerged, and is a little rigid
  c It does not take into account the possibility of a pre-analysis reflection stage
  d It was established without taking Freud properly into account and is too rigid

11

Working with dreams

Jung was initially unimpressed by what would become one of Freud's seminal works, *The Interpretation of Dreams*, when it was first published in 1900. He would, however, come to greatly appreciate the ideas Freud put forward, and dream work became of central significance to the Jungian approach.

This chapter begins with a brief explanation of distinctions between Jung's approach to the nature and significance of dreams compared to Freud. We will consider the compensatory and synthetic nature of dreams, supported by brief examples. The use of amplification, particularly where archetypal themes arise, will also be highlighted.

Royal road to what?

The notion that dreams were an unrivalled route, a 'royal road', into discovering what strong unconscious influences may be at work in the human mind, was a powerful one. Jung adopted Freud's approach for a period, although eventually this became another area of psychoanalytic theory and practice where their views diverged. Why was this?

For Freud, the dream is essentially a *wish fulfilment*: dreams enable repressed sexual drives and impulses to be discharged while the conscious mind rests (Rycroft, 1995). He saw this as a manifestation of an evolutionary imperative for humans to repress sexualized impulses (including those expressed aggressively), in order to prevent their uncontained and potentially destructive expression towards other people, or themselves. He also saw the dream as a guardian of sleep, because the sublimation of strong desires, via apparently meaningless dream images, meant the dreamer would not be woken up by them. The dream provided a mechanism for this potentially overwhelming libido to find an outlet, safely.

Spotlight: Freud, Jung and dreams

Freud analysed Jung but, according to Jung, Freud would not countenance such an arrangement in reverse. This included dreams, and one of Jung's most famous dreams about the house with many floors (see Chapter 4), and their conflicting interpretations of it, helped to illuminate a fundamental area of difference between them. For Jung, the layers of the house represented different historical collective 'layers' (the collective unconscious), whereas for Freud, the skulls in the underground cave represented Jung's unconscious wish to 'kill the Father' (the Oedipus complex).

Freud's exclusive emphasis on the psychosexual significance of dreaming became too narrow for Jung, who came to see dreams as pointing to a kind of intelligence in the way the unconscious works. He proposed that our dreams tell us something about ourselves to keep us on track in the individuation process. Jung also extended his conviction, about the presence in psyche of archetypal influences and the collective unconscious, to dreams, in a further distinction between him and Freud.

Jung's perspective on dreaming

'The dream is a spontaneous self-portrayal in symbolic form of the actual situation in the unconscious... The dream is a little hidden door in the innermost and most secret recesses of the psyche, opening into that cosmic night which was psyche long before there was any ego consciousness...'

Jung, 2011, p. 263)

For Jung, dreams convey the intimate relationship between the personal present and the vast collective dimensions of psyche that stretch back to before human consciousness developed awareness of self, others and the natural environment. They also give an insight into what is going on within us at any given time, and serve a function on behalf of our development and individuation. It is clear, then, that dreams for Jung are certainly more than a collection of random images.

Spotlight: What might Jung think of a neurobiological perspective on dreams?

A purely neurobiological explanation argues that the brain processes the images concerned during the night, in order to clear out the system from all it has been bombarded with the day before. Although Jung would accept neurobiological ways of looking at what dreams 'do' for the psychosomatic health of a person (Rosen, 2005), he believed that, if one spends time pondering a dream, however random the imagery and structure of it, then something valuable will come out of this (however limited).

Key idea: Symbol formation

This was another area of difference between Jung and Freud. Jung came to the view that, when Freud used the term 'symbol', say the 'snake for a penis' (phallic) example mentioned above, he was not using the term in its full sense but rather as a 'sign' of the latent psychosexual meaning beneath the surface. Instead, Jung saw symbols as intuitive representations of what has not yet been consciously recognized by the dreamer.

For Jung, symbols do not primarily portray what drives and impulses currently influence us, though this will be 'in the mix' of a dream. Rather, they represent what has not come fully into our conscious awareness yet; symbols can be said to describe what is waiting under the surface to show itself to us for the purpose of strengthening our self-knowledge and alerting us to what we may need, in a compensatory way, to address in our conscious attitude. They are charged with archetypal energy but are formed in the personal unconscious. See below for an example of how a current personal theme the dreamer may be overlooking here (the likely ending of a relationship or phase of life) is charged by an archetypal essence (of 'endings'/'death') to create a compensatory dream symbol (a fallen tree), to alert the dreamer.

How archetypal and personal influences create a symbol to alert the dreamer

Dream symbol	Fallen tree – *personal unconscious*
Archetype	Endings/death – *collective unconscious*
Meaning	The end of a phase or relationship in life – *conscious mind*

Our task is to notice what symbols may mean, and this involves *work*: a symbol will often not make it clear at first glance what it is trying to convey, as it needs us to reach out with a conscious, if lightly held, attitude of inquiry to make sense of it, drawing on our felt, sensed, intuited and thought responses to the dream images. This way we can work with the *synthesis* of archetypal, unconscious personal and conscious symbolism present in a dream to notice and apply the apparent message we are receiving.

From a Jungian perspective, dreams have the following four main functions:

▶ **Dreams as a snapshot**
The way a dream provides a picture of what is happening within us at the time we are having it via our *imago* (or 'dream ego', which awakens at night while our daytime *ego* slumbers), means our task is to see this as a kind of 'gift'. If we can allow it time and space, this gift can help us see the significance of this 'picture'.

▶ **Dreams as synthetic**
A Jungian reading of a dream will consider its capacity for *synthesis*, whereby elements of conscious memory, either from the day just finished, or older influences, get blended with unconscious personal and archetypal elements. This *synthetic* approach is forward-looking and recognizes that a dream, like a complex, has a number of key elements in it. This contrasts with a *reductive* approach as found in Freud's tracking of causation in the psyche. In order to understand the *synthetic* approach better, we need to look at the process of *symbol formation* which, in Jungian thinking, is a crucial element enabling us to become aware of unconscious influences through dreams.

▶ **Dreams as compensatory**

> '... we must remember the working hypothesis we have used for the interpretation of dreams: the images in dreams and spontaneous fantasies are symbols, that is, the best possible formulation for still unknown or unconscious facts, which generally compensate the content of consciousness or the conscious attitude'.
>
> Jung, 1970, para. 772

We have already touched on Jung's principle of *compensation*: the idea the unconscious compensates for our conscious attitude, all in the service of maintaining balance, or *homeostasis*, in the psyche. Where our ego gets carried away with its own self-importance, for example, then the aspects

of self which are buried in the unconscious will find a way
of letting us know this needs to be addressed or we will be in
trouble, as the first case study below illustrates. Or, where our
typological make-up leads us, say, into over-relying on objective
facts to support our *extraverted thinking*, then our *introverted
thinking* will trip us up by leading us into over-emotional
reactions to criticisms of our approach to hopefully alert us to
the problem.

The man who forgot who he was

Jung reported an analysis with a middle-aged man who had risen
to a position of power and influence in the world from humble
and impoverished beginnings. He reported suffering from anxiety
and dizziness, and brought a couple of dreams which seemed to
highlight what lay behind this.

As well as noting the parallel between mountain sickness
(provoking a kind of vertigo and nausea to do with being 'too high')
and the man's reported symptoms, Jung observes how the first
dream reinforces a sense of the man forgetting from how far
'down' he had come. In the dream he is back in the village of his
birth and there are lads there commenting on how rarely he comes
back to visit.

In the second dream, there is a more dramatic narrative in which
the dreamer is running to the station to catch a train; but he
realizes he has forgotten his briefcase and so dashes back home
to get it. As he races back to the station, the train is already pulling
out. Worse still, he sees that the track has sharp bends in it and
the train will surely come off the rails if it goes too fast. Sure
enough, the driver picks up speed and the man watches in terror
as the train comes off the track and crashes. As Jung puts it:
'since the engine-driver in front steams relentlessly ahead, the
neurosis happens at the back… his ambition drives him on and
on, and up and up into an atmosphere which is too thin for him…
Therefore his neurosis comes upon him as a warning' (Jung, 1966,
paras. 300–1).

Jung reports that this analysand appeared to struggle to accept
this reading of the situation and went on to suffer serious health

problems. This example in some ways is more clear-cut than many presentations will be in analysis. However, it provides a good example of where dreams offer a compensatory message – in this case about the need to 'slow down' and to get back to one's roots, which the dreamer is then at liberty to choose to hear, and adjust their conscious attitude in response – or not...

▶ Dreams as archetypal; and amplification

'... amplification is a way of connecting the content from a dream or fantasy with universal imagery by way of using mythical, historical and cultural analogies.'
Casement, 2001, p. 80

As will be clear from the discussion in this chapter, archetypal imagery can present in dreams. Sometimes it seems to break through into otherwise more mundane dreams, such as when a familiar scene from a person's life is suddenly populated by famous religious or historical figures, or perhaps 'invaded' by aliens.

In analysis, Jung referred to working with this aspect of dream work as 'amplification'. The role of the analyst is to facilitate the analysand as they come up with associations, but in this case the analyst might offer some links to archetypal themes that, in turn, could help the analysand play with connections to her or his own experience and understanding. For example, someone dreams of two planets apparently on a collision course – Earth and Mars – so the 'home' or 'mother' planet on the one hand and the 'red/fiery' and 'warlike' one (Mars as the Roman god of war) on the other. Then Pluto is spotted in the corner of the night sky, and the two planets slow down, though they are still close to collision. Pluto, in Greek mythology in particular, is ruler of the underworld, and links to the border territory between the above and below, life and death, conscious and unconscious.

Much would depend on the personal associations of the dreamer, but this dream seems to suggest an impending collision or conflict, possibly one that involves people, or inner influences; and where a serious clash of values is implied (Earth vs Mars, passive vs aggressive, feminine vs masculine?).

However, the slowing down of the planets, and the appearance of Pluto, with its link to 'the underneath', suggests it is possible that something else can happen. If the unconscious is listened to, perhaps a new way through, which supersedes the apparently imminent conflict, can be found? By its nature, this aspect of dream analysis has a speculative dimension, but by always following psyche and the associations of the dreamer, the way a dream offers up archetypal aspects for amplification can enrich and enlighten.

Key idea: Repeating dreams

Some people report experiencing the same dream a number of times, sometimes over a long period of their life. A classic example is dreaming of being in a familiar house – usually a home one grew up in – and discovering a part of the house one has never seen before. This often points to some aspect of our selves which has been overlooked and not lived out (though it could, among other explanations, also be to do with difficult memories that have been repressed). The image of a house, home or building is often seen symbolically in Jungian terms as representing the whole of the psyche which we 'live in' (or the *temenos*, to give it its Latin term).

The structure of a dream

Jung identified four archetypal stages (as he had done for analysis in general) of a dream. In brief, these are as follows:

1 **Exposition** – The opening scene, which introduces the characters, the setting and the problem symbolically portrayed by the dream.

2 **Development** – How the plot in the dream emerges.

3 **Culmination** – Something significant happens.

4 **Lysis** – This is the conclusion and the most important stage, as it suggests how the dreamer might attend to the problem portrayed in the opening scene.

While it is important to acknowledge the sometimes chaotic and variable structure of our dreams, this can nevertheless be a useful frame of reference for working with dreams. Likewise, none of the ways of looking at dreams portrayed in this chapter is straightforward, and the maxim of treating every dream, dreamer and dream analysis as individual is pivotal. There is also a risk that we may uncritically accept whatever the unconscious seems to be saying to us. As Samuels et al. put it (1986, p. 49):

> 'Jung repeatedly cautioned against overrating the unconscious and warned that such a tendency impairs the power of conscious decision. In this regard, an exceptionally beautiful or numinous dream may have an unhealthy seductive attraction until one looks more closely at it.'

This therefore calls for an open but critical attitude to collaboration with the unconscious in deciphering dream meanings. It should also not put too much weight on theory but, rather, treat the dream as a 'friend' who needs to be allowed to speak their truth, because:

> 'we must renounce all preconceived opinions, however knowing they make us feel, and try to discover what things mean for the patient... if the practitioner operates too much with fixed symbols, there is a danger of his falling into mere routine and pernicious dogmatism, and thus failing his patient.'
>
> Jung, 1966, para. 342

Instead, Jung advocates an attitude of *circumambulation*. That is, to hold the dream in mind and 'walk around' it, revisiting aspects of the dream where this is pertinent to more fully understanding its meaning(s).

Jungian dream analysis

Soon after Jolanta begins analysis, she reports the following dream:

'I am standing in a wide corridor in an airport. In front of me I can see the horizontal moving walkways which will take me to the exit of the airport (in the UK) but I cannot carry all my bags, which are very heavy, and I've forgotten to put them on a trolley. I drop one bag, which has a wig of long curly hair pointing out of the zipped top of the bag, on to the escalator which heads back up towards the baggage hall I have come from. I watch as it disappears from view and think, "Now I will have to buy some new hair."'

The analyst asks Jolanta to share any general associations she might have; which she does in terms of remembering how she felt (scared, alone but excited) when she first arrived in the UK, that she lost an important item of luggage, which included some correspondence with a woman she had been close to in Poland, and she found the horizontal walkways/escalators at airports 'irritating because they are so slow'. She said it felt as if the 'hair' had something to do with her relationships and sexuality (she mentions pubic hair).

Then the analyst invites Jolanta to explore the dream using Jung's four-stage model (though she uses her own words to explain how the dream might be worked with this way). So the dream is broken down as follows and Jolanta is invited to reflect on each stage:

Exposition: The dreamer stands in front of the walkways towards the airport exit but she has too many bags to carry. **Jolanta (J):** 'Reflects my problem, too much baggage from the past and I can't adapt well to changing circumstances and complicated relationships.'

Development: The dreamer notices she has no trolley and has dropped a bag with her 'hair' in it on the reverse escalator back to the baggage hall. **J:** 'Carrying too much... have dropped what really matters...' (she sobs a little here).

Culmination: The dreamer watches the bag with the 'hair' disappear out of view. **J:** 'Feels like it will slip out of my hands again, like the last two relationships I messed up.'

Lysis: The dreamer is telling herself she needs to buy some 'new hair'. **J:** 'Not sure, other than I feel the need to do something about how I deal with people I care for and have sexual relationships with.'

There are further reflections on the dream but Jolanta's responses here demonstrate the value of breaking a dream down into stages, though some dreams fit this better than others.

Reflective exercise

If you want to, and have a dream in mind, try writing it down, following the four-stage approach used above, and noting your responses. You may also consider keeping a dream diary: jot down in a few words the main elements and developments in your dreams, as you remember them each day.

The key bit of advice here is to do this as soon as you wake up (best to keep a pad and pen next to the bed). If you don't, it may all be lost by the time you brush your teeth! Then, when you have a moment, play around with what it might mean. You could even try putting yourself into the place of each character or object in the dream; this can illuminate the part of you they represent.

As with all work with the unconscious, dream material needs to be handled with care, so do not work with dreams unless you have a good grip on reality and feel settled in yourself. If a dream disturbs you, it helps to talk it through with someone you trust. Also, remember that other people's dreams belong to them, however much we might feel like interpreting them on their behalf!

Working with dreams

This chapter has illustrated some key aspects of how dreams are perceived and worked with from a Jungian perspective. The exploration has been by no means exhaustive – for example, space precludes a full discussion on how far dreams may be *prospective*, which means how dreams may show us what 'future conscious achievements' we might manage, thus helping us move out from where we are stuck in the present (Whitmont and Perera, 1989, p. 56). However, this chapter should have provided you with a sense of how much potential there is in this area for therapeutic and personal development.

Key terms

Amplification: To explore associations and meanings relating to all archetypal aspects of a dream, in order to draw out valuable associations which deepen the meaning of the dream.

Circumambulation: To 'walk around' something in order to see it from all angles. With dreams, this involves revisiting elements and exploring fresh angles, to deepen insights.

Compensation: In dream work, where deficient or mistaken conscious attitudes are pointed out, in order for the dreamer to address them for their own protection or individuation.

Four stages of a dream: Four archetypal stages of a dream (according to Jung): 1. Exposition, 2. Development, 3. Culmination, 4. Lysis.

Prospective: Where dreams may show us something of where we may be heading: not a 'prophecy' as such, more suggestions of what could be to help us make choices.

Symbol: Something representing something else. In dreams, symbols represent what has not yet come to conscious awareness, portrayed in a related, but still obscure, form.

Synthesis: How dreams often combine archetypal and unconscious personal symbolism, to convey meaning(s). Jung advocated a *synthetic* approach to work with analytic material – focusing on meaning and purpose, rather than a *reductive* or purely causal approach.

Dig deeper

Casement, A., *Carl Gustav Jung,* Ch. 3 (London: Sage, 2001)

Freud, S., *The Interpretation of Dreams* (Ware: Wordsworth Classics,1997)

Jung, C. G., 'The Practical Use of Dream Analysis' in *The Practice of Psychotherapy,* CW16 (London: Routledge, 1966)

Jung, C. G., *The Undiscovered Self: with Symbols and the Interpretation of Dreams* (Oxford: Princeton University Press, 2011)

Rosen, M., *Sleep and Dreaming (Grey Matter)* (Broomall, US: Chelsea House, 2005)

Rycroft, C., *A Critical Dictionary of Psychoanalysis* (London: Penguin, 1995)

Samuels, A., Shorter, B. and Plaut, F. (eds.), *A Critical Dictionary of Jungian Analysis* (London: Routledge, 1986)

Whitmont, E. C. and Brinton Perera, S., *Dreams, A Portal to the Source* (London: Routledge, 1989)

Fact-check (answers at the back)

1 Why was Jung's approach to dreams different from Freud's?

   a He thought dreams fulfilled sexually based wishes, unlike Freud

   b He believed dreams were a product of the ego

   c He thought dreams could support individuation and revealed archetypal process

   d He believed dreams were sent by God and always revealed the numinous

2 Why are dreams more than just a neurobiological 'offloading' to Jung?

   a They portray what is happening in our psyche as well as collective influences

   b Every element in a dream is worth its weight in gold

   c They portray what is happening in the collective psyche not the personal one

   d Every element in a dream goes back into the psyche

3 How can dreams be similar to complexes?

   a They are hard to understand like complexes

   b They grip the psyche and take control of it, while we are asleep

   c They portray archetypal influences

   d They contain a range of influences, like a complex

4 What is meant by a 'compensatory dream'?

   a A dream which points out how a person can claim compensation

   b Where a dream makes up for the person not having dreamed the night before

   c A dream which points out something a person is overlooking in their conscious attitude

   d Where a dream makes a person feel better

5 What is the role of symbols for Jung and why is this different to Freud's approach?

   a Symbols are purely random, while Freud saw them as representing deeper processes

   b Symbols reflect the conscious attitude; Freud saw them as representing the unconscious

   c Symbols represent what is not yet known; Freud saw them as 'signs' of latent material

   d Symbols come direct from the collective unconscious; Freud disagreed

6 How are archetypal images in dreams 'amplified' in analysis?

   a By helping the analysand associate to archetypal images and generating relevant links

   b By the analysand drawing the images as large as possible to clarify archetypal themes

   c By encouraging the analysand to closely explore every detail of the dream

   d By the analyst repeating back to the analysand the archetypal themes for them to reflect on

7 What mistaken assumptions can impede successful work with dreams?

   a That dreams can be treated like complexes

   b Deferring uncritically to the unconscious, and trying to interpret others' dreams for them

   c Treating the unconscious as if it is our friend

   d Working with symbols too much, and failing to interpret others' dreams for them

8 What are the four stages of a dream, in the right order?

   a Development, Exposition, Culmination, Lysis

   b Exposition, Culmination, Development, Lysis

   c Development, Exposition, Lysis, Culmination

   d Exposition, Development, Culmination, Lysis

9 What does it mean to 'circumambulate' a dream?
- **a** Walk around it, in the sense of looking at it more than once and from different angles
- **b** Draw images of the dream within a circle so that all the parts can be seen together
- **c** Imagine within a dream in decreasing circles until the centre of the 'mandala' is reached
- **d** Explore dream meanings while riding in circles on a bike, to free up the conscious mind

10 In what sense are some dreams 'prospective'?
- **a** They accurately predict the future
- **b** They give us a sense of what may be possible
- **c** They help us to assess our career prospects
- **d** They show us in the exposition what will happen in the lysis

12

Active imagination

This chapter will look at ways of working therapeutically with the unconscious with an emphasis on archetypal imagery. Jung's important notion of the transcendent function as the driver of meaning making, arising from work with the unconscious, will be described. Second, we will explore the powerful ways in which active imagination can enable us to benefit from encounters with the unconscious, including how it can better help us understand dreams. We will also consider the place of active imagination in analysis, plus potential pitfalls and ethical implications. The case study will apply these ideas.

Working with image, archetype and the transcendent function

Archetypal images do not just arise in our dreams, but also from spontaneous fantasy in our waking life. A key concept in unlocking the Jungian approach to working with image and archetype is the **transcendent function**. Jung used this term to describe the capacity of the psyche to hold both conscious and unconscious activity at the same time, and enable a blend of the two to emerge, though this was not a straightforward process and it involved a good deal of wrestling and confrontation, as well as negotiation, between ego and the unconscious. However, the way in which symbols can activate this function means new insights, and transitions into new psychological states, are made possible. This principle links to the one of *homeostasis* mentioned previously – Jung's emphasis on the self-regulating priority of the psyche, which works to try to keep us 'in balance'.

Jung describes the key role of the *transcendent function* thus:

> 'the harmonizing of conscious and unconscious data is...
> an irrational life-process which expresses itself in definite
> symbols... In this case, knowledge of the symbols is
> indispensable, for it is in them that the union of conscious
> and unconscious contents is consummated. Out of this union
> emerge new situations and new conscious attitudes.
> I have therefore called the union of opposites the
> "transcendent function".'
>
> Jung, 1968, para. 524

Note his emphasis on the value of 'knowledge of the symbols'. He is suggesting the value of an analyst having an understanding of archetypal imagery so they might help an analysand see possible links from images in night or day dreams to their own situation (or to their individuation process in general). Inherent in this approach is also a valuing of experiencing and engaging with images arising from the unconscious.

The *transcendent function* operates to enable us to do this so we can 'transcend' our current psychological position (e.g. feeling stuck). We take the conscious decision to engage with what is coming at us from the unconscious; and out of this engagement, this struggle, something new emerges which 'transcends' the previous impasse and enables change and growth to happen. The influence of the dialectical philosophy of Hegel (1770–1831), described in Chapter 3, can be seen here. This is not a function of the psyche that 'transcends' in a spiritual or religious sense of encounter with something 'transcendent' (which is a confusion that sometimes creeps in when *transcendent function* crops up as a term, considering Jung's association with the spiritual or numinous).

Spotlight: Jung and mathematics

Jung borrowed the term *transcendent function* from mathematics. It refers to the notion of a 'transcendental' number – in other words, one that cannot be derived from an algebraic equation (as 'pi' can be) but rather one that implies an 'irrational' number emerging unpredictably within its own logic, not unlike the workings of the unconscious.

Working with active imagination

Jung developed an approach to accessing the contents of the unconscious via the use of fantasy, because, as Casement (2001, p. 2) points out:

'Unconscious material is needed for the transcendent function to be activated but Jung thought that dream material does not have sufficient energy for this purpose. Nor do unconscious slips because these are too fragmentary. Instead, fantasy is necessary and this must be allowed free play while the individual remains as conscious as possible.'

Jung had come to the conclusion that the predominating influence in modern, Western, humanity – rationalism and the use of directed thinking to preserve and expand the knowledge and well-being of civilization – had significantly suppressed the capacity to be open to unconscious influences. Therefore a conscious *effort* is required to open oneself up to them. This is in contrast to work with dreams. Here, the imagery is initially experienced passively, when asleep, while waking fantasy enables active engagement in the present. The active conscious effort involved has a moral aspect. We have a responsibility to ourselves (literally to our *self* and how it prompts us towards individuation), as well as to our place in the collective development of human consciousness, to engage with our unconscious and from it derive insights we can apply to our lives.

'Active imagination' is essentially Jung's term for the use of guided fantasy that can activate the transcendent function, and his formulation for describing the underlying process sets the scene well:

> *'firstly, extending the conscious horizon by the inclusion of numerous unconscious contents; secondly, of gradually diminishing the dominant influence of the unconscious, and thirdly, of bringing about a change in personality.'*
>
> Jung, 1966, para. 358

From this formula for describing what happens when a conscious effort is made to expand our awareness of our unconscious, Jung devised a method for 'actively' working with imagination that could fulfil this aim. This was derived initially from his own confrontation with the unconscious, described in Chapter 1. He applied a clear sequence to this, which we shall come on to. This in turn was based on his theoretical formulation of how the activation of the *transcendent function* effectively shifts the active centre of the psyche from the ego to a position which is on the mid-point between conscious and unconscious and between ego and self, as shown in the following diagram.

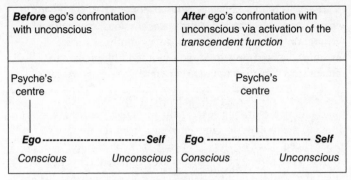

Before ego's confrontation with unconscious	**After** ego's confrontation with unconscious via activation of the *transcendent function*
Psyche's centre *Ego* ----------------------------- *Self* *Conscious* *Unconscious*	Psyche's centre *Ego* ----------------------------- *Self* *Conscious* *Unconscious*

The effect of activating the *transcendent function*

THE STAGES OF ACTIVE IMAGINATION

As Chodorow (1997) points out, Jung's initial formulation from 1935 has been developed beyond the initial two stages he proposed, and the value of working in this way with the unconscious has spawned a number of applications that can support personal development in general, as well as being used as a tool in the analytic context. An example of this is Robert Johnson's application to 'inner work' (1986; see 'Spotlight' below), and comparisons can be made with the use of guided imagery in the Humanistic field (e.g. Natalie Rogers, 2000).

Jung drew on his formula for activating the *transcendent function* to identify two stages wherein a person first allows the unconscious to take the lead. This requires an attitude of careful attention to the unconscious, and is not the same as common definitions of daydreaming, whereby we may choose a theme we want to daydream about so we are initiating the process and then guiding ourselves through it. In fact, Jung meant the opposite. He described it to be like dreaming but with our eyes open. We find a quiet space and sit and wait for fantasy to emerge, noticing the emotions being generated by this process.

Once images form, we allow them to show us what they want us to see, not what we might consciously be seeking out. Jung, and others following him, discovered that using creative expressive methods can support the spontaneous expression of what is coming forward from the unconscious: spontaneous writing, drawing, painting (or through another creative medium), or by simply holding it in mind (taking care to remember as much detail of what we have seen as we can).

The second part of the process involves the conscious mind taking the driving seat, as the ego takes the lead in noticing themes and insights emerging from the fantasies experienced. This, for Jung, is where the ethical obligation comes to the fore. As the insights are evaluated, they must be integrated and lived out, otherwise one has effectively decided to ignore the messages arising from the unconscious. Having said this, as with dreamwork, the indications revealed are not to be simply swallowed uncritically, but need to be scrutinized and evaluated to check their validity.

Once those aspects that genuinely do not seem authentic, or connected to current challenges and themes, have been tested and set aside, what is left does often require adjustment on our part to a new attitude to life, sometimes significantly, but often in a subtle but important way. We may recognize that we no longer need to reach after unrealistic ambitions, or realize we have taken a completely one-sided attitude towards an aspect of our lives, such as our closest relationships, and adjust accordingly.

One of the later models for active imagination which has become well established is that of Marie-Louise von Franz (1979). She set out Jung's model in four clear and elegant stages:

1 Empty the 'mad mind' of the ego

2 Let unconscious fantasy image arise

3 Give it form of expression

4 Ethical confrontation: apply it to ordinary life

As you will have noticed, this is a similar sequence but laid out in four stages, with an initial emphasis on the work needed to clear the 'mad mind' – by which she meant the generally full and frenetic mind we are all used to experiencing on a daily basis – full of worries, ideas and the fantasies we generate. Jung referred to the Taoist principle of 'wu wei' here, which is a fundamental state of 'non-action' that has to be *actively* cultivated. So, the work our conscious mind has to do is based on an attitude that prioritizes 'wu wei' so the unconscious fantasy images can arise from their own volition, not from our habitual tendencies to generate and control them.

Spotlight: Active imagination and personal development

Johnson (1986) proposes an adaptation of the Jungian model which can be used to support personal development. The four stages he proposes are:

1 **Invite the unconscious**
   Consciously wait for, or even ask, the unconscious to show itself.
2 **Dialogue and experience**
   Allowing spontaneous images to appear and experiencing them. Beginning to dialogue with these (e.g. asking 'what do you have to say to me?')
3 **Add the ethical element of values**
   Thinking carefully about implications arising, and applying them to our lives.
4 **Make it concrete**
   Taking the essence of what has been discovered and bringing it into life, e.g. by changing a habit or making something that physically represents this essence.

Key idea: Handle with care

This kind of use of active imagination has potential value for personal development, but needs to be handled with care. One's state of mind is the most important consideration to check prior to using such approaches, as Jung was rightly concerned to point out. Any concerns about someone's current, or long-term, capacity to engage with active imagination safely would render the use of active imagination inappropriate.

Active imagination in Jungian analysis

Within Jungian analysis, active imagination can be used to facilitate the analytic process. It may be, for example, that a theme relating to a complex keeps coming up and may feel stuck. Inviting the analysand to clear a space and see what images come up, supported perhaps by the use of drawing materials, can unlock the situation via the images and associations arising. It can also be fruitful to do active imagination around a dream, whereby key themes and characters within a dream can be revisited and actively engaged with. An example of this is given in the case study below.

Often, the use of this tool will become pertinent once the analysis has developed for a period and the analysand is ready to engage more actively with the unconscious. This can then be used to facilitate the process, for example by inviting the analysand to play with an image which they report is present as they talk with the analyst, or one which may have cropped up, unbidden, in between sessions. The analyst may also invite them to draw the image using the paper and crayons or pencils that they keep available in their consulting room.

This, then, provides an immediacy to material from the unconscious for both involved to look at, and for the analysand to associate to. There may also be scope to set up a dialogue, in the room, between the analysand and the figure or object(s) portrayed.

THE ANALYST'S ACTIVE IMAGINATION

Sometimes spontaneous images are generated in the analyst's countertransference. Shaverien (2007) describes examples in her work, such as the image of a wolf appearing over the shoulder of the analysand, and how this gave her clues about what was happening for the analysand as well as between both of them in the room. This is an example of the analyst being active with the appearance of imaginal material, and there is a choice for them as to whether to offer such an image back to the analysand or just to hold it in mind as a potentially valuable tool for better understanding what psyche is 'saying'.

THE PITFALLS OF ACTIVE IMAGINATION

In terms of where active imagination can be counter-productive, the risk of triggering strong psychological reactions (and even 'possession' by the imagery) in the analysand has to be watched for consistently. It might be that their fascination with the imagery means they avoid confronting what is being presented. However, where used appropriately and in a way that is attuned to the process and dynamics emerging in the analysis, active imagination can provide powerful access to the unconscious.

Jolanta plays with her dream

After doing some initial amplification of the connections and possible meanings associated with her 'airport' dream (see Chapter 11), the analyst senses intuitively that the dream could reveal more if Jolanta were given the chance to 'play' with and explore it more freely than merely thinking about what its elements might mean.

After explaining briefly how active imagination works, the analyst invites Jolanta to consider using this approach, having first assessed her readiness to do so. The analyst feels that, although they have not been working together long (about four months), they have formed a strong working alliance in their twice-weekly sessions. Jolanta agrees, and the analyst invites her to clear her mind and then invite the dream about the airport back in. She is then invited to explore it however she wants, and spend time 'walking around' (in her imagination) inside it, maybe talking to different elements in it.

Jolanta finds it hard to get into this activity at first, it feeling a touch artificial, but once she fully relaxes in her chair she finds herself 'in the airport' and spends a few minutes walking around by the walkways, enjoying standing in them with her trolley as they move slowly towards the exit.

She then makes her way to the escalator behind her, which is taking the bag she accidentally dropped on to the 'up' escalator back to the baggage hall. She decides to try and retrieve the bag, but realizes, as she stands behind it, that she just wants to follow it and the tousle of her hair sticking out of it. She follows its move on to the baggage claim area and realizes that at any moment it will disappear from view and end up back on a plane to Poland. So she walks quickly forward and scoops the bag up and holds it in front of her eyes. She then asks it the question: 'Why are you taking my hair back to Poland?' Eventually the bag 'says' *'Because you did not say goodbye properly.'*

This feels very powerful to Jolanta and she starts breathing deeply and fast. The analyst notices this and invites her to come back from the airport and out of the dream, if she wants to. Jolanta nods and allows herself time, with the analyst's help, to find her way back into her bodily awareness. The analyst says that, if it is helpful, she can look around the room and notice carefully all the furniture and objects in it, to help her 'come back' to reality. But Jolanta says she is fine.

She smiles and says it has been powerful and has helped her understand how much she has left behind, and that she's 'left the people that really mattered to me too quickly' so it was 'no wonder I keep being horrid to people I get close to here'. Jolanta also says it feels as if there is also something more to it, 'something from way back... family...' which they both agree they could explore. In a prospective sense, there is also something important about not trying to cut off the past (as her hair got separated from her in the dream) in order to go forward. 'I have to bring the past with me, or my hair will keep falling out!'

This active engagement with the imagery in a dream has proffered some valuable insights for the analysand. It has also given her agency in engaging with unconscious material. She is also beginning to apply its psychological and ethical implications to her life situation. This is not 'pure' active imagination, as the analyst has set the scene by suggesting she engage with the dream in this way rather than literally seeing whatever came into her mind once she had cleared it, but this example illustrates how the active imagination sequence can be adapted to meet the needs of the situation and individual.

Spotlight: Watching a film as active imagination?

Jungian writer John Izod (2002) suggests that, when we fully engage with a work of fiction, especially film, it can be like active imagination. By playing with what we would like to happen as we are watching a film, for example, we are taking an active role in shaping the material 'coming at us'. As Izod observes, this is a way of describing how we can use the symbols and narrative on the screen to deepen our awareness of self, just as Jung proposed active engagement with the unconscious, via our imagination, can do.

Key terms

Active Imagination: Allowing spontaneous fantasy to arise from the unconscious and then engaging with it consciously to uncover fresh insights, which should then be applied to life.

Transcendent function: The capacity in the human psyche to facilitate engagement between conscious and unconscious contents and to synthesize these to create a new situation in the psyche that promotes balance and the individuation process.

Dig deeper

Casement, A., *Carl Gustav Jung* (London: Sage, 2001)

Chodorow, J. (ed.), *Jung on Active Imagination* (London: Routledge, 1997), pp. 1–20

Hannah, B., *Encounters with the Soul: Active Imagination as developed by C. G. Jung*, 'One Beginning Approach to Active Imagination' (Cambridge, MA: Sigo, 1981), pp. 52–65

Izod, J., 'Active imagination and the analysis of film', *Journal of Analytical Psychology*, pp. 267–85 (April 2000)

Johnson, R., *Inner Work: Using Dreams and Active Imagination for Personal Growth* (New York: Harper & Row, 1986)

Jung, C. G. (1958), 'The Transcendent Function', CW8, paras 131–93

Jung, C. G. (1928), 'The Technique of Differentiation between the Ego and the Figures of the Unconscious' in *Two Essays on Analytical Psychology*, CW7, 2nd ed. (London: Routledge, 1966)

Jung, C. G., 'Conscious, unconscious and individuation' in *The Archetypes and the Collective Unconscious*, CW9i (London: Routledge, 1968)

Rogers, N., *The Creative Connection: Expressive Arts as Healing* (Ross-on-Wye: PCCS Books, 2000)

Schaverien, J., 'Countertransference as active imagination: imaginative experiences of the analyst', *Journal of Analytical Psychology*, 52(4), 413–31 (September 2007)

Von Franz, M-L., *Alchemical Active Imagination* (Boston: Shambhala, 1979)

Fact-check (answers at the back)

1 What does the transcendent function allow us to do?
  a Access the transcendent via the unconscious
  b Synthesize unconscious and unconscious material in a meaningful way
  c Transcend the conscious mind in order to access archetypal imagery
  d Explore the collective unconscious as fully as we want

2 What do the workings of the transcendent function allow to happen?
  a Conscious and unconscious to disengage so that the unconscious can come through
  b The person to rise above whatever problems they are experiencing
  c Conscious and unconscious to engage and promote balance and healthy change
  d The person to experience the transcendent

3 How did the philosopher Hegel influence Jung on the transcendent function?
  a By suggesting that all of reality is really transcendent
  b By constructing a synthesis of Kant's noumenal and phenomenal
  c Through his idea of thesis and synthesis producing a transcending antithesis
  d Through his idea of thesis and antithesis producing a transcending synthesis

4 Why is a dream not so effective for activating the transcendent function?
  a It is experienced passively and so does not allow for conscious confrontation
  b It leaves us in a state of inactive sleepiness
  c It is already transcendent so we cannot apply it to reality
  d It activates a symbolic function

5 What do the two fundamental stages of active imagination involve?

   a First, us becoming thoroughly conscious of ourselves and, second, unconscious

   b First, allowing the unconscious to overwhelm us and, second, to repress it

   c First, allowing consciousness to fade by us choosing a fantasy to follow, then seeing what the unconscious does with this

   d First, allowing the unconscious to take the lead in fantasy and, second, consciously evaluating this and applying it to life.

6 What specific stages of active imagination have other authors emphasized?

   a Artistically recording the experience; writing about it to a trusted person

   b Filling the mind at the start; emptying it afterwards

   c Emptying the mind at the start; doing a ritual at the end to embody the experience

   d Inviting in a fantasy of our choosing at the start; dismissing it at the end

7 What does 'wu wei' mean and why is it ideal for active imagination?

   a A state of complete relaxation which helps us to notice our deeper thoughts

   b A state of 'non-action' which is also alert and dynamic

   c A state of relaxation that helps us to dream

   d A state of 'non-action' so we fall into an unconscious state

8 How can active imagination be utilized to support the analytic process?

   a In work with complexes, dreams and spontaneous images arising in the transference

   b In helping to form the working alliance in the early stages of the analysis

   c In identifying the personality type of the analysand

   d In helping to work with repressed psychosexual roots of neurosis

9 The use of active imagination can be counter-productive if the analysand does what?

   a Becomes scared of the imagery and avoids talking about it

   b Gets too fascinated by the imagery and avoids the complex it symbolizes

   c Becomes confused because they think it is a dream

   d Gets overconfident and tells the analyst they completely understand what it means

10 What ethical considerations need to be applied to active imagination?

   a The analysand must understand it in detail before they undertake it

   b The analysand needs to practise imagining things regularly before they are ready

   c The analysand must be fully conscious of their imagination first

   d The analysand must be stable enough psychologically to encounter the unconscious

13

Alchemy and analysis

Jung arrived at some of his most profound insights into the therapeutic process as a result of his studies of alchemy. His extensive research into its traditions and practices, across many centuries and cultures, led him to apply its underlying principles that he discovered to analysis. This chapter will explain these principles and illustrate how influential they remain in post-Jungian thinking. It will also demonstrate how alchemical principles can be applied in analysis, particularly in relation to the archetypal transference, via the case study.

The influence of alchemy on Jung

> 'For... [Jung]..., the alchemical goal of extracting gold from base metal is mirrored in analytical work in the gradual extraction of the unconscious gold from the base metal of consciousness to lead to the higher union of the two.'
>
> Casement, 2001, p. 54

Alchemy is a vast topic, with current cultural manifestations having their historical roots in the work of the alchemists, which, as Schwartz-Salant points out (1995, p. 7) was built up by 'many groups and individuals from Egypt, Arabia, Iran, Greece, India, China, England, Germany and France... (and)... was a kind of applied mystico-philosophical system'. Jung initially found what he read about alchemy to lack relevance to the importance of archetypal influences, not least because of the apparently futile and fanciful attempts to literally produce gold from leaden dregs (base metal), which alchemists, at first glance, seemed to have pursued.

Spotlight: Harry Potter and alchemy

The most obvious example of where alchemy crops up in contemporary culture is in the hugely popular *Harry Potter* books (Rowling, 2007) and films. These feature alchemical ideas and terms such as the 'philosopher's stone'. Rubeus ('red') Hagrid and Albus ('white') Dumbledore have first names derived from alchemy. Alchemy is also an optional subject on the curriculum at Hogwarts.

Jung's interest in alchemy was prefigured by a dream he had in 1926. In this dream, he found himself in the seventeenth century, stuck in a courtyard, the door to it having slammed behind him. He later realized, after reading *The Secret of the Golden Flower* (an ancient Chinese alchemical text Richard Wilhelm sent him in 1928), that this dream was about alchemy, with the unconscious pointing him towards the later Middle Ages, the source of some important alchemical texts. He thought he might be 'let out of the courtyard' once he had properly examined alchemy, and drawn from it what was germane for the present time, and for the Jungian analytic framework. It was then his exploration of the work of Paracelsus (1493–1541) – who laid the foundation for the study of alchemy as a representation of important underlying psychological processes – that helped Jung make sense of the connections between alchemy and the principles underpinning psychotherapy (as well as collective psychological and religious ideas and structures).

In *Psychology and Alchemy* (1980), Jung sets out what he thinks happened to him during his 'creative illness' (1913–17), following his break with Freud, in alchemical terms. He saw his experiences of descent into chaotic and often dark encounters with the unconscious as the necessary 'base metal' required for him to uncover the 'gold' which lay therein, enabling him to construct the theory and practice of analytical psychology. He also conveyed his perception of the significance of the work of the alchemists as being their projection of the unconscious into matter, as he explains here:

'The real nature of matter was unknown to the alchemist: he knew it only in hints. In seeking to explore it he projected the unconscious into the darkness of matter in order to illuminate it. In order to explain the mystery of matter he projected yet another mystery – his own psychic background – into what was to be explained: Obscurum per obscurius, ignotum per ignotius! *This procedure was not, of course, intentional; it was an involuntary occurrence.'*

Jung, 1980, para. 345

Spotlight: Roots of the word

The word 'alchemy' can be traced back via Middle English, French and Latin to roots in Arabic *al-kīmiyā'*, where *al* means 'the' and *kīmiyā;* means the 'art of transmuting metals'.

Alchemical principles

What were the alchemical principles from which Jung derived these insights?

The word *alchemy* is usually defined in two ways. It is:

▶ a historical phenomenon predating chemistry that aimed to transmute base metal into gold

▶ a descriptive term for an almost magical process that can bring about something new, through combining or mixing two or more substances or influences.

It is the second of these definitions which provided Jung with the most potent application to his thinking. Alchemy helps to describe the process which happens when a person consciously confronts the unconscious, enabling a new situation, and consequent level of awareness, to emerge in the psyche.
In this respect, Jung's influences from alchemy helped him formulate his ideas about the **transcendent function** and **active imagination**.

ALCHEMY AS A METAPHOR FOR CHANGE

The key to working with alchemical ideas, of course, is to see them as both archetypal and metaphorical. The alchemical process – whereby different substances are placed in a container (variously named as crucible, retort or *vas*) and then heated and mixed together, with the hope of new 'gold' emerging as a result – is a good metaphor for the therapeutic process. In analysis, the analysand and analyst are 'in the work together', and the developing working alliance, process and transference relationship can generate something 'new' and of real value. The influence of alchemy could also be described as archetypal, because these parallels apply more or less to all therapeutic work.

Also, in working with difficult material, such as what gets tied up with the *shadow*, *inferior function* and *complexes* of the analysand, the analysis could be said to work with the 'base metal' from which psychological 'gold' can be drawn out, rather like the principle of finding 'the diamond in the rough'.

Finally, there is a relevant parallel around the 'containing' role of the analysis: the regularity of setting and time, and the reliable presence and therapeutic skills of the analyst, act as a suitable 'container' within which the analysand can feel securely 'held', and change can occur. This is similar to the alchemical *vas,* without which the elements could not be mixed, and hopefully transformed.

'SEEDING' THE GOLD AND ANALYSIS

As Mathers (2014) observes, the alchemists usually put a little gold into the crucible at the beginning to 'seed' the process (usually by dissolving a little of what their patron had initially paid them into a risky combination of sulphuric and nitric acids), meaning some gold at least could be found at the end of the process. Mathers (op. cit., p. 6) highlights the parallel with therapy:

> *'Fortunately, neither they nor their patrons knew much about measuring... Like counsellors / therapists / analysts and those who work creatively, they didn't precisely know what they were doing; it "just happened".'*

Likewise, some 'gold' needs to be present at the beginning of the therapy in order for some to emerge later, in deeper and stronger form. This could be described in terms of the quality of the initial psychological contact made 'in the room' between the analyst and the analysand, and in relation to the nature of the unconscious connection between them. Overall, one could call the attitude of the analyst a crucial 'seeding' factor, one that is open to the direction the analysand's psyche seems to be pointing towards, and to the workings of unconscious process generally – plus certain faith shifts can happen for the analysand.

ALCHEMY, ARCHETYPAL PROCESS AND TRANSFERENCE

Jung proposed that the full 'journey' through analysis could be framed by a model drawn from a text written by the medieval alchemists – the *Rosarium* – and he used this as the basis for his description of the largely hidden unfolding of the transference between analyst and analysand. As we have seen, Jung subscribed to the general principle of the psychoanalyst becoming, in effect, a key parental figure for the analysand, who then projects unconscious contents relating to early influences on to the therapist. However, his distinction between the personal and collective unconscious led him to make a parallel one about the transference.

Jung developed the idea of 'archetypal transference' alongside the 'personal' version, believing that strong transferences could build up which led the analysand to project archetypal figures on to the analyst (e.g. an evil monster or a wonderful healer). He also proposed there are archetypal dynamics at work in all analytical relationships (e.g. the initial awareness of the analysand about their problems and how resistances can get in the way of working on these). Jung also posited that there is *direct communication* between the unconscious of the analysand and of the analyst (and vice versa). This principle, which Jung suggested builds up as the analysis proceeds, is key to his description of the alchemical influences on the archetypal transference.

In his paper 'Psychology of the Transference', Jung (1966) describes the archetypal transference as an unfolding pattern of unconscious stages that govern the therapeutic process and lead the analysand towards a fuller, individuated, state of being. This state relies on the full involvement of the analyst, whose unconscious interacts with that of the analyst to provide a fundamental alchemical component in the analysis.

Full analysis involves passing through all key stages of the alchemical cycle towards a new 'concunctio' (marriage/union) between opposites in the psyche; this is replicated by the evolving therapeutic relationship. These stages, with their associated titles from the *Rosarium*, are described below. Each stage is portrayed in a woodcut from the *Rosarium* featuring female and male elements representing the encounter and blending of opposites in the psyche.

The 'Mercurial Fountain' from the alchemical *Rosarium* text; the solar and lunar streams represent male and female elements

Spotlight: Did Jung adapt the *Rosarium* to suit?

Jung seems to have been somewhat selective, in that he utilized only 10 of the 20 stages and associated images from the original document when he wrote about alchemy's application to the therapeutic relationship. His approach could therefore be criticized for adapting alchemical principles to fit his thinking rather than using the exact archetypal principles and stages handed down across the centuries. However, the stages he drew on in the *Rosarium* were the most obviously relevant ones for crucial stages of change (or 'stuckness') in both the alchemical and therapeutic process. He thereby identified key points of development which, he argued, feature in all fully fledged analyses.

We will now look at each of these ten alchemical stages with a brief description of each, and of the process experienced by Jolanta across a lengthy analysis, which seems to reflect how these unfolded.

The archetypal transference	Jolanta's alchemical path

1. The mercurial fountain

This represents the start of the analysis as the analyst and the analysand meet for the first time and begin to get a sense of one another.

At the beginning of her analysis, Jolanta feels uncertain of what to expect but is open to explore how it might feel when with her analyst, Liz.

2. King and queen

Here the relationship develops, as framed by the working alliance, as persona influences diminish.

Jolanta explores her situation and feelings. Liz senses that Jolanta is engaged and open to the process, if a little anxious.

3. The naked truth

Work with shadow...

Jolanta shares the difficulties experienced in her close relationships and notices discomfort, even shame, about this.

4. Immersion in the bath

With the greater transparency from the analysand, a descent into the unconscious can now happen.

As Jolanta goes further into her difficulties, she notices strong feelings emerging about Liz, and at one point gets angry with her. The image of a witch from a storybook starts to appear in her mind during sessions. She eventually shares this with Liz and they explore this. Liz has felt angry herself in her countertransference, and has a recurring image of a tiny girl running scared through the woods.

5. The conjunction

The erotic imagery conveys an unconscious 'union' between the analyst and analysand. This may be reflected in anima–animus dream imagery. However, this is not a definitive resolution of the process.

Powerful feelings move around the analytic space. Jolanta notices some attraction towards Liz, who in turn finds herself taking a mix of angry and erotic feelings to discuss with her supervisor. Jolanta has the dream about the airport and working on this brings deeper insight.

6. Death

Also termed 'the nigredo', this is a point in the analysis where everything seems to come to a halt – the energy goes out of the work as the cycle of unconscious development goes from life to death.

Jolanta feels exhausted after her sessions with Liz. She tells Liz, who has also found herself dreading the sessions with Jolanta, who seems demanding and critical. Liz feels sleepy at times and Jolanta increasingly thinks of ending the analysis. After nine months she leaves, saying that there is no more to gain.

The archetypal transference	Jolanta's alchemical path

7. The ascent of the soul

This is a stage of acute vulnerability, as the level of ego strength has fallen in response to the unconscious depths revealed. A kind of psychological decomposition occurs, so the analysand is vulnerable to disorientation. With the analyst's help, conscious awareness is focused on, while some new life is awaited (comparable to the phrase 'it is always darkest just before the dawn').

Jolanta's departure does not last long. She calls Liz two weeks later and asks to return, which is a relief for Liz as she has been worried that Jolanta is vulnerable. Jolanta explains that although she was 'fed up' with the analysis being 'stuck', she realized that she had not finished with it and felt 'wobbly' without it.

8. Purification

Here, what is termed 'the sprinkling of the dew' comes in and brings unexpected but welcome new life to the analysis. The emergence of a new consciousness in the analysand has an unconsciously led feeling base. Meaningful shifts can only arise beyond and beneath cognitive awareness and process. This is a principle mirrored in thinking on therapeutic change (e.g. Greenberg, Rice and Elliot, 1993).

Once she is back in the analysis, Jolanta explains that she has had a dream that made her 'wobbly', in which she was on a plane flying without a pilot. They fruitfully explore this. There seem to be links to the transference ('a pilotless plane'), her past (the plane as connection to her home and the quality of care she received) and archetypal links to the theme of flying unsafely (the 'eternal child').

9. The return of the soul

The imagery denotes a reintegration of previously split-off, or dissociated, aspects of psyche. The analysis is now moving towards a defining and refining of what really matters: of what makes the analysand the person they fully are.

Here, just over a year into the analysis, Jolanta describes being able to see more clearly her pattern of defending against intimacy. She also comes to realize that what she has 'left behind' may actually be available to her if she nurtures it: her value and integrity.

10. The new birth

Finally, the conjunction of opposites can come to its fulfilment, and this is reflected in the image of a hermaphrodite which fully combines masculine and feminine in balance (syzygy). The work is 'completed' through a realization of the self, whereby the analysand will notice, at however subtle a level, that something important has happened, or at least been revealed, within them. The analyst, too, will notice a sense of having been changed in some way by the process. The analyst will help the analysand reflect on ethical and practical implications arising.

The analysis draws towards its conclusion as Jolanta professes that she has 'done the work' and feels better about seeking out a close relationship based on a secure sense of her own worth, including her sexuality. She has worked on the underlying fragility of her loving relations to each of her parents, although Liz senses that there is more to explore here. Liz can see Jolanta's strengthened sense of self, as a more relaxed and mature personality. Liz, too, felt affected by the analysis, questioning her capacity to sit with strong feelings and complexes, but she has emerged with greater self-knowledge. Jolanta notes the need to allow herself time to reflect on what she has gained from the work and what it will mean for her life.

Limitations and possibilities

It is important to recognize that Jung's portrayal of the archetypal transference and the process it is meant to facilitate is rather an idealized one. In order for analysis to generate this process in full, a lengthy and intensive analysis is required, something which demands very significant investment in time and money, and is less common nowadays unless it is in the training analyses that trainee analysts undertake. This model could also be critiqued for being too formulaic. Most analysts would say from experience that, although this archetypal template is valuable, the 'order' in which change might happen cannot be predetermined. This author, for example, has experience of working with male analysands where the nigredo, or 'death' stage, appears at the outset of the work and needs to be revisited over and over again to enable a shift to occur (Goss, 2014). A looser, more general application of alchemical ideas sometimes seems to work better, such as where a shift in the alchemical 'colouring' is described (Martin, 2006): from the blackening of the vessel (nigredo), through a whitening (albedo) and yellowing (citrinas), to the reddening (rubedo), where life has fully returned.

Also, as highlighted, the 'outcome' of the process is very difficult to call, as an analysand may withdraw from the analysis at any point (especially at the nigredo, or 'death' stage) and the work can get stuck or snarled up by the power of the complexes at work, or by difficult dynamics in the transference–countertransference. Finally, there is rarely a 'complete' resolution as portrayed in the new birth stage. Rather, the analysand may arrive at a powerful awareness of who they are, flaws and all, and have something valuable to take with them from the analysis.

We are all 'works in progress', as Jung would agree, so regarding the archetypal transference as a valuable archetypal template but acknowledging the uncertainties of therapeutic work is often best. However, the alchemical framework Jung discovered is clearly germane to personal development and long-term therapy. Despite its apparent irrelevance at first sight, it is now something which Jungian analytic practice and related academic and clinical studies value and take very seriously.

Key terms

Alchemy: The long tradition of mystical–philosophical thinking and practice which aims at transmuting base metal into gold; the mystery or 'magic' of this process, which is sometimes applied to other cultural settings.

Archetypal transference: Refers specifically to Jung's application of the *Rosarium* to analysis, but can also refer to where archetypes come up in projections in analysis, as well as to inner relationships ubiquitous in depth psychological work.

Vas: The container in which the alchemists mixed their 'materials', also sometimes called the crucible or retort. A metaphor for the 'container' of analysis.

Dig deeper

Casement, A., ,*Carl Gustav Jung* (London: Sage, 2001)

Goss, P., 'Masculinity and Claustrum as Shadow Vas', Ch. 13 in Mathers, D. (ed.), *Alchemy and Psychotherapy: Post-Jungian Perspectives* (London: Routledge, 2014)

Greenberg, L., Rice, L. and Elliot, R., *Facilitating Emotional Change* (New York: Guilford Press, 1993)

Jung, C. G., 'Psychology of the Transference' in *The Practice of Psychotherapy*, 2nd ed. (London: Routledge, 1966)

Jung, C. G., 'The Psychic Nature of the Alchemical Work' in *Psychology and Alchemy*, CW12, 2nd ed. (London: Routledge, 1980)

Martin, S., *Alchemy and Alchemists* (Harpenden: Pocket Essentials, 2006)

Mathers, D. (ed.), 'Introduction' in *Alchemy and Psychotherapy: Post-Jungian Perspectives* (London: Routledge, 2014)

Rowling, J. K., *Harry Potter Box Set: The Complete Collection* (New York: Levine Books, 2007)

Shwartz-Salant, N., *Jung on Alchemy* (London: Routledge, 1995)

Fact-check (answers at the back)

1 What did alchemists try to do with metals?
- **a** Turn base metal into silver
- **b** Turn silver into gold
- **c** Turn base metal into gold
- **d** Turn gold into base metal

2 Why did Jung think alchemy was relevant to his 'creative illness' of 1913–17?
- **a** He had dialogued with a number of alchemists in his encounter with the unconscious
- **b** The unconscious is like an alchemical 'crucible' to mix ideas in
- **c** His experiences were an alchemy of illness and sanity
- **d** His 'base' experiences made it possible for him to extract theoretical and clinical 'gold'

3 Following his studies of Paracelsus, what did Jung see that the alchemists had done?
- **a** Come up with an explicit formula for working with the unconscious
- **b** Projected the unconscious, collective and personal, into matter
- **c** Deliberately connected the numinous and personal unconscious
- **d** Deliberately tried to trap spirit in matter

4 Why is the therapeutic process like alchemy?
- **a** It involves work with difficult material that can produce valuable psychological outcomes
- **b** It does not always work and is often futile and fanciful
- **c** It involves working with changes in the 'psychic temperature' of the analysis
- **d** It works best where both participants are familiar with alchemical principles

5 Why is the 'analytic container' like the alchemical *vas*?
   a   It needs to take place in an environment with lots of old artefacts around
   b   It provides a safe and consistent space in which the process can take place
   c   It generates a lot of heat which can get out of control
   d   It provides opportunities for mystical experiences

6 Why is the 'seeding' of gold in the alchemical process like analysis?
   a   The analyst is paid to provide the process for the analysand
   b   Analysis sometimes has 'golden' breakthrough moments
   c   The analyst and the analysand generate gold from the start
   d   The analyst needs to be open to the potential for change and growth from the start

7 What does the archetypal transference between analyst and analysand refer to?
   a   The fact there is always a transference between them
   b   The unconscious connection between them, and archetypal projections arising
   c   The unconscious projection of parental figures on to the analyst
   d   The awareness of transference cropping up in the analysis at key points

8 Why does the *Rosarium* provide a template for the archetypal transference?
   a   It portrays the relationship between opposites through a natural cycle of change
   b   It portrays the erotic relationship between the masculine and feminine in the psyche
   c   It portrays the alchemical process, which is archetypal
   d   It portrays the archetype of the masculine and feminine syzygy

9 Between the mercurial fountain and nigredo ('death'), what happens?

   a The analysand disappears into their unconscious

   b The analysand and analysts share difficult experiences until the work gets stuck

   c The analysand explores their shadow, then there is deeper union with the analyst until the work deadens

   d The analyst helps the analysand explore what gets them stuck in life, and so that is what happens

10 Between the ascent of the soul and new birth, what happens?

   a The analysand is first vulnerable to the unconscious but eventually integrates it

   b The analyst looks at the analysand's spiritual beliefs to help their soul develop

   c The analysand 'ascends' in a transcendent way and the analyst helps the 'new birth'

   d The analyst is also affected and 'ascends' and has a new psychological birth

14

Working with children and lifespan development

Jung proposed four life stages, each of which has a particular purpose within the individuation journey of the human being. The task, according to Jung, is for each of us to recognize what 'belongs' in each life stage and attend to this as best we can, in order to become as fully 'who we are' as we can manage in our lifetime.

All these stages, including childhood, have significance for Jung in terms of psychological development and therapeutic approaches. In this chapter exploring Jung's archetypal model of the life stages, the importance of the *child* archetype for Jung, and his perspective on childhood, will be contrasted with Michael Fordham's developmental model and the nature of Jungian child analysis. A case study will illuminate the practice of Jungian child analysis and address the question of lifespan development.

Jung and the 'child' archetype

Jung took the view that childhood was not the right stage of life to concentrate our efforts to understand the individuation process. He thought the child's unconscious was dominated by the unconscious of the parents, and therefore children did not become properly self-aware, and therefore able to begin to individuate, until puberty (at the earliest). This principle may ring true where a child finds themselves living out what a parent did not achieve (e.g. someone realizing that their career choice was actually what their mother or father had wanted to do but had not) but, as we shall see, Jung's proposition has not held up as an overarching principle.

Spotlight: The child and the collective unconscious

Jung proposed that the child is 'nearer' the collective unconscious than the adult. This idea seems to be supported by children reporting vivid fantasies and dreams, or becoming thoroughly identified with a character from a story – a Snow White or a Harry Potter – who enthrals them.

Imagination can be so vivid it is not uncommon for a child to experience a real sense of the presence of monsters or ghosts in their darkened bedroom. However, was Jung making assumptions based on *his* unusually active imagination and openness to dreams as a child?

The *child* archetype is not to be exclusively identified with childhood. This can be seen as an archetypal influence which enables us all, at whatever stage in life, to get in touch with our capacity for childlike play and creativity. It also has its problematic side, wherein the linked archetype of the 'eternal child' (*puer aeternus*: male; *puella aeturnus*: female) can come to dominate an adult's psyche. This is characterized by a deep (often hidden) longing to still be a child and not wanting to grow up ('Peter Pan'), with all the attendant implications of taking responsibility and leaving the 'safety' and 'magic' of childhood behind. The positive side to this is where the *eternal child* archetype facilitates access to extensive resources of imagination, play and creativity, enabling the adult to produce, for example, a powerful piece of art or music.

For Jung, the *child* archetype also represents important dimensions of the developments of collective consciousness, reflecting the struggle for integration and completion which has hallmarked human evolution. As he puts it:

> 'The "child" is all that is abandoned and exposed and at the same time divinely powerful: the insignificant, dubious beginning, and the triumphal end. The "eternal child" in man is an indescribable experience... an imponderable that determines the ultimate worth or worthlessness of a personality.'
>
> Jung, 1968, para. 300

As Shiho Main (2008) argues, the *child* archetype represents an important collective influence around the evolution of human consciousness. It challenges the overly 'grown-up' rational aspects of the scientific empiricism and positivism that are the basis of the modern world.

Jung's model of the life stages

Before outlining Jung's model of archetypal life stages, within which a Jungian approach to working therapeutically with children can be set, a couple of contextual points. First, why did Jung propose such a framework? The answer lies with his notion of a prospective individuating process that we can all engage with, and succeed in doing to varying degrees.

Likewise, there is a purpose to the division he made between the first and second half of life, something we explored in relation to typology in Chapter 9. He used the metaphor of the sun's trajectory across the sky over a day to provide a metaphor for this. The first half of our life is the 'morning', when the sun dawns in the eastern sky and rises up to its highest place at midday. This, for Jung represents our fundamental task in the first half of life: to find our place in the world and fulfil our 'outer' potential.

Then, once we reach mid-life, we change direction. Like the sun, once it arrives at the zenith of its ascent, we begin our 'descent' towards the end of our lives, a shift that can be imperceptible, but irrevocable once it is begun. This movement inwards implies a need to come back to who we are in a fundamental sense, and includes spiritual aspects of our sense of self. This is a time when we are being called to work on our self-development and consolidation rather than our responsibilities for others or our *persona* in the world. Finally, we ready ourselves for death (and beyond?).

Although linear and clear-cut, the Jung's life-stage model recognizes that each person will experience and 'perform' their path through life in their own unique way, so any generalizations like these need to be seen as archetypal but not *fixed* templates to describe life's patterns. He would accept the evidence of people bursting into extroverted life in the second half of life through a new work or creative venture, or following a deeply introverted path, as say a solitary researcher or religious contemplative, in the first half. These principles are there to help us get an overall sense of the shape of archetypal influences on our passage through life, not to prescribe and limit how this might be lived out by individuals. Rather, it can be argued that the idea of lifespan development being a movement first 'out into the world', then 'back into self', is a valuable one.

The four specific life stages Jung proposed are:

1 Childhood

2 Adolescence and early adulthood

3 Full adulthood and mid-life

4 Old age

Each stage is described below, with particular thought given to the particular purpose of each one in relation to the individuation process.

LIFE STAGE 1: CHILDHOOD
Jung thought the child did not really have an identity separate from its parents because their unconscious, and the collective

unconscious more generally, was the dominant influence. For Jung, the child's ego has not properly separated from the self. This means that she or he, up until puberty, is not properly aware of themselves (we can compare this to Jung's personal experience of 'stepping out of the mist' at the age of 11, described in Chapter 2, and possibly critique this aspect of his model as too closely influenced by his own subjective experience).

This perspective has been amended significantly by post-Jungian thinkers. In particular, Michael Fordham (1994), has proposed a model for understanding child development from a post-Jungian perspective. He based this on rigorous and extensive infant observation, and it is more in accord with psychodynamic theorists such as Klein (in particular), Winnicott, Fairburn and Guntrip (see Gomez, 1997), who recognized the autonomous development of the child from the very beginning of her or his life. (The model and its influence on child analysis are described further below.)

LIFE STAGE 2: ADOLESCENCE AND EARLY ADULTHOOD

This stage carries archetypal connotations of 'the hero's journey' (Campbell, 2012), since it first involves the young person trying to break free from the overarching influence of parents and other authority figures. For Jung, this is where the individuation process 'proper' begins, and this has a prospective purpose (Frankel, 1998). The extroverting impulse to get out into the world and find one's place in terms of work and relationships (possibly starting a family) then continues to hallmark the period through to the late twenties, when for Jung, the person becomes properly 'adult' (rather than as early as 18, or even 16, as current convention puts it).

LIFE STAGE 3: FULL ADULTHOOD AND MID-LIFE

The thirties, forties and beyond should see the individual consolidate their *persona* place in the world and fulfil their personal and professional aspirations – although learning to deal with the disappointments and broken dreams of adulthood are also part of the individuation process. At mid-life, as highlighted above, Jung proposed that psyche makes a turn inwards and the *introverted* function usually takes precedence. This can take the dramatic form of a mid-life crisis (new relationship, job or way of life) or show itself in a more subtle but real shift towards self-reflection and the spiritual side of life.

LIFE STAGE 4: OLD AGE

Here, the introverting impulse moves the individual further towards reflection and contemplation about the meaning of their lives – what they have achieved or have regrets about, as well as underlying themes pointing towards deeper purpose or spiritual connections. Sometimes this may be about an existential struggle with life's 'meaninglessness'; sometimes it may have a clear root in a religious tradition or spiritual search. Either way, the task of reconciling oneself to who one is, as well as preparing for the end of life and what may or may not lie beyond it, is central to this period of life.

APPLYING THE MODEL TO ANALYSIS

It should be clear, from the discussion so far, that this framework has implications for the therapeutic setting. The analyst takes carefully into account the 'life stage' of their analysand, alongside all other factors described in previous chapters, such as complexes, transference–countertransference and typology. Jolanta, our fictional analysand, for example, is 28 and therefore crossing the stages between early and full adulthood. Using Jung's formulation for this, it does seem as if she is wrestling with questions of belonging as well as the struggle to find and sustain a rewarding long-term relationship.

MICHAEL FORDHAM AND CHILD DEVELOPMENT

Michael Fordham radically reshaped Jung's initial thinking on the nature of childhood and therapeutic work with children (Astor, 1995). Jung showed no interest in applying analytic principles to children – because of his conviction the child was not a proper 'individual' but dominated by parental and collective influences. Fordham, on the other hand, though analysed by Jung, was also strongly influenced by the thinking emerging from Object Relations theorists. In particular, the ground-breaking play-therapy-based approach of Melanie Klein (e.g. 1946) made a deep impact on him, while he developed his interests in paediatrics and in psychoanalysis with children.

The theoretical base for Klein's work arose from Freud's psychosexual formulations, but she condensed these – believing that all fundamental aspects of Freud's model, including the Oedipal complex, were present from birth, and so even the play of very young children conveyed unconscious patterns which portrayed *desire, envy* and *greed*, for example.

Fordham was taken with these insights, and thought Klein had understood some very important psychic processes, such as **splitting** – a universal human tendency to split experience into 'good' and 'bad' – as well as her powerful insights into **projection** and **introjection** (Klein, 1946). He also appreciated the work of Donald Winnicott in identifying pivotal ideas about stages of development in infancy and beyond. Winnicott also highlighted how crucial the quality of care provided by the primary carer is for healthy child development (and the corresponding need for 'good enough mothering' (Winnicott, 1965)). These ideas were also developing in the context of Bowlby's (1999) research into attachment and separation, which reinforced the critical role of early relationships in shaping the inner life of the young child, as well as the patterns of relationship that could come pervasively to influence adolescence and adulthood.

Fordham conducted extensive observations of very young children, carefully noting their responses to the world around them. He was particularly struck by the capacity of babies, right from their entry into the world, to make their needs known – crying repeatedly, for example, until they got the soothing sensation of mother's nipple in their mouth, and her milk filling their stomach, to assuage their hunger. Slightly older infants, he noticed, could both physically reach out for what took their interest, and catch their mother's attention with a sound or a smile. It became clear to Fordham that Jung's notions about children having a passive relationship to inner and outer influences were not borne out by how they operated. While they might be strongly influenced by parental and collective influences, it was also clear that deeply psychological and relational forces were at work in them.

From these insights, Fordham constructed his own theoretical model for understanding early child development, which in turn enabled him to evolve a clinical framework for child analysis. Fordham proposed that at birth the self was whole, but as soon as the baby comes into contact with reality, beyond her or his own skin and mother's womb (which had been the whole of their prenatal 'world'), the self begins to 'de-integrate'. What Fordham meant by this is a healthy process whereby, as the baby engages with the sight, sound, smell and touch of their environment, they find themselves psychologically having to let go of the sense of being completely contained within their own skin (fused to mother) and instead 'reach out' or 'towards' their environment, in order to get their needs met.

Thus, when an infant cries because it is hungry – to get a response from mother – it is de-integrating (and their cry is a de-integrate). They are letting go of their basic integration of self, in order to reach out and get what they need. If the mother hears and responds to this by picking the baby up and giving them the milk they are craving, this enables re-integration for the infant, whereby the de-integration by the infant has been satisfactorily met. Fordham proposed this as the basis of ego formation: the cycle's promotion of the child's autonomy enabled ego to separate from self and establish the ego–self axis (described in Chapter 5).

This process, Fordham believed, enabled the child to develop the necessary reflective capacity to develop a sense of self, which could then be expressed through their play, behaviour, creativity or explicit use of language. Where the infant is not provided with the responses she or he seeks, and where this happens regularly – or the primary carer responds in an inconsistent way – then there is a risk of dis-integration rather than de-integration–re-integration. If the infant's efforts to be heard and seen and get the need for a cuddle or a feed are not met, she or he may slowly give up trying, or their behaviour may become uncontained and reactive. If the re-integrates are offered inconsistently by mother or other carers, the child may desperately try to control the situation by becoming very rigid in its responses. All these responses reflect the efforts of psyche not to disintegrate and thus generate significant mental health problems which remain into adulthood.

Spotlight: Child observation

The training organization Michael Fordham was instrumental in establishing, the Society for Analytical Psychology in London, is one of a number that place strong emphasis on the value of infant observation as a precursor to training as a Jungian analyst. Trainees are encouraged to visit a volunteer family once a week for two years to observe closely and meticulously record what they observe happening between the infant and mother for one hour. They then present their observations to the student group. This is a very good way to promote observational skills and tease out unconscious dynamics inherent in early relational patterns, including those of de-integration–re-integration.

Post-Jungian theory and practice

Valuable work continues to build on Fordham's thinking. Maria Sidoli (2000) places emphasis on the constellation of archetypal figures in the psyche of the child which represent bodily experienced suffering and sometimes trauma. She uses the example of the child producing an image of a witch in their spontaneous drawings, which comes to stand for acute disruptions to the *de-integration–re-integration* cycle. Jean Knox (2003) has elucidated the strong links between attachment patterns and archetypal process, while Margaret Wilkinson (2006) has provided important insights into the impact of these influences, from a neuroscientific perspective, on child development and adult experience and relationships. In this respect, post-Jungian thinkers are making valuable contributions to this area.

The boy who couldn't find the top

Mahmut, a four-year-old boy, was referred for Jungian child analysis after his family and the staff at his day nursery reported his lack of verbal communication. His vocabulary was limited to under 40 words (which he could use in both Turkish and English), and there was one word, 'top', which he repeated regularly, especially when he was distressed. He would sometimes accompany this word by pointing up above his head, or putting both his hands on the top of it. His formal developmental assessment by an educational psychologist had confirmed there was no developmental delay that might have affected his speech.

The analyst spent a number of sessions mainly observing his play. Mahmut seemed to be particularly interested in building towers and then pushing down on them from the top until they were broken into lots of separate bricks on the floor. His drawings often involved shapes without a top to them – for example, he would draw a house or a car without a roof. When the analyst asked him about this, he would usually say 'top' and point at the picture.

From information the parents and others had given about the boy's early life, the analyst wondered how much disruption there might have been to the *de-integration–re-integration* process. Mahmut had been affected by a lengthy period when his parents visited ill relatives in Turkey, so his grandparents had looked after him; they had been having major building work done while he was staying with them. While it was unclear how directly the latter factors related to how Mahmut presented in analysis, they seemed to have a bearing on his capacity to express himself and relate to others. The lack of a 'roof' in his drawing suggested this, too – Fordham had noticed a child's natural tendency to move towards drawing complete circular shapes after their formative use of individual straight lines – and the analyst wondered whether the incomplete houses and cars reflected where *re-integration* in response to his *de-integrates* had not been consistently offered.

In the light of this hypothesis, the analyst focused on engaging in reciprocal play and verbalization with Mahmud, to offer him a reparative experience of *de-integration–re-integration*. Over 18 months of analysis (twice a week), Mahmut came to develop further spoken language and to express unconscious Influences through a fuller range of play as well as some 'complete' drawing of houses, cars, etc. The nursery and Mahmut's parents agreed to take a similarly responsive approach to Mahmut's communications of feelings and thoughts, and gradually he became more settled and engaged in his relationships with others.

Key idea: Jungian play therapy

Play therapy lends itself well to a Jungian approach, with its emphasis on working symbolically and creatively. Eric Green (2014) has provided a clear overview of the ways in which this can be implemented, e.g. via sand play or drawing, to work in a variety of applications including abuse and bereavement, as well as presenting conditions such as ADHD and autism. Jungian approaches to counselling children are also influential (Allen, 1989).

Key terms

Child archetype: The constellation in the human psyche of collective representations of wholeness, as well as the past and future of human consciousness. In individuals this represents these influences of past development and future potential in the individuation process.

De-integration–re-integration: Fordhams' ego-formation process whereby the infant engages with their environment and lets go of the sense of being completely contained and instead 'reaches out' or *de-integrates* in order to get their needs met. When the primary carer(s) respond to this need, the child can *re-integrate* a new experience securely.

Good enough mothering: Winnicott's term to describe what the infant requires to develop ego strength, independence and capacity for relationship.

Introjection: Klein's term for the way the infant unconsciously 'takes in' versions of part-objects (e.g. mother's breast or face) and in healthy development this eventually becomes a full version of 'mother' (whole object).

Projection: Where we put unconscious aspects of ourselves onto the other person.

***Puer* and *Puella aeternus*:** The eternal child archetype (eternal boy – *puer*; girl – *puella*) which Jung proposed could affect a person's capacity to fully 'grow up' and accept responsibility, but which could also be a source of creativity.

Splitting: Klein's term to describe the fundamental tendency of the infant to split experience into 'good' and 'bad' in an all-or-nothing way. This gets resolved when the infant realizes that mother, like themselves, is a mix of good and bad.

Dig deeper

Allen, J., *Inscapes of the Child's World: Jungian Counselling in Schools and Clinics* (New York: Spring Publications, 1989)

Astor, J., *Michael Fordham: Innovations in Analytical Psychology* (London: Routledge, 1995)

Bowlby, J., 'Attachment' in *Attachment and Loss*, (vol. 1), 2nd ed. (New York: Basic Books, 1999)

Campbell, J., *The Hero with a Thousand Faces*, 3rd ed. (San Francisco: New World Library, 2012)

Fordham, M., *Children as Individuals* (London: Karnac, 1994)

Frankel, R., *The Adolescent Psyche: Jungian and Winnicottian Perspectives* (Hove: Brunner-Routledge, 1998)

Gomez, L., *An Introduction to Object Relations* (New York: New York University Press, 1997)

Green, E., *The Handbook of Jungian Play Therapy with Children and Adolescents* (Baltimore: Johns Hopkins University Press, 2014)

Jung, C. G., 'The Child Archetype' in *The Archetypes and the Collective Unconscious*, 2nd ed. (London: Routledge, 1968)

Klein, M., *The Writings of Melanie Klein, vol. 3.* (New York: Free Press, 1946)

Knox, J., *Archetypes, Attachment, Analysis: Jungian Psychology and the Emergent Mind* (Hove: Brunner-Routledge, 2003)

Main, S., *Childhood Re-imagined: Images and Narratives of Development in Analytical Psychology* (London: Routledge, 2008)

Sidoli, M., *When the Body Speaks: The Archetypes in the Body* (London: Routledge, 2000)

Wilkinson, M., *Coming into Mind: The mind–brain relationship: a Jungian clinical perspective* (London: Routledge, 2006)

Winnicott, D., *The Maturational Process and Facilitative Environment* (London: Karnac, 1965)

Fact-check (answers at the back)

1 Why did Jung not see child analysis as worthwhile?
   a Children could not understand therapeutic language
   b The unconscious of a child was dominated by parental and collective influences
   c Children found it hard to concentrate
   d The unconscious of a child is flooded with childish, not mature, things

2 What does the child archetype do, according to Jung?
   a It always tries to stop us growing up
   b It represents the regressions and fragmentation of the psyche
   c It shows us what we were like as a child
   d It represents wholeness, and humanity's past and future

3 What can be problematic about the 'eternal child' archetype?
   a It can lead us to avoid adult responsibility and regress to an unrealistic 'childishness'
   b It can make us obsessively religious
   c It can stop us treating our own children in a caring and respectful way
   d It can make us wish it could be Christmas every day

4 What influence does the archetype of senex (wise old man) have?
   a It encourages us to pass through the life stages quickly
   b It stops us from grounding our creativity in something real
   c It generates wisdom and order but is sometimes too impatient and excitable
   d It generates wisdom and order but sometimes is too conservative and reactionary

5 What is the correct order of Jung's four life stages?
   a Childhood and adolescence; early adulthood; full adulthood and mid-life; old age
   b Childhood; adolescence and early adulthood; full adulthood and mid-life; old age
   c Childhood; adolescence and early adulthood; full adulthood; mid-life and Old Age
   d Childhood and adolescence; early adulthood; full adulthood; mid-life and old age

6 What is the emphasis/task of adolescence and early adulthood?
  a To be introverted while still establishing our identity
  b To establish who we want to be when we grow up
  c To be extroverted in establishing our identity in the world
  d To extrovert completely so we become totally identified with our personas

7 What is the emphasis/task in old age?
  a To reflect in an introverted way on our life's meaning, and prepare for death
  b To try and push our regrets away from consciousness
  c To rest and look after our physical health
  d To keep working and remain extroverted for as long as we can

8 How are the life stages relevant to analysis?
  a They provide a metaphor for the process of analysis
  b They help work with the age difference between analyst and analysand
  c They provide a framework for understanding challenges the analysand may be facing
  d They provide a way to help get the analysand to focus specifically on the 'here and now'

9 For what reason was Fordham influenced by object relations theory on child development?
  a It could explain observable autonomous behaviour and unconscious processes
  b It offered a way of describing why a child could not make use of analysis
  c It provided an updated rationale that supported Jung's views on childhood
  d It helped Fordham interpret his own relationships to his parents

10 How does understanding de-integration–re-integration help the child analyst?

a It helps them notice where the child is too influenced by their parents' unconscious

b It provides ways to understand where the child's development may have got disrupted

c It allows the analyst to re-integrate what they have forgotten about the child

d It offers a specific model for analysing the child's dreams

15

Working with mental health difficulties

Through his work on schizophrenia (see Chapter 3), Jung was able to identify underlying psychological processes that demonstrated unconscious influences on mood and behaviour and establish an approach to the workings of the human psyche which could facilitate resolution, or at least partial resolution, of presenting obstacles to mental health (e.g. complexes). The template Jung established in this respect hallmarked his later work in a number of areas which remain highly relevant today. Specific themes such as addiction and depression continue to be explored from a Jungian perspective and to benefit from the application of Jung's key principles regarding self-regulation and the capacity of the unconscious to facilitate healing.

This chapter explores the origins of Jungian approaches and how they are applied today to therapeutic work with people experiencing mental health difficulties. Theory and clinical applications of work with depression trauma, addiction and personality disorders are also discussed.

Jung and the mind–body connection

What motivated Jung's early work in psychiatry was his desire to understand the workings of the unwell psyche so as to alleviate the suffering of the individual patient, which, in the case of those at the Burgholzi, was generally pervasive and debilitating. Jung would move away from the Freudian notion of 'cure' and towards the principle of 'healing', which he thought better captured the need for a more holistic approach to addressing influences in the mind–body (or **psyche–soma**) dynamic which perpetuated discomforting and harmful effects on health and well-being.

Other Jungian writers have built on his emphasis on the importance of the body–mind connection, in influencing the well-being of psyche. Melanie Costello in her book *Imagination, Illness And Injury: Jungian Psychology and the Somatic Dimensions of Perception* (2006), illustrates with case studies how cognitive and affective processes can create bodily ('somatic') manifestations, e.g. where depressive, anxious or self-critical states contribute to illness. This is located within an archetypal framework for understanding how our perception of ourselves (influenced by our complexes) can create the conditions for this.

Jung's approach to depression

The angle Jung took towards working with depressed people was rather different from the current emphasis on structured, often short-term therapeutic interventions for depression and anxiety, such as those deployed by a cognitive behavioural approach (Beck and Alford, 2008). Jung wrote about depression in relation to his theory of archetypal opposites and compensatory mechanisms in the psyche. One case from his practice which he described involved a wealthy businessman who had been able to retire early to enjoy all the benefits of his financial situation. However, he discovered that this drove him into a state of hypochondriac anxiety and depression, which did not abate when he decided to start working again. Jung made a link between this apparently regressed psychological state and his need to be attended to by his mother, which inevitably dated back to early life.

Jung tried to help this analysand by getting him to recognize the presence of the opposite to the overflowing riches which he (materially) possessed. This opposite was the neediness of the boy within who had not had his needs met and was now manifesting this through psychosomatic symptoms and a deep despair. Jung characterizes the approach required in terms of the 'downward gradient' trapped energy needs in order to be able to flow naturally again (like a stream seeking a downhill route in the landscape):

> 'It has become abundantly clear to me that life can flow forward only along the path of the gradient. But there is no energy unless there is a tension of opposites: hence it is necessary to discover the opposite to the attitude of the conscious mind... Seen from the one-sided point of view of the conscious attitude, the shadow is an inferior component of the personality and is consequently repressed through intensive resistance. But the repressed content must be made conscious so as to produce a tension of opposites, without which no forward movement is possible.'
>
> Jung, 1966a, para. 78

In this case, the analysand was not ready to work with his *shadow* to uncover what lay behind his neurotic and depressed state. Jung reports that the analysis, and likewise the man's process of healing, was not able to move forward.

Another example that builds on this approach to working with depression is Judith Hubback's (in Samuels, 1989) discussion of working with people whose depression is intimately linked with early experiences of familial disruption or unhappiness. She demonstrates how the unconscious will split in defence against this and in turn how this can make the archetypal inner *coniunctio* (or 'inner marriage', as described in alchemical terms in Chapter 13) needed for healing, unavailable. Intensive work in the transference–countertransference is needed. The analyst picks up how the analysand is unconsciously fantasizing about the inner life/lives of their parents so these fantasies can be properly processed, to clear the way for the trapped energy in the depression to be released.

A further example of a Jungian approach is provided by David Rosen (2002), who emphasizes the healing potential of working with the unconscious. Individuals experiencing the deepest of depressions, he argues, can gradually transform their misery into creative energy by working with symbols that arise from their suffering. This approach tallies with Jung's premise that we need to identify and work with repressed *shadow* contents in the psyche, to release, step by step, the trapped energy which can slowly improve the person's state of mind.

Addiction: a sickness of the spirit

Jung provided a framework for understanding addiction from an archetypal perspective, which has come to be influential. His proposal that addiction – and in particular alcoholism – has its roots in an absence of *spirit*, or the spiritual in a general sense, was picked up by the founders of Alcoholics Anonymous (AA), and provided the foundation for the work of that organization (as well as other 'Anon' groups such as Narcotics Anonymous). The principle of there being a 'gap' in the psyche which alcohol or another drug can fill led to the emphasis in AA on 'handing over' the task of giving up alcohol to something with more 'spiritual power' than the drink.

As Jung put it (1961) in a letter to Bill Wilson (one of AA's founders):

'(the)... craving for alcohol was the equivalent, on a low level, of the spiritual thirst of our being for wholeness, expressed in medieval language: the union with God... "alcohol" in Latin is "spiritus" and you use the same word for the highest religious experience as well as for the most depraving poison. The helpful formula therefore is: spiritus contra spiritum.'

The Latin phrase here translates roughly into 'spirit against the ravages of spirits'. So, for Jung, the domination of alcoholic spirits (and by implication, other addictive substances) in the life of the addict needs to be replaced by something 'spiritual'. Jung may have had religious belief in mind for some people. However, like AA's '12 steps', a Jungian approach emphasizes the individuality of the pursuit of meaning in life. So this could also be a wider or alternative version of spirituality rather than being part of a faith community. Equally, it could be a deeper grasp of life's existential value and struggle, or a humanistic/atheistic framework.

Whichever form this takes, the key point here is that addiction comes to be seen as an attempt to fill the gap in meaning in someone's life. This gap may be triggered by trauma or loss, or generated by a more low level, long-lasting sense of unease and emptiness. In this sense, one could describe addiction as a kind of complex, which grips the psyche by the way it perpetuates the sense of lack, that then gets temporarily 'filled' by alcohol or other drugs. As well as the AA framework, the principle of 'filling the gap' which supposedly stimulates the draw towards drug dependency is a familiar one in some of the literature associated with 'Recovery' (e.g. Adams and Greider, 2005). Presentation of addiction in Jungian analysis tends to be viewed through this frame, although other perspectives on treatment of addiction, as well as the specifics of the analysand's way of presenting with this, will be incorporated properly into the approach taken.

Luis Zoja (2000), a Jungian thinker, has taken this thinking a step further by locating addiction in a collective context. He argues that addiction (whether to drinking, eating, gambling, smoking, sex or shopping) is prevalent in westernized societies because it is a response to an important *lack* in the Western, consumerist psyche. This lack he associates with the need for *initiation*:

'We appear to live under conditions that are, for the most part, desacralized. However, it is enough just to scratch the surface of the situation to rediscover many elements of a real religious state, the survival of which manifests itself indirectly, especially in a need for esoteric and initiatory experiences.'

Zoja, 2000, p. 2

Zoja points out that, in so-called primitive societies, drugs were used in a controlled way as part of initiation rituals. In particular they would play their part in the following sequence, where an adolescent was being initiated into the mysteries and responsibilities of adulthood:

1 Experiencing the transcendence of meaninglessness

2 An initiatory death, involving a kind of renunciation of one's previous identity and 'the ordinary world'

3 Initiatory ritual, e.g. through controlled use of drugs

Step three is generally unavailable, as the second step is not provided for in Western societies – there is no established provision for people to refrain from behaviour that is consumer led, other than in some religious or alternative lifestyle communities. What Zoja suggests happens instead is a kind of misguided attempt (partly conscious but mainly unconscious) to 'arrive' in a new or 'other' state which fulfils an archetypal need for initiation. So the gambler keeps gambling, the drinker keeps drinking, etc., in an attempt to experience a proper sense of initiation. However, the fantasy of reaching the new/adult state via the use of the drug becomes the thing that sustains the addiction. Without the 'initiatory death' first, the use of the drug becomes a thing of addiction, not initiation.

WORKING WITH ADDICTION IN ANALYSIS

In the therapeutic context, naming and owning the *shadow* of addiction in a person's life, then the reflective search for what really matters to them (existential, spiritual, practical or religious), followed by the nurturing and conscious integration of this in their life via concrete steps or inner commitment to what is important, can make a real difference in supporting abstinence or moderation of addictive behaviour, as those who have successfully implemented the '12 steps' of AA can testify. David Schoen (2009) provides an archetypal Jungian critique of why these seem to work more than many other interventions. He suggests that more than personal *shadow* needs to be overcome – addiction, he says, is a struggle with **archetypal shadow** (or 'evil'?). Work with dreams and other unconscious material is needed to tackle the deep roots of addiction, he argues.

However, other writers have stressed the need for a science-based understanding of the nature of addiction and sobriety (e.g. Sheff, 2014), and Jung's initial formula can seem a little simplistic, relying on his own emphasis on the 'religious problem'. In this respect, the possibly one-sided solution he proposes needs to be placed in the wider context of what can influence addictive behaviour, such as the way the craving for the addictive substance can get hard-wired into the brain. However, Schoen's and Zoja's formulations provide powerful insight into what perpetuates the apparent epidemic of addictive behaviour in Westernized societies.

Addiction: finding the will to stop

Jolanta had been aware for some time that her habit of having a beer and a few glasses of wine just about every night after work, sometimes complemented by smoking cannabis, had got out of hand. Sometimes it would be a whole bottle of wine (or more) and at the weekends there would often be parties with the friends she had made from work, as well as from the gym she worked out at most days of the week.

Curiously (at first glance), it was the gym that alerted Jolanta to the problematic cycle she seemed to have got into. She would go to the gym straight after work and go for the burn – push herself as hard as she could on the running machine and the weights, before showering and then heading home. She was often on a high anyway, with the endorphins kicking in, but she deliberately did not drink any water. When she got home she'd open a cold beer, relishing it as she drank it quickly, and then go on to the wine, as well as smoking cannabis some evenings.

Jolanta knew this cycle was starting to dominate her life; she would be thinking about the high-octane workout–drink–smoke sequence at regular intervals during the day at work, and had got to the point where she was turning down social invitations in order to get her buzz at the end of each day. She sensed an emptiness behind all this and shared this with her analyst. She described a dream where she was standing in an empty classroom in her old school in Poland.

When they explored what this might be about, it became clear how powerful the sense of disconnect between present and past was for Jolanta. She had left so much behind, including some deeply unhappy family dynamics that remained unresolved. She spoke of having come to the UK to escape this but also to 'grow up'. After a number of sessions around this theme, she resolved to go home in her next holiday – 'to get back in touch with who I am'. Whatever it was she had tried to escape from, but which she inevitably carried in her *shadow,* needed to be faced. She also resolved to cut back on her substance use, but was unsure whether she had the will to manage this. But by not renewing her gym membership for a few months, she could change the routine that supported this. She would jog instead, and drink water afterwards, and restrict her weekend drinking to moderate levels.

Jolanta's emerging awareness of her reliance on the previous routine, which seemed to have an addictive quality, enabled her to recognize the feeling of 'lack' behind it. She saw the importance of finding a more meaningful sense of who she was and what really mattered to her (Jung's 'spirit' to counter the 'ravages of spirits'). She also recognized the need to root her movement into full adulthood, in both a proper recognition of past influences and a conscious effort to control her drug consumption. Here, *ego* had begun to listen to *self*: but would Jolanta be able to sustain this?

Trauma: an archetypal approach

An important contribution to clinical work with severe mental health problems has been made by Donald Kalsched (1996). Rather than trying to understand the impact of childhood trauma only in neurobiological or psychodynamic terms (though both of these are crucial), Kalsched proposed that a deeper psychic process is activated by trauma. This is archetypal, in terms of how psyche responds to the overwhelming terror and threat of destruction, inherent in trauma induced by physical or sexual abuse, or some kind of shocking experience of loss or disaster. Kalsched drew on Jung's pertinent observations on how the consequences of trauma manifest in the psyche:

'a traumatic complex brings about dissociation of the psyche...
it forces itself tyrannically upon the conscious mind...
I have frequently observed that the typical traumatic affect is
represented in dreams as a wild and dangerous animal – a
striking illustration of its autonomous nature when split off from
consciousness.'

Jung, 1966b, paras 266–7

Like Jung, Kalsched noticed in his practice how analysands who
had been on the receiving end of deeply disturbing traumatic
experiences in childhood presented with nightmarish dream
material involving not just dangerous animals, but scenes of
utter brutality – murder, beheadings and vicious attacks on the
dreamer or other figures in dreams.

Kalsched made sense of these phenomena by considering the
workings of what he named 'archetypal defences'. He posited
that the psyche has a natural tendency to defend itself in
proportion to the scale of the attack it experiences. Where abuse
or other trauma involving primary carers occurs, these defences
are caught in an impossible position, as the child cannot expel
the bad experiences, for they have been created by an intimately
loved figure. The energy remains trapped and, instead, the
very defences that also hold the child's brittle psyche intact in
the face of devastating assault assume a position where they
attack the self, because they cannot attack the external figure
which has inflicted the damage. Hence the dissociation occurs,
which means the psyche splits into separate domains, causing
inner disturbance and conflict. Kalsched argues that this is an
archetypal response, manifested in archetypal imaginal figures,
to early trauma and loss.

The analyst utilizes the (archetypal) transference to enable the
intervening, disrupting defences to slowly transform, as well as
taking the empathic stance needed for healing. Dream material
is pivotal to noticing where and how the internal 'figure'
maintains the split, and for any symbolism which might indicate
a shift in this. Kalsched gives an example of a black sword
held by a monstrous figure which became double-edged with

a red tinge, reflecting the alchemical move in the analysand's unconscious from the darkness of *nigredo* to the life-bringing *rubedo* (redness), a move which showed itself in the settling and integrating of psychic elements, as the healing process ensued. Kalsched (2013) more recently deepened his conceptual framework in terms of describing where trauma interrupts not just personal development but also the archetypal level of human experiencing – the level of 'soul'.

Because of how deeply pervasive these influences are, meaningful work with them takes time. Careful attention to the process of the analysand is needed, from ethical as well as therapeutic standpoints. Likewise, the analyst also needs to attend to their own self-care, as they contend with disturbing material (supervision plays an important role here).

Key idea: Trauma and countertransference

The analyst needs to attend to their countertransference when working with trauma, as with all clinical work. Wilkinson (2003) has elucidated this in terms of a neuroscientific understanding of how important it is for the right-brain of the analyst to connect to the right-brain of the analysand, as this is where the connections to deeper trauma buried in the unconscious can be found. The dissociative defences can be broken down via the transference–countertransference, drawing on dreams and other material, with important shifts resulting for the analysand.

Personality disorders and other mental health needs

The Jungian approach can be caricatured as being suitable only for the 'worried well' (people who have the time and money to explore their inner processes in analysis). However, analysts are geared up to practise with the full range of mental health difficulties. This is supported through their training (where a placement in a psychiatric setting is usually a prerequisite) and, often, previous experience (many trainees will have worked in the mental health field, or already be qualified psychotherapists or practitioners in this area).

Analysts are required to keep up to date with developments in the mental health field throughout their professional lives, and integrate this into their practice (an example is Wilkinson's work (2003), above). They will also often take a number of low-fee analysands who cannot afford the full fee but are presenting with significant needs. The work of an analyst also includes situations where decisions need to be taken about referral of those presenting with very significant mental health problems. These can require a more cross-disciplinary approach than pure analysis, to protect the psychological stability, and even the safety, of the person concerned, and those around them.

In relation to personality disorders, the work of Nathan Shwartz-Salant is a good example of this. With respect to borderline personality disorder, and its hallmark of unpredictable and difficult ways of relating to others, Shwartz-Salant (in Samuels, 1989), starts from the premise that:

> 'Often, psychotherapy reveals bewildering and bizarre introjects stemming from the patient's early childhood experiences... (for which)... An imaginal focus is required if one is to engage the borderline person effectively.'
> Shwartz-Salant in Samuels, 1989, p. 159

He advocates a willingness on the part of the analyst to 'go mad' with their analysand. This does not mean that the analyst abdicates responsibility for the containment and professional boundaries of the work – rather, they hold to Jung's principle that the analyst must be in the archetypal transference with the analysand, and allow the alchemical process of change to happen. This experience of psychological connection, held by the analyst within the maintenance of professional boundaries, then provides the basis for greater personality stability, and capacity for relationship.

In relation to narcissism and narcissistic personality disorder, while other Jungian writers like Jacoby (1991) stress the convergence with ideas from psychoanalysis and object relations, Shwartz-Salant (1982) again deploys an archetypal approach. The need for deep mirroring by the analyst for the analysand, who, like Narcissus, has previously only known themselves as the mirror, is a key feature of his approach. The incorporation of feminine and masculine archetypal influences to facilitate a new awareness of the presence and needs of the 'other' is another.

Spotlight: Typology and narcissism

Aron (2004) suggests that the concept of 'narcissism' would be better understood by exploring deep typological influences from a Jungian perspective, such as levels of sensitivity in introverted personalities.

The approaches described in this chapter demonstrate how a Jungian approach to significant mental health difficulties can provide fresh and profound insights into the ways in which psychic disturbance, and the human suffering associated with it, arise, and how they can be ameliorated.

Key terms

Borderline personality disorder: A presentation of personality that is often characterized by unstable, sometimes hostile, relations with other people and dramatic switches in mood. It is sometimes portrayed as sitting in the 'border territory' between neurosis and psychosis.

Narcissistic personality disorder: A presentation of personality that is hallmarked by a dominant focus on self and a severe difficulty in making and sustaining reciprocal relationships.

Psychopathology: This term refers to the study of the origins of mental health in the individual – psychological, biological, genetic and social. It is also used in a generalized way in psychiatry and psychotherapy, for example in case discussions, to direct attention to these origins.

Dig deeper

Adams, N. and Greider, D., *Treatment Planning for Person-Centred Care: The Road to Mental Health and Addiction Recovery* (Amsterdam: Elsevier, 2005)

Aron, E., 'Revisiting Jung's concept of innate sensitiveness', *Journal of Analytical Psychology*, 49, 337–67 (2004)

Beck, A. T. and Alford, B. A., *Depression: Causes and Treatment*, 2nd ed. (University of Pennsylvania Press, 2008)

Costello, M., *Imagination, Illness And Injury: Jungian Psychology and the Somatic Dimensions of Perception* (London: Taylor & Francis, 2006)

Jacoby, M., *Individuation and Narcissism: The Psychology of Self in Jung and Kohut* (Hove: Routledge, 1991)

Jung, C. G., Letter to Bill Wilson regarding alcoholism, 30.1.1961. Copy at http://www.silkworth.net/aahistory/carljung_billw013061.html

Jung, C. G., *Two Essays on Analytical Psychology*, 2nd ed. (London: Routledge, 1966a)

Jung, C. G., *The Practice of Psychotherapy*, 2nd ed. (London: Routledge, 1966b)

Jung, C. G., *Psychology and Religion: West and East*, CW11, 2nd ed. (London: Routledge, 1969)

Kalsched, T., *The Inner World of Trauma: Archetypal Defences of the Personal Spirit* (London and New York: Routledge, 1996)

Kalsched, D., *Trauma and the Soul: A psycho-spiritual approach to human development and its interruption* (London and New York: Routledge, 2013)

Rosen, D., *Transforming Depression: Healing the Soul Through Creativity* (Newburyport, MA: Hays (Nicolas), 2002)

Samuels, A., *Psychopathology: Contemporary Jungian Perspectives* (London: Karnac, 1989)

Schoen, D., *War of the Gods in Addiction* (New Orleans, LA: Spring Books, 2009)

Sheff, D., *Clean: Overcoming Addiction* (Lyndhurst, NJ: Houghton Mifflin Harcourt, 2014)

Shwartz-Salant, N., *Narcissism and Character Transformation: The Psychology of Narcissistic Character Disorder* (Toronto: Inner-City Books, 1982)

Wilkinson, M., 'Undoing trauma: contemporary neuroscience. A Jungian clinical perspective', *Journal of Analytical Psychology*, 48(2), 235–53 (April 2003)

Zoja, L., *Drugs, Addiction, and Initiation: The Modern Search for Ritual*, 2nd ed. (Einsiedeln, CH: Daimon, 2000)

Fact-check (answers at the back)

1 Why did Jung prefer the term 'healing' to 'cure'?
- **a** Unconscious processes could not cure, as Freud argued
- **b** This made therapeutic language easier to understand
- **c** Unconscious processes, which facilitate well-being, are more holistic than Freud argued
- **d** Jung saw his work as 'spiritual healing'

2 Why is work with shadow important in tackling depression, according to Jung?
- **a** Because it enables the trapped energy creating the depression to be released
- **b** Because it helps to see why the person might choose to be depressed
- **c** Because it meant the analysand would stop projecting their low mood on to the analyst
- **d** Because it allows the trapped energy in the shadow to relax the body

3 What is meant by a 'synthetic' approach to working with the unconscious?
- **a** The early stages of analysis where the work is rather synthetic rather than real
- **b** Conscious and unconscious influences are worked with together to facilitate healing
- **c** The way in which an analyst positions themselves in relation to the analysand
- **d** Conscious and unconscious influences are analysed separately, then together

4 How did Jung think religion or other meaningful influences helped alcoholics?
- **a** By helping them forgive themselves for their addictive behaviours
- **b** By taking them away from reality so they would not turn to drink
- **c** By providing them with genuine 'spirit' to replace damaging alcoholic spirits
- **d** By offering contact with 'spirits' of the dead rather than those of the bottle

5 Why does Zoja think addiction is related to a collective Western problem?

   a Because it sometimes replaces religion, as Jung argued

   b Because it is something people do to copy others and gain acceptance

   c Because there are too many consumers with spare cash to buy drugs

   d Because it reflects our consumerism, which stops proper initiation into adult society

6 What happens when psyche dissociates in response to trauma?

   a It splits into separate parts and produces imagery which is hostile and frightening

   b It refuses to associate with other people in case they criticize them when vulnerable

   c It splits into mind and body and these are then in conflict with each other

   d It refuses to engage with the analyst or the therapeutic process

7 Kalsched argued that trauma creates an archetypal pattern. How?

   a By triggering a warped alchemical process in the unconscious

   b By creating archetypal images which help the person forget the trauma

   c By dropping the individual through their defences and into the unconscious

   d By creating defences against psychic collapse which generate violent imagery

8 What part do the monstrous figures in dreams and fantasies play?

   a They draw the analysand towards the healing process in therapy

   b They symbolize the split in psyche and keep the person away from healing the trauma

   c They guide the analyst towards their own splits and so stall the process

   d They provide images from childhood which help the analysand remember the trauma

9 What are the expectations of analysts regarding work with mental health needs?
   a They are expected to take a classical Jungian position with all needs presented
   b They can always choose what sorts of mental health needs they want to work with
   c They are expected to work with a wide range and keep their knowledge up to date
   d They must work with psychiatric inpatients only

10 What does Shwartz-Salant's approach to borderline personality disorder involve?
   a The analyst imagining they are the analysand, to promote unconscious union
   b The analysand imagining they are their parents, to promote unconscious union
   c The analyst imagining they are mad, to promote unconscious union
   d The analyst allowing their own 'mad' images to arise, to promote unconscious union

Section 4

Jung's legacy: culture, spirituality and therapy

16

Jung's legacy in the arts and sciences

Jungian thinking has influenced a number of areas within our culture, including academic, clinical and spiritual ones. This chapter begins with Jung's approach to science, his valuing of scientific empiricism and his parallel critique of scientific orthodoxy – via, particularly, the concept of synchronicity. We will consider why the Jungian viewpoint has not found it easy to gain acceptance in the scientific world. Then we will explore how Jung's valuing of creativity as an important contributor to the individuation process has helped spread the influence of his ideas to writers, artists, filmmakers and musicians.

Jung's grand project

'... Jung's conceptions of the archetypes, libido and the collective unconscious represented a confluence and synthesis of a number of philosophical, physiological, biological and psychological conceptions at the end of the nineteenth century. Since then the increasing autonomy and fragmentation of psychology, together with the diversification and specialization of sciences of the body, has unravelled even the possibility of such a synthesis.'

Shamdasani, 2003, p. 271

Jung, as we have seen, saw the 'big picture'. As he built on his initial ideas about the human psyche and developed effective treatments and therapeutic interventions for a wide range of presenting mental health conditions, a larger canvas came into view. However, his ambitious framework for influencing scientific thinking has not penetrated academia in the same way as his ideas have generally infiltrated Western culture. As we explore one or two key concepts relevant to Jung's approach, it is important to hold in mind how the position he took left him at times on the perimeters of mainstream empirical scientific study.

By 'thinking outside the box', Jung found himself out on the fringes of mainstream acceptability in the wider psychological and scientific fields. Although there was interest in Jung's ideas, such as by the zoologists Friedrich Alverdes and Konrad Lorenz (more details in Shamdasani, 2003), these tended to be short-lived.

Spotlight: Archetypes and animal behaviour

Konrad Lorenz was a Nobel Prize winning ethologist (i.e. he studied animal behaviour) who, in the mid-twentieth century, noticed Jung's ideas on archetypes and linked these to his understanding of instinctual processes in animals, such as innate release mechanisms (Lorenz, 1970). He demonstrated how such processes are imprinted on animals (e.g. when a baby goose responded to him as 'mother', after encountering him first after hatching from the egg).

Though he argued that Jung may have over-generalized, he also acknowledged the value of his (and Freud's) thinking for developing an approach that tried to explain deep-seated instinctual behaviours. More widely, further specific investigation of such areas drew science towards detailed investigatory research, and away from Jung's tendency to try to synthesize ideas.

Jung was concerned about what he saw as a deep split in Western culture, one that others were highlighting. A contemporary of Jung's, the scientist and fiction writer C. P. Snow, delivered a lecture in 1959 in which he identified the 'two cultures' (Snow, 2001, p. 3) of the sciences and the humanities, and a deep rift between them within intellectual life across all Western societies. Jung saw this split as indicative of how Western culture had got out of touch with its own *soul*, a perception which led him to entitle, in 1933, one of his more deliberately populist books *Modern Man in Search of a Soul* (Jung, 2001). He argued that Western culture had fallen into thrall with the principles of scientific empiricism and a positivistic fixation on provable, measurable, facts. This had driven citizens of these societies away from the search for deeper meaning in life, and hence created a malaise that was individual but also collective.

Humanity was divided against itself, as Jung saw it, because of a split between two fundamental sides of human nature – the rational and the irrational. By sweeping away centuries of religious and other traditions outside the realm of orthodox science, especially those which maintained an investment of meaning in humanity's relationship with the natural world, Jung saw a dangerous one-sidedness emerging in Western culture. He saw the rise of fascism and communism and the growing despoiling of the natural environment in this light. People, and governments, had become over-confident in their own ability to generate wealth and develop the knowledge base of civilization. With the spectre of nuclear destruction of this very 'civilization' looming over the post-war world, Jung warned of the dangers of this exponential growth in the ability to both create and destroy (Freeman, 1959).

Jung thought he had found what he was looking for in order to bridge the divide between religion (and the arts) on the one side, and science on the other, when he began to explore the phenomenon of **synchronicity**. We shall explore this sometimes misunderstood, and even maligned, principle below, as a basis for understanding more fully how Jung saw the creative possibilities for individuation via engagement with both arts/humanities (and religion) and science.

For him, the holistic nature of the individuation process demanded a willingness on our part to embrace and engage with both sides of this 'coin'. When we made one-sided choices to focus on one side at the expense of the other, we were promoting the collective one-sidedness that was tilting us towards danger. Jung embodied this principle in how he sustained a keen interest in scientific matters, developed his own artistic sensibility in his painting (and 'imaginative play' with the stones on the shores of Lake Zurich), and made the psychological and experiential exploration of religious experience fundamental to his framework.

Synchronicity as connecting principle

'Both views, the materialistic as well as the spiritualistic, are metaphysical prejudices. It accords better with experience to suppose that living matter has a psychic aspect, and the psyche a physical aspect... The "acausal" correspondences between mutually independent psychic and physical events, i.e. synchronistic phenomena, and in particular psychokinesis, would then become more understandable, for every physical event would involve a psychic one and vice versa.'

Jung, 1970a, para. 780

Jung did not properly articulate his ideas about synchronicity until 1952, after he had been working with the eminent physicist Wolfgang Pauli (1900–58) and further refined his thinking about the possibility of a close, and mutually influential, psychic relationship between nature and psyche.

Jung's idea was based on observations of what he came to see as meaningful coincidences. He thought these might not be explicable in rational terms, but that they pointed towards something at work under the fabric of familiar consciousness which seems to generate such phenomena. This hypothesis certainly fell into the kind of territory where he could lay himself open to criticism for being 'unscientific' or even 'mystical' – not epithets he and analytical psychology needed, as it tried to establish its credibility.

However, having taken the (brave?) step of putting these ideas in writing, Jung was able to offer modernity a potential tool for acknowledging the appearance of the mysterious in ordinary life. His **acausal connecting principle** (Jung, 1970b, p. 8) was one Jung thought people could relate to, even if his embellishments about the significance of this might not be of interest. This principle proposed that where something which happens in outer reality resonates in some unexpected way with a thought or intuition within, *synchronicity* is at work (e.g. we are thinking about a person we know, and the phone rings, and it is them).

More generally, the ways in which synchronicity can occur can be described as falling within one of three main categories:

1 Events or factors which coincide in time and space and seem to have some meaningful link but are not connected in a causal way (such as the 'phone call' example just given)

2 Events or factors that do not coincide in time and space but for which there seems to be some kind of meaningful link (e.g. we discover that the person who owned a car before we bought it had previously sold a car to another member of our family some time ago, in another part of the country)

3 Events or factors which link the outer, physical world with the inner, psychic one; Jung's example of the 'scarab beetle' described below, fits into this category

All these phenomena, according to Jung, suggest that the fabric of reality is not as easily defined as some scientists would want to make out. The 'ruptures of time' which synchronicity represents can not only provide insights which support the therapeutic process on occasion, but as Main asserts (2004, p. 142):

'By virtue of the simultaneously individual and social nature of the self and the microcosmic relationship of the individual to the macrocosm of the world, beneficial 'effects' can also come about acausally or synchronistically.'

As Main (2004) argues, 'synchronicity' is more than a term Jung deployed to try to explain meaningful coincidence. Rather, he sets it up as a source of *insight*, where we might be able to make some meaning about the connections suggested; and of *mystery*, in a world where this term can otherwise be reduced to describe gaps in scientific knowledge. As Main further remarks, by bringing a dimension of the indeterminable to science, based on his 'acausal' experiences:

'... precisely this alien and subversive character is what fits synchronicity to underpin Jung's radical critique of the scientism, soullessness, and authoritarianism of modern western culture, as he perceived it.'
Main, 2004, p. 143

In this respect, an argument can be made for seeing synchronicity as thoroughly relevant for postmodern attempts to loosen the West's historical tendency to adopt fixed explanations for what makes our world the way it is. Rosemary Gordon (1993) also makes a useful point: the acausal nature of synchronicity does not have to be seen as problematic in how it seems to contradict or undermine causal thinking. Rather, the two can complement each other, once we accept the paradox of their co-existence.

Jung and the famous 'scarab beetle'

The most well-known example of synchronicity referred to by Jung involved an analysand of his who reported a dream in which she was given a golden scarab. You might recognize this word from Chapter 1 and Jung's vision that included a giant black scarab beetle swimming in an underground stream, which in turn he related to an Egyptian myth of rebirth.

In this case of a woman who dreamed about receiving a golden scarab, Jung described how firmly she would tend to cling to the rational, and not allow its opposite into her awareness (he thought she had a 'rigid *animus*'). Jung reports, just as the woman was describing the dream image above to him in his consulting room, there was a knocking sound on the window behind him. He saw a flying insect trying to get into his consulting room. He opened the window and caught the creature in his cupped hands. He realized that, on closer inspection, this was a *scarabaeid* beetle – the closest type of beetle to an African scarab to be found in central Europe – and, not only this, but it is an insect that would not usually choose to fly into a darkened room from the brighter environment outside.

Jung came to see meaning in this event, as it seemed as if his well-defended analysand was affected by this eruption of nature into the analytic space. She had shown a little loosening of her hardened intellectualism while describing the dream, but this unexpected manifestation, in an instinctually alive form, of the irrational, seemed to allow her to open up to deeper influences. It signified a long-awaited shift in her attitude towards the analysis and her own process within it.

The key point here, which illustrates the fundamental principle of synchronicity is, two things that were happening simultaneously – in this case a woman reporting a dream about a scarab and a scarab-like insect flying nearby and colliding with the window of the room she was in – were not *causally* connected. The telling of the dream did not make the beetle fly into the window, and the beetle flying into the window did not prompt the woman to describe the dream. These two aspects of the situation were not 'logically' connected but there does seem to be a relationship between the two, represented by the commonality of the presence of a scarab in both elements of the equation.

This kind of example, which Jung uses to 'evidence' the veracity of his theory, could be criticized as reflecting confirmation bias, whereby a person seeks out the so-called 'evidence' to confirm what they have already decided is the case. This criticism holds up when applied to an earlier study of Jung's, which purported to show an 'acausal connection' between a person's star sign and their choice of partner, not least as participants were self-selecting supporters of this idea.

The idea of synchronicity has also been seen in certain quarters as another example of how Jung generated a mystical edge to his conceptual framework and clinical practice. Richard Noll (1994), for example, made a forthright argument that the Jungian project as a whole was more like a cult, with Jung as its leader, which had built up a view of the contemporary world which owed more to religious fervour than intellectual rigour and proper psychological investigatory practices. For Noll, synchronicity fitted this critique of Jungian thinking well, as it tried to provide a quasi-scientific rationale for what was in his view, Jung's cult of personality, disguised as analytical psychology. However, whatever view one takes about *synchronicity*, Jung's use of examples such as the scarab one can provide beguiling food for thought in the face of the difficulty in 'proving' its validity.

Science and Jungian thought

Post-Jungian thinkers have taken Jung's ideas and blended these with recent theoretical developments. Hester Solomon (2007) adopts the theory of 'emergence', which draws on complexity and chaos theory to help us understand how deeper structures may be at work behind the apparent unpredictability of molecular and other activity. As she puts it (op. cit. p. 284), 'Under the right conditions, a structural transformation into a more complex pattern or meaning may occur…(and)…then genuinely novel properties and processes may emerge.'

She makes the comparison in psychological terms with Jung's idea of the *transcendent function* powering the individuation process –

an underlying dynamic which generates something new out of the often messy interface between conscious and unconscious influences. She demonstrates how Jungian thinkers such as Cambray (2009) deploy emergence theory to provide perspectives on the interaction of psyche and matter. This aims to complement orthodox scientific frameworks and deepen understanding about how physical matter might intersect with subtle psychic influences, within a post-Newtonian framework. This fits with Jung's adoption of the medieval idea *unus mundus* (all of reality is united as one).

Spotlight: Evolutionary psychology

Links between the field of evolutionary psychology and Jung's thinking on archetypes can be found in the work of MacLennan (2005), who sees them as embedded in a person's genotype (their genetic make-up). Theories on personality traits also build on the focus Jung gave to typology, although influential thinkers in this area have developed their own frameworks for making sense of this (Cervone and Pervin, 2007).

Jung's influence on the arts

We have seen how Jung drew on his own artistic and creative capacities to produce the graphic illustrations for *The Red Book*, as well as to support his own engagement with the unconscious. He and other Jungians (e.g. Jaffe, 1964) have identified the importance of art where it reveals symbols evocative of archetypal and unconscious influences. However, Jung cautioned against overvaluing the aesthetic quality of art produced in therapy, as it would distract from its therapeutic meaning. Jungian ideas have also influenced a number of important artists, musicians and writers, not to mention filmmakers.

Spotlight: Abstract expressionism

Two artists who developed their style of painting under the influence of a Jungian perspective are Jackson Pollock (1912–56) and Mark Rothko (1903–70). Their 'abstract expressive' work followed the way surrealist artists (e.g. Salvador Dali, 1904–89) painted responsively to the flowering interest in psychoanalysis.

Pollock undertook Jungian analysis and fostered a close interest in Jung's symbolic and archetypal approach. This became reflected in his painting. One piece, *Bird* (1941), seems to portray his *individuation* process, with a dominant eye overlooking the whole picture, with a flavour of his apparent *negative anima* difficulty in the more conflicted elements elsewhere in the picture.

In Rothko's case, his broad aim was to portray the inner world, as a reaction to what he saw as the overemphasis on appearance in the modern world. Rothko came to see the purpose of producing works of art as experiential more than aesthetic – his later work with its huge canvasses washed in shades of colour were designed to evoke emotion and reflection, even a kind of 'spiritual' experience. He proposed that the unconscious could be projected on to the pictures and generate conscious awareness of deeper influences. For both Pollock and Rothko, Jungian principles acted as a resource and stimulus for their art.

MUSIC AND WRITING

Other areas of creative expression in the public domain have been touched by the power of Jung's ideas. The British classical music composer Sir Michael Tippett reports in his autobiography (1991) how reading Jung's works inspired him to dig deeper into his own psyche (he spent nine months in 1939 analysing his own dreams), and how this helped infuse his compositions with richer layers of meaning. His *Midsummer Marriage* (1955), for example, has alchemical and individuation-related themes.

The German author Herman Hesse was analysed by Jung and the archetypal resonances of his writing reflect this (for example in *Demian*, 2006). The Irish poet Seamus Heaney also draws on Jungian archetypes, for example the *Great Mother*, in his poem 'Bog Queen' (1976).

FILM, FILM CRITICISM AND POP CULTURE

There is also a blossoming school of film criticism which applies Jungian symbolism and ideas (e.g. Hauke, 2013), recognizing how film operates like a kind of viewfinder into the human psyche. Concepts such as *shadow* possession, for example, are graphically portrayed in films such as *Lord of the Rings* (Jackson, 2001–3), where Frodo wrestles with the problem of the ring's power and whether he can overcome it. *Shadow* also crops up in classic filmmaking (e.g. *Psycho* by Alfred Hitchcock, 1960) as well as in contemporary films such as *V for Vendetta*, where collective *shadow* of an oppressive dystopia is represented by the subversive 'V' (McTeigue, 2005).

A more populist example is the American film franchise *Star Wars*. Although George Lucas, who created and produced the hugely popular series of films, described the key influence on the structure and themes he used as Joseph Campbell's (2008) 'hero's journey' framework, this in turn was strongly influenced by Jung's theories.

Another example from popular culture is the British pop/rock group The Police, who released an album in 1983 entitled *Synchronicity*. This proved to be their most successful record and the title was a direct reference to Jung's theory. This also reflects how, while notions such as synchronicity have not been recognized in many parts of the academy as scientifically or psychologically significant, Jungian ideas have attracted interest and creative energy in those who influence, and enjoy, popular and higher cultural life.

Key terms

Emergence: Theory arising from studies in physics, which postulates the presence of underlying patterns that generate new structures from apparent chaos.

Synchronicity: Jung's 'acausal connecting principle', which, as this phrase implies, refers to two (or more) disconnected phenomena apparently being connected where there is no causal explanation for this. Jung suggested this happened outside ordinary time and space, while also bridging psyche and matter in how it manifests itself.

Unus mundus: A phrase Jung borrowed from medieval philosophy, which refers to the idea that all of reality is united as one. Synchronicity operates as it does because the relationship between psyche and matter is intimately interconnected, according to Jung.

Dig deeper

Cambray, J., *Synchronicity: Nature and Psyche in an Interconnected Universe* (Texas: A & M Publications, 2009)

Campbell, J., *The Hero With a Thousand Faces* (Novato, CA: New World Library, 2008)

Cervone, D. and Pervin, C., *Personality Psychology* (Hoboken, NJ: John Wiley, 2007)

Freeman, D., *Face to Face,* episode on C. G. Jung, 22/10/59 (BBC Productions, 1959)

Gordon, R., *Bridges: Metaphor for Psychic Processes*, Ch. 24 (London: Karnac, 1993)

Hauke, C., *Visible Mind: Movies, Modernity and the Unconscious* (London: Routledge, 2013)

Heaney, S., 'Bog Queen' in *North* (New York: Oxford University Press, 1976)

Hesse, H., *Demian* (London: Peter Owen Modern Classics, 2006)

Jaffe, A., 'Symbolism in the visual arts' in Jung, C. G. and Von Franz, M. (eds.), *Man and His Symbols* (Garden City, New York: Doubleday & Co., 1964)

Jung, C. G., 'Flying Saucers: A Modern Myth of Things Seen in the Skies' in *Civilisation in Transition*, CW10, 2nd ed. (London: Routledge, 1970a)

Jung, C. G., *Synchronicity: An Acausal Connecting Principle* (London: Routledge, 1970b)

Jung, C.G., *Modern Man in Search of a Soul* (London: Routledge Classics, 2001)

Lorenz, K., *Studies in Animal and Human Behaviour*, vol. 1. (R. Martin, transl.) (Cambridge, MA: Harvard University Press, 1970)

MacLennan, B. J., 'Evolution, Jung, and Theurgy: Their Role in Modern Neoplatonism' in Berchman, R. M. and Finamore, J. F. (eds.), *History of Platonism: Plato Redivivus* (New Orleans, LA: University Press of the South, 2005)

Main, R., *The Rupture of Time: Synchronicity and Jung's Critique of Modern Western Culture* (London: Brunner-Routledge, 2004)

Noll, R., *The Jung Cult: Origins of a Charismatic Movement* (Princeton, NJ: Princeton University Press, 1994)

Shamdasani, S., *Jung and the Making of Modern Psychology: The Dream of a Science* (Cambridge: Cambridge University Press, 2003)

Snow, C. P., *The Two Cultures*, 2nd ed. (Cambridge: Cambridge University Press, 2001)

Solomon, H., *The Self in Transformation* (London: Karnac, 2007)

Tippet, M., *Those Twentieth-century Blues* (London: Hutchinson, 1991)

Films (directors named):

Hitchcock, A., *Psycho* (Hollywood, CA: Paramount Pictures, 1960)

Jackson, P., *Lord of the Rings Trilogy* (Wellington: Wing Nut Films, 2001–3)

McTeigue, J., *V for Vendetta* (Hollywood, CA: Warner Brothers, 2005)

Fact-check (answers at the back)

1 Why has academia not widely accepted Jung's ideas on science?
- **a** They are too complex for many people to understand
- **b** They suggest a view of reality not wholly based on measurable research outcomes
- **c** They are too critical of conventional science
- **d** They imply that reality can be manipulated by people into any shape they want

2 Why did Jung believe that humanity was generally divided against itself?
- **a** Because Westernized thinking was different from Eastern ideas
- **b** Because people kept going to war
- **c** Because Westernized thinking in arts and science split the rational and the irrational
- **d** Because fascism and communism split politics and nations into left and right wing

3 Why did Jung call synchronicity an 'acausal connecting principle'?
- **a** Because it involves two unrelated events that do not cause each other but are meaningfully connected
- **b** Because it involves two events which try to influence each other but do not manage to do so
- **c** Because it involves two events, one of which causes the other, but the connection is not clear
- **d** Because it involves two unrelated events which do not connect unless we impose a meaning on this

4 Why did Jung see synchronicity as bridging arts/religion and science?
- **a** It provides a spiritual language to explain quantum physics
- **b** It ruptures time and therefore allows us to experience creative processes
- **c** It brings meaning to science and can link numinous experiences to it
- **d** It helps us visualize a bridge between famous scientists, and writers and gurus

5 What are the three meaningful but acausal ways in which synchronicity coincides?

   a Events coinciding in space and time, and those which do not, and those disconnected across inner–outer dynamics

   b Events in time and space, those which connect to events not coinciding in time and space, and those linking the inner physical world with outer psychic events

   c Events coinciding with inner images, time stopping, and events repeating in a pattern

   d Events coinciding in time and space, those not coinciding in time and space but linked, and those linking the outer physical world with the inner, psychic, one

6 How can synchronicity be helpful to the therapeutic process?

   a It can create a powerful awareness of unconscious influences for the analysand

   b It breaks up the monotony of predictable analyst–analysand dynamics

   c It helps the analysand notice coincidences in their daily life

   d It helps the analyst understand how the collective unconscious operates

7 How does Jungian thinking link with emergence theory?

   a By demonstrating the importance of our emerging individuation process

   b By the transcendent function's generation of new patterns from conflicting old ones

   c By highlighting ways in which the collective unconscious emerges archetypally

   d By the underlying influence of Jung's theory of synchronicity on science

8 How can focusing on aesthetic qualities of an analysand's art affect therapy?

   a It might help to understand how a person's creativity could help them grow

   b It might provide the basis of an interesting illustrated case study

   c It might stop the analysand from listening to what the analyst says

   d It might distract the analysand from the artwork's meaning for their development

9 How did Jung's thinking influence the abstract expressionist school of art?

a His abstract thinking provided a good model

b His ideas on archetypes and symbolism were expressed within this school

c His colourful approach to art as reflected in *The Red Book* impressed them

d His ideas about the transcendent function helped them transcend older art forms

10 How did Jung influence George Lucas's creation of the *Star Wars* movies?

a Because Lucas read Jung's ideas on the Hero, which inspired the series

b Because Lucas based the character of Yoda on Jung

c Because of his 'archetypal' influence on Joseph Campbell's writing on the Hero

d Because Lucas based the character of Obi-Wan Kenobi on Jung

17

Jung's legacy in religion and spirituality

Jung's focus on the place of religion in the human condition, and the importance of meaning in life, has been highlighted more than once in this book. Here, we will consider his psychological exploration of the nature of religion as experiential phenomena. While noting his influential interest in Eastern spirituality, the focus is on his important arguments for a post-Christian approach to Western religion, particularly his ideas on the evolution of relations between the human and the numinous described in *Answer to Job*. The debate around Jung's association with the 'New Age' movement is explored, and a brief case study illustrates how the numinous can have an impact on the therapeutic process.

Jung's religious grand project

> 'It is not ethical principles, however lofty, or creeds, however orthodox, that lay the foundations for the freedom and autonomy of the individual, but simply and solely the empirical awareness, the incontrovertible experience of an intensely personal, reciprocal relationship between man and an extramundane authority which acts as a counterpoise to the "world" and its "reason".'
>
> Jung, 1964, para. 510

It will be clear from previous discussions how important the place of religion in the human psyche was for Jung. The imprint of his father's influence in this area was described in Chapter 2. Also, we have noted the way in which the young Carl's awareness of the depths within him – via vivid dreams, the encounters with spiritualism facilitated by his mother and cousin, and the split between his personalities number one and two – led him inexorably towards a fascination with the spiritual/religious dimension of the human condition. It was more than a fascination, though – for Jung there was something about the 'religious problem' that needed resolving.

The rigid dogmas and deadened spirituality (as he saw it) of the Christian Church spoke to how out of kilter this institution was with the spirit, the zeitgeist, of the times. Jung perceived a malaise at the heart of Western life – an absence of meaning, a *lack* of 'spirit' in the human 'soul'. For Jung, the falling away of organized religion had left people without a compass with which to navigate the irrational, profound and traumatic domains of life. Hunger for meaning, he came to think, required engagement with the *numinous*, and he took the view that for many people a religious faith could act as a conduit and container for this need. So what did Jung mean when he used the term 'religion' in relation to the term 'numinous'? He explains:

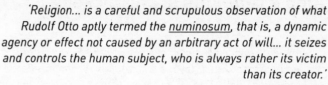

> 'Religion... is a careful and scrupulous observation of what Rudolf Otto aptly termed the <u>numinosum</u>, that is, a dynamic agency or effect not caused by an arbitrary act of will... it seizes and controls the human subject, who is always rather its victim than its creator.'
>
> Jung, 1969a, para. 6

As with so many of Jung's lines of thought, there were paradoxes at work in his perspective on religion. On the one hand, he might recommend to an analysand that they return to the faith they might have left behind in their youth; on the other, he was intensely critical of how versions of such faith were being promulgated by the religious establishment. In this respect, he would also follow the lead of the analysand where they were engaged in a search for meaning that arose from the *numinous* promptings of the unconscious. This could lead to a fresh engagement with a previously held belief, or a new spiritual or existential framework altogether.

Jolanta, spirituality and therapy

In her previous analysis sessions, Jolanta had been trying to get to grips with addictive tendencies which, with the help of her analyst, she had come to recognize as acting as a kind of substitute for an emptiness in her life around 'meaning'. She had decided to take a trip back to her homeland in order to get back in touch with what really mattered to her.

When Jolanta took this trip, she had a mixed experience: some contacts with members of her family, and with friends, had been awkward or disappointing, while others had been touching and enjoyable. She had also revisited places of significance – standing outside a church and a school she had attended, and walking down a favourite lane in the town where she had been born. She also went to a secluded valley that she now realized had come to represent something important to her. As she reported the experience of walking down a footpath, she remembered believing (as a 12-year-old) that she had been the only person to walk along it 'for hundreds of years '... maybe ever...' Her analyst noticed

Jolanta's eyes widen and mist over, seemingly looking past, or through, her.

The analyst noticed how still Jolanta had become, in her chair, and a stillness in the room. After a lengthy silence, Jolanta's gaze returned to focus on her, and she said: 'I've just been down that path again, as we've been sitting here, and I've realized that, even if other people have walked down the path in that valley, the *real* path belongs to me.' Her analyst noticed how deeply expressed this observation felt to her as she received it from Jolanta. Something had shifted – in Jolanta, and in the therapeutic relationship. Something of a new depth was present in the work, and Jolanta said: 'I feel I am on the right track now... don't know what happened there, but it was something which connected the past, present and future for me. It's gone now, but somehow it feels it is still here too, and available to me...'

Jolanta had been touched by something at depth which had an unknowable but influential quality – a numinous movement of the self which speaks to what Young-Eisendrath (2004, pp. 184–5) terms 'the unconscious striving for spiritual development' which can generate such moments in therapy, and also in wider, lived experience.

In *Aion* (Jung, 1968) he described how limiting the medieval version of the Christian faith of his father had become, in the face of the overpowering presence of scientific empiricism. Jung also observed the ways in which the Church might overlook the darker side of the human condition (and of religion), and the place of the feminine, in favour of an emphasis on the 'goodness of God.' Jung regarded this as indicative of the impending end of an era: the Christian age (the age of the 'fishes' or *Pisces*) was coming to a close, and the age of *Aquarius*, where the feminine would emerge to take its proper place, was on the rise. More than this, the evolution of human spirituality was also intimately linked with the evolution of the *archetypally* spiritual. Jung argued that the numinous (or 'God') evolves, too. Jung explained this in *Answer to Job*.

Answer to Job and the evolution of the God Image

> 'Jung's understanding of the answer to Job implies that the universal truth of death and resurrection describes the process at work in the healing of the divine split which created human consciousness... As this process repeats in individual and societal life, a consciousness... for Jung, would be forced to evolve by the dynamic itself, in which ever more aspects of the divine antimony would be united in human historical consciousness.'
>
> Dourley, 1992, p. 26

In *Answer to Job*, Jung utilized the Biblical figure of Job to illustrate what he saw as the evolution of humanity's relationship with the archetypal divine, or the numinous. In the story, Job is tested *in extremis* by Yahweh, the father God of the Torah/Old Testament, losing everything he cherishes, with God waiting to see whether he will maintain his faith despite this. For Jung, this story represented how the God archetype is itself wounded and capable of destructiveness, and how God needs humanity to help heal 'his' wounds.

Jung's proposal that, like human consciousness, Gods evolve over time reflects the carefully *psychological* way he went about trying to understand religious experience and imagery as archetypal. This approach has influenced key Jungian ideas such as Erich Neumann's symbolic evolution of consciousness (1954). Here, Jung came to equate such movement of the numinous/God with a movement of the *self*. As human is to divine in conventional religious thinking across many faith traditions, so ego is to self. This is because the self holds a deeper wisdom about us and our path through life, which we are called to listen to (as described in Chapter 5) if we want our ego to stay more on less on track and our psyche in balance. In this respect, the implications for our relationship to the numinous are significant. Not only should we see established images of God as representations of the self, but, in the same way, the workings of ego can influence self, so humanity can influence the nature of God.

Spotlight: Can humanity influence the evolution of God?

This is not a wholly original idea of Jung's. The Kabbalistic tradition (Dan, 2007) speaks of the need to heal the 'broken vessels' within which the divine should have been contained. It thus becomes our task to repair these.

Jung wrote *Answer to Job* in 1951, aged 75, while he was ill, with the narrative for it seeming to come to him from his unconscious, as he reported it. In essence, the central thesis is that God (or the 'God archetype'), in the form of *Yahweh,* did not provide an answer to the question posed by the story in the book of Job – why could he be so cruel and destructive towards a character who is clearly a good person? In moral terms, the story places the creator in the position of ethical transgressor, while the person he has created occupies the moral high ground for putting up with this persecution stoically, and apparently without malice. So the question arises, why does God do this? Does this God have some kind of neurosis?

For Jung, the answer was 'yes', and the unfolding of the relationship between God and humanity required the latter to play its crucial part in offering the creator healing. Edward Edinger helpfully outlines Jung's 'answer' to this problem by situating it under three headings:

1 The God Image as pictured in the Old Testament – Yahweh

2 The God Image as pictured in Christianity via Christ – the God of Love

3 The God Image as experienced psychologically by modern people (Edinger, 1992, p. 11)

Edinger (1986) also draws on the visionary paintings of William Blake to highlight how the story of Job can be seen as a portrayal of the dynamics of an encounter with the *self*.

Notice the term 'God Image' – Edinger is describing the evolving way God (or Gods) appears to us as humans in our thoughts, dreams and fantasies. We have already discussed the first version of these – Yahweh. Jung's psychological postulation was that the God archetype's response to Job's questioning of the creator's one-sided oppression of his faithful servant was to take the symbolic shape of Jesus.

Psychologically speaking, the God archetype, as a version of the *self*, realized that a move was needed towards *ego* by taking human form to help heal the split between divine and human. Hence the symbolism of the crucifixion and resurrection, where the barrier to conjunction with the divine death is 'overcome'. It is important, in Jungian terms, to see these processes in a symbolic way. The implication of the presence of a destructive side to God, which needs a redemptive move by the divine, is that the God archetype is *split* and, like us, has a *shadow*.

As we move to the third of the headings above, it is the very capacity for self-reflection, and symbolic thinking, which characterizes the approach of contemporary women and men. As Robert Segal (1992) puts it, 'contemporary' refers to people whose consciousness has moved beyond an 'ancient' tendency to project the image of God outwards (often into the sky for Abrahamic religions), and also beyond a 'modern' tendency to be over-rational and discount the relevance or presence of the God Image in the lives we lead. Instead, a 'contemporary' is someone who accepts the factual evidence of science but also seeks and senses a deeper layer of meaning to life.

Jung is arguing that, as in all other areas, nothing in the religious/spiritual dimension of life is fixed. He encourages us to play our part in the divine drama – which in other terms can be seen as a process of trying to resolve an unresolved set of dynamics between the archetypal and personal within each of us, as well as across the collective development of human experience. Jung's prompting for us each to be as awake as we can be to our individual place in this process is summed up well when he writes:

> 'Whoever knows God has an effect on him.'
> Jung, 1969b, para. 617

This statement and the whole thrust of his argument about 'the evolution of the God archetype' reflects Jung's interest in Gnosticism (Segal, 1992), the movement that arose in the second century after the death of Jesus, and which believed the creator of the world was not God but a 'demi-urge' who is a mixture of good and evil, and therefore from a Jungian perspective could be said to have a *shadow*.

The position Jung took on this led him into controversial waters and some significant debates, especially with Father White (Conrad-Lammers and Cunningham, 2007) who appreciated Jung's ideas but thought he went too far with *Answer to Job*. In turn, Jung disagreed with White's defence of the Church's doctrine of *privatio bono*, which does not subscribe to the notion of evil as an entity but rather as being 'the absence of good'. Jung saw evil as something real *(psychologically and spiritually)*, which led to human suffering. Jung therefore set himself apart from the Christian mainstream, but in doing so he stimulated debates on church doctrine.

Spotlight: UFOs as representations of the self

Edinger (1986, p. 9) has remarked: 'There is in the unconscious a transpersonal centre of latent consciousness and obscure intentionality. The discovery of this centre, which Jung called the self, is like the discovery of extra-terrestrial intelligence. Man is no longer alone in the psyche and the cosmos.'

This links to the commentary Jung (1977) provided on a phenomenon that characterized the Westernized psyche after the Second World War. He argued that the regular sightings of unidentified flying objects were manifestations of the 'otherness' of the self that people were unconsciously seeking out (because of its unavailability to the modern mind). Thus, UFOs were projections of unconscious psychic contents and symbols of the psychic wholeness of the self.

East and West

Jung also laid the ground for a reconsideration of the value of Eastern spirituality, such as through his psychological commentary on seminal writings such as *The Tibetan Book of the Dead* (1969c). Jung saw Eastern thought as offering a compensatory holism to the patriarchal religion of the West. This is now seen as a precursor of the Western adoption of Eastern traditions such as mindfulness (Germer et al., 2005). The interest in links between psychotherapy and Eastern spiritual traditions, which he initiated, remains strong today (Mathers, Miller and Ando, 2009).

JUNG AND THE 'NEW AGE'

David Tacey, in his book *Jung and the New Age* (2001), explores the phenomenon of 'New Age' spirituality, which has been particularly popular in the US but which has also influenced developments in Europe and elsewhere in Westernized societies. These have included:

▶ a flowering of an individualized approach to spirituality

▶ an appetite for exploring alternative ways of thinking about religion, spirituality and personal growth.

There is considerable evidence for this shift towards an individual emphasis in spiritual quest and practice, with all sorts of meditative, contemplative and more ritualistic frameworks and practices to pursue; sometimes these are characterized by the flavour of consumerism so prevalent in our societies (Heelas, 2008).

Tacey's analysis of these developments in the late twentieth and early twenty-first centuries provides a critique for the way in which the ideas of Jung can be appropriated. His ideas are used to support the notion of there being a significant underlying shift in Westernized consciousness which is somehow leading us towards a 'new age' in which a more holistic spirituality fills the 'gap' left by the supposedly 'fading' religions of the modern and pre-modern eras.

Tacey argues that, however well-intentioned the New Age movement may be, it can lapse at times into a self-delusion of holistic integration, whereas it really wants to discard the struggle for wholeness via the work which needs to be done to integrate archetypal opposites. In this respect, he sees some contemporary spiritual approaches as adopting a sort of

'Jungian fundamentalism... (the adherents of which)... only approach Jung at second – or third – hand, that is, after he has been put through a New Age wash that makes him almost unrecognizable to serious readers of Jung'.

Tacey is directing his critique towards writers and those engaged in 'New Age' activity who he thinks are idealizing and even concretizing some of Jung's most prominent concepts, such as the collective unconscious, active imagination and the archetypes. One example he gives in this area concerns the 'men's movement' which has been prominent on both sides of the Atlantic as a manifestation of a perceived need for men to rediscover their authentic masculine identity in the wake of feminism. He quotes Moore and Gillete (1990, p. 7) who describe Jungian psychology as providing 'good news for men' in how this supports mythological insights into the presence of a 'blueprint... for the calm and positive mature masculine' in all men. For Tacey, this kind of approach oversimplifies the complexities of Jung's ideas about gender and the archetypal masculine (and feminine), in a way that might encourage the enthusiast for New Age thinking to get a picture of Jung as a kind of 'guru' whose influence can lead society towards transformation.

Key idea: Jung and New Age thinkers

Despite these criticisms of New Age thinking, Jung's insights into what he saw as the role of fresh psychological and spiritual awareness provide a response to a deeper collective call for change in our way of relating to symbolic and archetypal influences. He identified this era as a 'right moment for a metamorphosis of the Gods' (Jung, 1964, p. 585). Something is changing in the (Westernized) human condition, Jung believed, so, to this extent, what 'New Age' thinkers suggest may reflect a real strand in Jung's thinking.

What Tacey perceives in New Age philosophy is a wish to avoid really engaging with the full substance and challenge of a Jungian take on the malaise of the twentieth- and twenty-first-century mind. He makes the point that bringing about a deep psychological and spiritual change in response to social, moral, political, socio-economic and ecological challenges is, to say the least, hard work. He sums this up in this way:

> 'The New Age says, "It's easy",
> The Old Age says "It can't be done",
> But the prophetic voice says:
> "It can be done, but it's not easy."'
> Tacey, 2001, Frontispiece dedication

Key terms

God archetype: The archetype of the numinous/divine which evolves over time and cultures; it can be seen as a representation of the *self* in relation to the *ego*, as the deeper intelligence in the unconscious which guides the latter in life.

God image: The way the divine/numinous presents itself to humanity at one particular time; this evolves in relation to the dynamic between Gods/Gods and humanity and religions.

The numinous: An experience of something transpersonal, divine, religious or mysterious. Casement and Tacey (2006, p. vxvi) describe it as 'the emotional quality of religious experiences'.

The religious function: This refers to the human psyche's need for 'religious (i.e. numinous) experience' and a living spirituality which can help promote a deeper sense of meaning to life.

Dig deeper

Casement, A. and Tacey, D. (eds.), T*he Idea of the Numinous, Contemporary Jungian and Psychoanalytic Perspectives* (London: Routledge, 2006)

Conrad-Lammers, A. and Cunningham, A. (eds.), *The Jung–White Letters* (London: Routledge, 2007)

Dan, J., *Kaballah: A Very Short Introduction* (Oxford: Oxford University Press, 2007)

Dourley, J., *A Strategy For a Loss of Faith: Jung's Proposal* (Toronto: Inner City Books, 1992)

Edinger, E., *Encounter with the Self: A Jungian Commentary on William Blake's 'Illustration of the Book of Job'* (Toronto: Inner City Books, 1986)

Edinger, E., *Transformation of the God Image: An Elucidation of Jung's 'Answer to Job'* (Toronto: Inner City Books, 1992)

Germer, C., Siegel, R. and Fulton, P. (eds.), *Mindfulness and Psychotherapy* (New York: Guilford Press, 2005)

Heelas, P., *Spiritualities of Life: New Age Romanticism and Consumptive Capitalism* (London: Blackwell, 2008)

Jung, C. G., 'The Undiscovered Self' in *Civilisation in Transition*, CW10 (London: Routledge, 1964)

Jung, C. G. (1968), *Aion*, CW9ii (London: Routledge, 1991)

Jung, C. G., 'Psychology and Religion' in *Psychology and Religion: West and East*, CW11 (London: Routledge, 1969a)

Jung, C. G., 'Answer to Job' (ibid, 1969b)

Jung, C. G., 'Psychological Commentary on the Tibetan Book of the Dead' (ibid, 1969c)

Jung, C. G., *Flying Saucers: A Modern Myth of Things Seen in the Sky* (London: Ark, 1977)

Mathers, D., Miller, M. and Ando, O., *Self and No-Self: Continuing the Dialogue Between Buddhism and Psychotherapy* (Hove: Routledge, 2009)

Moore, R. and Gillete, D., *King, Warrior, Magician, Lover* (San Francisco: HarperCollins, 1990)

Neumann, E. (1954), *The Origins and History of Consciousness* (London: Karnac, 1989)

Segal, R., *The Gnostic Jung* (London: Routledge, 1992)

Tacey, D., *Jung and the New Age* (Hove: Brunner-Routledge, 2001)

Young-Eisendrath, P., *Subject to Change: Jung, Gender and Subjectivity in Psychoanalysis* (Hove: Brunner-Routledge, 2004)

Fact-check (answers at the back)

1 Why was the religion of Jung's father problematic for Carl?
  a It was too complicated
  b It only took the Swiss experience of Christianity into account
  c It was caught up with creed and tradition but not genuine religious experience
  d It portrayed Christianity as rational

2 What does the numinous refer to?
  a Numerical representations of transcendence
  b The highest point of experience in a meditative or similar state
  c Images of the Church as portrayed in important rituals
  d The emotional quality and impact of religious experience

3 Why did Jung think the Christian era was coming to a close?
  a It referred to a medieval conception of God and left out the feminine
  b It believed in a model of the divine which was too similar to other religions
  c He had a vision where the 'fish' of the Piscean era were swept away
  d He thought the rational mind was now clearly superior to the religious one

4 Why did Jung think the Old Testament God was 'neurotic'?
  a Job generated a good deal of anxiety for God
  b God refused to relax about his creation
  c Job was God's therapist but God refused to pay the fee
  d God reacted to Job's goodness by persecuting him

5 What did Jung think was our task in relation to the God archetype?
  a To worship it/him/her
  b To help heal the split in it/him/her
  c To ask forgiveness for our shadow frailties
  d To try and portray the image of it/him/her

6 The 'God Image' has had three stages according to Jung. What are they?

   a Yahweh, Christ and our psychological grasp of it/him/her now

   b Christ, Science and Contemporary

   c Yahweh, Job and Christ

   d Yahweh, Jehovah and psychological grasp of it/him/her now

7 What does Jung advocate we do regarding the numinous?

   a Keep trying to make it appear in our lives, and contextualize this in Jungian psychology

   b Stay open to numinous experience, explore it psychologically and contextualize it

   c Remain alert to it and keep a record of when we experience it for psychological research

   d Be open to the analysis of the numinous intellectually

8 In what way is the Gnostic approach to religion similar to Jung's?

   a It emphasizes the goodness of God

   b It believes in the collective unconscious as created by God

   c It advocates the idea that evil is real and part of the divine

   d It promotes the notion of a higher and lower world

9 Why did Jung disagree with the Church's doctrine of *privatio bono*?

   a He saw evil as a presence in its own right and not the absence of good

   b The church represented something repressive to him

   c He saw God as a many-faceted phenomenon which we cannot know

   d The influence of the church and his father interfered with his private ideas

10 Why is the 'New Age' movement drawn to Jungian ideas?

   a They are more logical than older religious ideas

   b Jung looks like a wise old man

   c Jungian therapy is newer than Freudian

   d Central concepts of a Jungian framework appear relevant to it

18

Jung's legacy in politics, ecology and education

It is not hard to see how a Jungian approach may have something to say about collective influences and developments, considering that the approach is founded upon the premise of there being a collective unconscious beneath the purely personal one. Jung's ideas about identity, nations and the collective form a starting point for a discussion about the relevance of Jungian thinking to politics and social issues. However, the legacy of Jung's dealings with Nazi Germany, as well as some of his thinking about the differing unconscious foundations of nations, raises the question: Was he racist? We explore the debates and the evidence. We will also consider how post-Jungian ideas on ecology, education, and political issues can provide valuable insights into the challenges faced by our world in the twenty-first century.

Peoples, politics and problems

In his biographical work written at the end of his life, *Memories, Dreams, Reflections* (1963), Jung warned of the destructive potential of the *shadow* of humankind. In the face of this he said:

> *'Today we need psychology for reasons that involve our very existence. We stand perplexed and stupefied before the phenomenon of Nazism and Bolshevism because we know nothing about man... If we had self-knowledge, that would not be the case.'*
>
> Jung, 1963, p. 363

Although the two movements Jung had in mind half a century ago no longer cast their *shadow,* his point remains pertinent. All expressions of potential tyranny, nationally and internationally, can be seen as expressions of the *shadow* of all of us. 'Self-knowledge' therefore becomes a prerequisite for individuals to contribute to the health of the 'body politic'.

The way human beings get into deadly conflicts, for example, can be seen as an archetypal pattern repeating itself over and over again, from the brutal battles that established and maintained the Roman Empire through to the huge wars of the twentieth century, which sucked in almost the whole world, as well as more recent conflicts in Europe, Asia and Africa. Likewise, the ways in which societies organize themselves to protect their members and provide for them has an archetypal resonance: monarchist, democratic and totalitarian approaches all reflect archetypal, ubiquitous forms of governance.

Jung was also interested in what might make different cultures and nations distinctive, as well as where they may have common features. It was an area he explored without the sensitivities and attitudes we now take as read. These were not on his radar and he did not steer clear of overgeneralizing, or even stereotyping, communities, nations and cultures.

WAS JUNG A RACIST?

Perhaps the greatest and most enduring controversy associated with Jung is the question of how he responded to the rise of the Nazis in Germany, as well as whether his approach to culture and nationality had a strand of what we might term 'racist' to it. Inevitably, Jungians have found this debate uncomfortable and some have steered clear of it, while others have defended Jung's 'innocence'.

Andrew Samuels, however, in his 1993 book *The Political Psyche* took on such questions head on. His aim was, by being as open, undefensive and thorough in his research as possible, to clear the air around this question. His approach was informed by his own experiences, as a Jewish Jungian analyst, of being quizzed about this, particularly by psychoanalysts from other traditions. Jung's ideas and approaches, however innovative and potentially valuable, have been somewhat tarnished by his alleged racism and anti-Semitism.

Farhad Dalal (1988) was clear, after investigating Jung's writings, that indeed he *was* a racist in the way we might understand this term (where this refers to someone who believes people of another race or culture are inherently inferior to their own race and culture). This view was based on the way Jung tried to group nations and races as part of a more layered model of the collective unconscious. Jung does indeed overgeneralize about the 'character' of groups of peoples (e.g. African) and individual nations, implying characteristics that are present in some but 'missing' in others. So one implication would be that African people are inherently less developed than their European counterparts because they lack some kind of civilizing aspects that 'the white man' may have.

To our eyes, this kind of thinking is clearly very dangerous territory for a psychologist to get into. As Samuels observes (1993, p. 309), Jung makes the mistake of trying to generalize about the psychology of nations, to the point where he lapses into a kind of *racial typology*, implying that 'superior' or 'inferior' characteristics are present in different national populations. However, does this make Jung a racist in a clear-cut way? Samuels invites us to consider, without in any way

excusing his approach, whether Jung has set himself a trap and
fallen into it, while trying to think creatively about the ways in
which culture, race and nationhood influence us as individuals
and societies. Jung tries to analyse this question solely through
an *archetypal* lens. As Samuels argues, it is a major error to leave
out crucial factors such as historical and cultural influences, as
well as socio-economic and political ones, when trying to make
sense of what generates nationhood. There is more to a nation
than longstanding, archetypal, influences, and this problem
pertains to Jung's relation to Nazism and anti-Semitism.

What did Jung do or say that might give cause for us to
wonder if he, at the very least, compromised his integrity or,
at worst, suggested fascist and/or anti-semitic leanings in his
attitude towards Jewish people in particular? In relation to the
latter, here's a quote from Jung's writings in 1918 in which he
describes 'the Jew' as:

> 'badly at a loss for that quality in man which roots him to
> the earth and draws new strength from below. This chthonic
> quality is to be found in dangerous concentration in the
> German peoples...'
>
> Jung, 1970a, para. 19

This kind of writing reflects the attempt by Jung to portray
essential features of different nations and races. In this case, he
also went on to portray the writings of Freud (and Adler) as
Jewish proponents of a particularly *Jewish* form of psychology.
He argued that the deterministic nature of Freud's approach,
for example, suited the 'Jewish characteristic' of needing to
bring psychological influences back to their material basics (in
his case, psychosexual roots), as a kind of compensation for
a supposed lack of 'roots in the earth'. In this respect, Jung's
approach to the nature of 'the Jewish psyche' may well have got
tangled up with his efforts to distance himself from Freud, and
the difficulties this split caused for him.

It is worth noting how Jung points out what he sees as a dangerous
flaw in the 'German psyche' in this quote as well; though, again, he
risks the precision of his observations in the way he makes such a

big generalization about a nation and its people. However, there is no getting away from the facts surrounding Jung's activities with the General Medical Society for Psychotherapy (GMSP), which was initially based in Germany (though it subsequently became international). This came, like all else in Germany, under the control of the Nazis after they took power in 1933.

In the same year, Jung became president of the GMSP. He took steps to make it still possible for Jewish practitioners to remain members of the society, although the Nazis had banned their involvement in a national society. Jung helped create an individual membership route instead. Nevertheless, how could someone who might profess real qualms about the rise of the Nazi party take and hold such an influential position in an organization beholden to that movement? This question applies in particular to his involvement and editorship of the GMSP journal, the *Zentralblatt*. This journal included statements of Nazi principles inserted by the president of the German section of the GMSP. Jung claimed later that he had been unaware of this because he edited this journal from Zurich, and these inserts were made afterwards ahead of wider distribution.

If this explanation seems a little lame, then what is harder to understand is why Jung would not have noticed how anti-Semitic several articles in the *Zentralblatt* were. 'Under his watch', contributors wrote articles criticizing the Jewish state of mind and lauding the Aryan one. 'Aryan' was a term consonant with Nazi ideology and Hitler's vision of a 'master race', which would be given its 'living space' by the conquests by the German army. The more this area is investigated, as Andrew Samuels has done, the clearer it becomes that Jung did not disown such material, even where his name was co-attributed to some of them. However, as Samuels asserts, it is also highly probable that Jung was focused on preserving his position as editor, and as president of the International GMSP, as he fought to hold his corner in the psychoanalytic world. Possibly he allowed his name, and his editorship, to be besmirched in order to maintain his influence in the world of psychoanalysis, as well as uphold the influence of psychoanalysis in Germany, from where Freud was forced to flee in 1939 as a despised Jewish intellectual.

While this argument carries weight, when seen in the light of Jung's priority of building influence both within and outside Germany, the discomfort surrounding how he chose to deal with the phenomenon of Nazism remains. He was clear about the dark, shadowy influences at work behind this movement, again attaching it to dark forces in the national German psyche, which he described, in rebuttal to Freudian theory, as possessing an 'unparallelled tension and energy… (which is)…anything but a garbage bin of unrealizable infantile wishes and unresolved family resentments' (Jung, 1970b: para. 354). However, his musings on nationhood provided writers supporting Nazi ideology – who we would have no trouble seeing as 'racist' in their attitude towards the Jews – with the ammunition to supposedly 'substantiate' their assertions, by referring to the theories of an eminent psychologist.

As Samuels (1993, p. 302) observes, if Jung, as president of the GMSP had:

'confined himself to the political and institutional arena, then the ingenious way in which his constitutional reforms permitted Jews, barred from the German national society, to practise as individual members would not require justification 50 years later. But at exactly the same desperate moment in history, Jung's interviews, papers and editorials of the period… could easily be misunderstood as supporting Nazi racial ideology.'

Key idea: Assessing Jung's legacy

Looking back from the vantage point of the twenty-first century, it is easy to assume we can see what was right or wrong about what Jung did, as well as what he seems to have overlooked. There is sufficient evidence to suggest that Jung was not an open Nazi/fascist or a 'scientific' racist, but at the same time he seems to have allowed his preoccupation with archetypal influences, as well as the power plays of his leadership of the GMSP, to allow significant criticisms to stick. As we shall see, Jung's legacy in generating valuable insights into pressing contemporary issues is a strong one, and this needs to be weighed in the balance against these criticisms.

Post-Jungian ideas in ecology

Jung's framework for reading archetypal influences into the human condition offers valuable ways of thinking about our relationship with nature, including challenges inherent to dealing with humanity's despoliation of the environment. One way in which this can be applied is through the use of *ecocriticism*. This term refers to the exploration and critique of literature, which can provide tools for considering how we can address problems such as global warming.

Susan Rowland (2012) writes from a post-Jungian standpoint, arguing that Jung's use of the symbol, and alchemy, can enable us to transform our consciousness of how these are rooted in nature. She does this by analysing the works of authors and playwrights. Examples include Jane Austen's portrayal of estrangement from nature in *Sense and Sensibility* (1811) and *The Tempest* (William Shakespeare, 1610–11). In both cases, 'civilized' humans come face to face with how nature can embody what human consciousness seems to be out of touch with – the *body,* and the animal in *our* nature. The implication is that such eco-critical explorations of literature can help us get back in touch with these characteristics and help us take better care of the environment.

Spotlight: Watching the detectives

An example Rowland uses is the *trickster* quality of the role of detective fiction, films and TV series. The detective both protects social norms and subverts them, getting inside the mind of the often-sociopathic criminals portrayed – and sometimes even behaving like them. So the detective symbolizes the instinctual pull towards 'hunting the wild' (the criminal), deeply rooted in our relation to nature.

Another writer (and analyst), Gottfried Heuer (2014), highlights the reciprocal problem of 'burn-out' as applied to ourselves as well as nature, arguing what we do to the natural environment mirrors the ways we can drive ourselves relentlessly through heavy workloads, and an unwillingness to face up to our full bodily based nature. He advocates a return to the holistic principles of alchemy, which values the latter, as well as the adoption of Lear's idea (2006) of 'radical hope'. Lear wrote about the experience of native Americans seeing their environment, cultural heritage and identity superseded by Western post-industrialized values. The 'radical hope' drawn on, in the face of such devastation, is for the *gold* of change in our relationship with the natural world (and ourselves), achieved by facing our collective *shadow* with courage and realism.

Post-Jungian ideas in education

The vexed question of how best to teach our children and young people is one that troubles governments, thinkers and the media across the Western world. Debates about academic and curricular freedom, versus prescription, and how to raise achievement versus tending to the personal and social development of pupils, are a hallmark of this area and can be seen in terms of archetypal polarities. The realization that depth psychology has something to offer debates about schooling and education is only now beginning to emerge. Biddy Youell's valuable book on schools from a psychoanalytic/psychodynamic perspective (2006) reflects this new thinking, but post-Jungians are also making their mark.

The edited collection *Education and Imagination* (Jones et al., 2008) provides good examples of this. It includes a valuable synthesis of Jung's ideas with those of educational thinker Lev Vygotsky (1896–1934). Vygotsky's theories (see Rieber and Robinson, 2004) are influential in teacher training but his emphasis on the need for schools to address the full nature of learning – a combination of nature and culture – is not always prioritized as central to the goals of educational systems in Westernized societies.

Matthews and Liu (2008) argue that Vygotsky's emphasis on the phylogenetic inheritance (i.e. the presence of images and psychological influences from across human history) in the developing mind of the child is analogous to Jung's collective unconscious. Vygotsky's teaching and learning approaches reflected this, with a balance advocated between more didactic, fact-based learning, and more creative, experiential, approaches. This could be said to mirror Jung's distinction between directed (i.e. focused on outer 'facts') and non-directed thinking (the allowing of imagination and free association).

The authors argue for a re-evaluation of the make-up of teaching and learning approaches in schools based on the 'balanced' approach of a Vygotsky–Jung bridge. As they put it:

> 'If we can culturally withdraw our inflation of ego in our belief that ego alone is responsible for rational advance, and respect the role of the archaic man in directed thought, then perhaps the way will become possible to give inner life its due as well... A theoretical framework that sustains such a position, such as arises through this synthesis of Jung and Vygotsky, is a worthy pursuit for pedagogical inquiry.'
>
> Matthews and Liu, 2008, p. 36

It is also potentially useful to apply Jungian concepts to the idea of 'special education' (as it is termed in the UK), and whether children and young people with significant learning difficulties may catch the *shadow* projections of the rest of us about our own 'learning difficulties'. The question of whether we need to keep them 'special', like the 'eternal child' *(puer/puella* in Jung's terminology) to represent our own wish to be 'the special child' also arises (Goss, 2008). Other contributions on Jungian applications include the use of storytelling (Jones, 2008) and software (Stratton, 2008) in learning institutions.

Politics 'on the couch'

In his writing on politics and the contemporary disenchantment about our democracies, Andrew Samuels takes the political arena and analyses it. He dissects the underlying roots of our political beliefs, inviting his readers to consider questions like: 'What was your first political memory?' – tying what first made a mark on us (e.g. a news story about national or international political events) to our formative psychological and familial influences.

Samuels sees the 'body politic' as in need of therapy, and extends the question of what needs challenging to include the problem of leadership. He argues the case for us to value the 'good enough leader'. He suggests that the well-worn 'heroic' leader model which relies on an archetypally driven idealized hero who will lead a community or nation to better times, or rescue it from the jaws of an enemy, is a source of potential danger, as borne out by the bloody events of the twentieth century (Samuels, 2001).

In turn, Samuels suggests we need to better understand what it is which works in 'good enough leadership', including the art of accepting failure and disappointment – in the same way parents can and do let us down, but can still be 'good enough'. He also argues that there is a place for 'erotic leadership':

> 'an erotic leader is not one who leaps in and out of bed... (but they) use their sexuality to convey to citizens that they (the citizens) are exciting, creative and autonomous people who can work co-operatively together.'
> Samuels, 2001, p. 85

Samuels asserts that political leaders need to truly relate to the people they represent and not be afraid to show their respect and appreciation for them: not leave them outside the heart of the decision-making process and convey a sense of 'putting up' with the electorate. This, in turn, Samuels relates to problems in our system that have patriarchal roots. As he points out, it is women who, all over the world, have indicated their distrust of the old, male, forms of heroic leadership. In this and other creative ways, Samuels diagnoses the 'sickness' in our politics and calls for a *resacralization of the culture*' (1993, p. 11) – an infusion of new life into how we 'do' politics.

Spotlight: A Jungian influence on politics

Andrew Samuels has worked as a political consultant for a number of governments around the world. In 1997 he proposed to Tony Blair, the new Labour Prime Minister of the UK, that there would be psychological and political value in offering public apologies for historical failures by the British government that might remain a source of hurt and anger. This included an apology for Britain's contribution to the disastrous events of the Irish potato famine (1845–52), which led to the deaths of at least one million people.

Samuels (2009) reports the experience of seeing parts of the media mock Blair for this move, and seeing first-hand how political good intentions can turn sour led him to recognize how difficult and complex the psychology of politics is. However, he argued that, by acknowledging the inevitability of failure and disappointment in politics and national life, we can begin to build new forms of political life:

'We should look for hope where we may least expect to find it, in the ordinary, the base and the abased – just as the alchemists of old did in their search for gold... Then we might resacralize politics in our time...'

Samuels, 2009, p. 2

Jungian thinking as a resource

The ideas discussed in this chapter indicate the richness of Jungian and post-Jungian ideas for thinking afresh about the challenges and possibilities of our postmodern, globalized culture(s): in particular the intractable (sometimes frightening) developments which can characterize local, national and international politics. In December 2014 an international Jungian conference in London, 'Analysis and Action', brought this rich potential for applying Jungian thinking to bear on topics such as refugee support, community building and conflict resolution. This event reflects the significant potential for further applications of Jungian thinking to social–political issues.

Key terms

Eco-criticism: The exploration and critique of literature which can provide tools for considering how we can address ecological problems.

Resacralization: Samuels' term to describe the need for numinously charged energy to return to our political and cultural life.

Dig deeper

Dalal, F., 'Jung: A Racist', *British Journal of Psychotherapy*, 4:3 (London: John Wiley, 1988)

Goss, P., 'Learning difficulties: *shadow* of our education system?' in Jones, R., Clarkson, A., Congram, S. and Stratton, N. (eds.), *Education and Imagination: Post-Jungian Perspectives*, Ch. 3 (London: Routledge, 2008)

Heuer, G., 'The Nature of Burnout and the Burnout of Nature' in Mathers, D. (ed.), *Alchemy and Psychotherapy* (London: Routledge, 2014)

Jones, R., 'Storytelling, socialization and individuation' in Jones, R., Clarkson, A., Congram, S. and Stratton, N. (eds.), *Education and Imagination: Post-Jungian Perspectives*, Ch. 6 (London: Routledge, 2008)

Jung, C. G., *Memories, Dreams, Reflections* (Glasgow: Fontana, 1963)

Jung, C. G., 'The Role of the Unconscious' in *Civilisation in Transition*, CW10, 2nd ed. (London: Routledge, 1970a)

Jung, C. G., 'The State of Psychotherapy Today' in *Civilisation in Transition*, CW10, 2nd ed. (London: Routledge, 1970b)

Lear, J., *Radical Hope: Ethics in the Face of Cultural Devastation* (London: Harvard, 2006)

Matthews, R. and Liu, C. H., 'Education and imagination: a synthesis of Jung and Vygotsky' in Jones, R., Clarkson, A., Congram, S. and Stratton, N. (eds.), *Education and Imagination: Post-Jungian Perspectives*, Ch. 2 (London: Routledge, 2008)

Rieber, R. W. and Robinson, D. (eds.), *The Essential Vygotsky* (New York: Springer, 2004)

Rowland, S., *The Ecocritical Psyche: Literature, Evolutionary Complexity and Jung* (London: Routledge, 2012)

Samuels, A., *The Political Psyche* (London: Routledge, 1993)

Samuels, A., *Politics on the Couch: Citizenship and the Internal Life* (London: Karnac, 2001)

Samuels, A., 'Transforming Aggressive Conflict in Political and Personal Contexts', *International of Journal Applied Psychoanalytic Studies*, 6(4), 283–99 (December 2009), published online in Wiley Inter-Science: http://www.interscience.wiley.com

Stratton, N., 'Learning assistants for adults' in Jones, R., Clarkson, A., Congram, S. and Stratton, N. (eds.), *Education and Imagination: Post-Jungian Perspectives*, Ch. 11 (London: Routledge, 2008)

Youell, B., *The Learning Relationship: Psychoanalytic Thinking in Education* (London: Karnac, 2006)

Fact-check (answers at the back)

1 Why can Jungian thinking provide original insights about social/political issues?
  a Because Jung saw himself as a social reformer
  b Because Jungian thinking on symbol formation has a social–political dimension
  c Because Jungian thinking on archetypes can illuminate social and political patterns
  d Because Jung had dubious political ideas

2 Why was Jung's thinking on nations and culture contentious?
  a It was too theoretical and influenced by assumptions about archaeology
  b It was too generalized and influenced by assumptions about race and culture
  c It was over-influenced by Freud
  d It was over-influenced by Levi-Strauss

3 What archetypal generalizations did Jung apply to Jewish and German people?
  a Jewish people are not properly rooted and German people are too driven by their roots
  b Jewish people have roots in Germany and German people have roots everywhere
  c Jewish people are too rooted and German people are not rooted enough
  d Jewish people like cooking root vegetables more than German people

4 In 1933, what did Jung become president of?
  a The General Medical Psychotherapy Society
  b The Society for General Medical Psychotherapy
  c The General Medical Society for Psychotherapy
  d The General Psychotherapy Society

5 Why did Jung's editorship of the *Zentralblatt* journal cause controversy?
  a He allowed contributors to edit their own papers
  b He banned Freudian contributions
  c He kept the profits from sales for himself
  d He overlooked the insertion of Nazi statements

6 Why might Jung's possible racism have been suggested?
   a He overlooked anti-Semitic articles and over-generalized about racial characteristics
   b His activities and omissions got blown out of proportion by his enemies
   c He ignored Freud and this meant that psychoanalysts accused him of anti-Semitism
   d His approach to the psychology of nationality was misunderstood

7 Why are Jungian ideas relevant to ecocriticism?
   a Jung was critical of ecological thinkers
   b Jungian symbolism and thinking are helpful in highlighting our relationship to nature
   c Jungian archetypes can be found in literature and these can be critiqued
   d Jung liked literature about nature

8 Why are alchemical influences relevant for thinking about the environment?
   a There is a need to understand the mutual relationship between nature and humanity
   b The alchemical process is full of natural materials
   c There is a need to directly apply the 'science' of alchemy to environmental crisis
   d The alchemical process is the same as solving the environmental crisis

9 How could a Jung–Vygotsky synthesis be helpful for school education?
   a High schools would benefit from teaching Jungian and Vygotskian theory
   b Jung's thinking on education reflects Vygotsky's pedagogic approach
   c School curriculums would be balanced between directed and non-directed thinking
   d Vygotsky's thinking on education was influenced by Jung's

10 Why does Samuels think politics 'needs therapy'?
- **a** Our politicians are psychologically disturbed
- **b** Politics has lost its connection with what matters and needs 'resacralization'
- **c** Our politicians have formally asked psychotherapists to give them therapy
- **d** Politics is too boring

19

Post-Jungian therapeutic developments

As with any school of thought or clinical practice, individual thinkers and practitioners who subscribe to a broadly Jungian approach have developed different ways of applying this. This chapter explores how Jung's clinical approaches have evolved since his death in 1961, and the different schools of thought within the post-Jungian field. Research findings on the effectiveness of Jungian psychotherapy will also be referred to, as well as where Jungian thinking has influenced other therapeutic approaches, such as creative ones. There is also a consideration of how Jungian approaches to working with the unconscious can be incorporated into an 'integrative' approach to therapy and counselling. The case study in this chapter will reflect this theme.

Diversity and commonalities

Samuels (1985) provided a valuable outline of how three main schools of thought before and after Jung's death emerged under the overall umbrella of 'Jungian'. These are the classical, the archetypal and the developmental. We will briefly consider each one, bearing in mind that each draws on Jung's original model significantly and differences are more a matter of degree.

Spotlight: Jung – 'I am not a Jungian'(!)

Jung is famously quoted (Sedgwick, 2003, p. 10) as saying, 'Thank God I'm Jung and not a Jungian.' He meant he did not approve of assigning generalized definitions of 'being Jungian', since it implied a kind of uniform set of principles and practices that everyone involved would adhere to in the same way. Jung was pointing out that this is not an individuated way of thinking, and that all so-called 'Jungians' or 'Post-Jungians' need to follow their unique, authentic, path.

CLASSICAL JUNGIAN

A classical Jungian approach adheres consistently to the framework established by Jung to understand the human psyche. However, one of the most prominent advocates of staying 'true' to Jung's approach, Gerhard Adler (1961), recognized the field had to evolve, proposing that the classical form would inevitably generate some variations from orthodox to unorthodox, while paying heed to important developments in psychoanalysis.

Nevertheless, key elements of a 'classical Jungian' approach to therapy can be identified, such as the centrality of the amplification of archetypal images, alchemy, full adherence to Jung's model of the psyche and the implications for therapeutic process (e.g. working with persona, then shadow, then anima–animus, then self as a natural analytic 'progression'). As Samuels (1985) notes, a classical Jungian sees the self as pivotal, supported by amplification of archetypal imagery and influences, with developmental personality factors as less significant (though still relevant). So, for example, there would be less emphasis on work with transference–countertransference and more on work with symbols of self and archetypes.

ARCHETYPAL JUNGIAN

There is crossover between the 'archetypal' and the 'classical' Jungians. The distinction, however, is around how archetypes are perceived and worked with. The main inspiration behind the archetypal approach was the American analyst and thinker James Hillman (1926–2011). Hillman proposed that images generated from archetypal operation create our experience of reality, and therefore our development and therapeutic growth depend on working with these images.

Hillman's writing reflects this position in how he explores closely all facets of image that arise from archetypal processes. Here is an example from his paper on the colour 'blue' and what it represents psychologically in the alchemical process between 'blackening' and 'whitening':

'The blue transit between black and white is like... sadness which emerges from despair as it proceeds towards reflection. Reflection here comes from or takes one into a blue distance... the Jungian notion of blue as "the thinking function"... (refers)... to blue's ancient association with the impersonal depths of sky and sea, the wisdom of Sophia, moral philosophy and truth.'
Hillman, 1980, pp. 1–3

There is an emphasis on guided fantasy and active imagination, and this chimes with Henri Corbin's (1972) concept of *mundus imaginalis* (imaginal world), which operates in us as an image-making cognitive function generated by sense impressions. Exploration of this provides elucidation of deeper meaning, and therefore growth and healing of the psyche. He often referred to our task in life as '*soul making*' (Hillman, 1980). This approach prioritizes the exploration and interpretation of archetypal imagery, followed by an emphasis on the self, then the development of personality and working with transference phenomena.

Spotlight: Hillman on the world's problems

In *We've Had a Hundred Years of Psychotherapy and the World's Getting Worse* (Hillman and Ventura, 1993), Hillman contributes to the debate about whether depth psychology can provide more input to social and political problems discussed in Chapter 18:

> 'By removing the soul from the world, and not recognizing that the soul is also in the world, psychotherapy can't do its job anymore. The buildings are sick, the institutions are sick, the banking system's sick, the schools, the streets – the sickness is out there.'
>
> Hillman and Ventura, 1993, p. 4

DEVELOPMENTAL JUNGIAN

This school provides a bridge into more integrative Jungian therapeutic approaches, which we will come back to. In Chapter 14 we looked at Michael Fordham's approach to Jungian child analysis and noted how influenced he had been by object relations thinking and practice (Astor, 1995). The incorporation of key ideas from Klein and Winnicott reflected a new emphasis on the importance of child development.

This new theoretical and clinical focus emphasized the central importance of healthy *de-integration* and *re-integration* by the infant, facilitated by key carers to enable the s*elf* to support healthy growth by the *ego*, and help the child to establish trusting relationships with others and find their place in the world. The focus on personality development, and the consonant need to focus on relationship and transference–countertransference in the analysis, is central. This elicits patterns of formative influence as well as drawing on archetypal imagery and symbols of the *self* where these might inform understanding of these patterns.

Psychodynamic thinking has touched the work of most Jungian practitioners to a meaningful degree, as it complements the 'bigger picture' of a classical Jungian model by locating early influences on the development of the analysand. In the UK, for example, learning how to work with object relations principles is a common feature of Jungian trainings. Meanwhile, the classical Jungian tradition in a 'purer' form is still at work, such as in the analytic trainings offered in the birthplace of this tradition, Zurich.

Is Jungian analysis effective?

It is generally recognized that the evidence base for depth psychological approaches (psychoanalytic, psychodynamic, Jungian) is limited and there is some way to go before this catches up with the extensive research provided to evaluate cognitive behavioural approaches to therapy (Dobson and Dobson, 2009). However, there has been some valuable and revealing research conducted about Jungian analysis that supports the arguments for its effectiveness.

For example (Roesler, 2013), the 2000–3 'PAL' research project in Switzerland involved 37 analysands and 26 analysts. Of the analysands, 57 per cent had depressive disorders and 47 per cent personality disorders. The average length of treatment was just under three years, and 90 sessions was the mean number of sessions involved.

Researchers, analysts and analysands were asked to evaluate progress at various points during the analysis with tools appropriate to each group: for example, analysands used the SCL-90-R, a widely used self-evaluation tool in psychotherapy research, as well as the Interpersonal Problems Inventory. Findings showed a very significant reduction of the Global Severity Index, which this tool measures for severity of presenting symptoms. In terms of the Inventory, there was significant reduction of personal problems. There were also consistently positive findings from the evaluations of the researchers: 90 per cent of analysands described the outcome as positive or better, and 75 per cent of the therapists likewise.

Although naturalistic research studies can be criticized as not being as robust as the 'gold standard' of random control trials, they are still comprehensive, valid and reliable in mapping progress and change in treatment. There is certainly more to be done to further test and demonstrate the efficacy of Jungian psychotherapeutic approaches. Nevertheless, as Roesler argues:

> 'Results of several studies show that Jungian treatment moves patients from a level of severe symptoms to a level where one can speak of psychological health. These significant changes are reached by Jungian therapy with an average of 90 sessions, which makes Jungian psychotherapy an effective and cost-effective method.'
>
> Roesler, 2013, p. 562

Expressive arts therapies

When Jung took time out, as a mature adult, to play with stones he had found on the shores of Lake Zurich, spontaneously building structures and allowing symbols and patterns to emerge and paying heed to his unconscious, he helped inspire the emerging fields of arts therapies (e.g. visual art therapy, drama therapy). Valuing a childlike stance, he illustrated why expressive arts therapies – spontaneously drawing a shape or a fuller picture, for example – can be so effective (Jennings and Minde, 1994). When we sit with an image, and notice associations and intuitions, insight and healing can result.

Natalie Rogers (2000) acknowledged the influence of Jungian ideas for her person-centred arts therapy. There is striking use of Jung's principles and 'play' in Japan, where *Hakoniwa* or sand tray therapy is a predominant influence in the work of analysts. This involves using miniatures to represent dynamics and archetypal influences, to help amplify and acknowledge these (Rogers-Mitchell and Friedman, 1994).

'Integrative Jungian' practice

An emerging '*integrative*' strand of post-Jungian practice, and even theory, reflects wider developments in the counselling and psychotherapy field, and there has been a growing move towards integrative models of psychotherapy in the past 30 or more years. Effective therapy across modalities tends to have the same hallmarks: a good-quality therapeutic relationship and a client/patient who is motivated to engage in the process (Cooper, 2008). This has gone alongside efforts by practitioner–theorists to establish ways of working and thinking, which draw together complementary elements of differing approaches to generate something more holistically effective (Norcross and Goldfried, 2003).

An example of this is cognitive analytic therapy (or CAT; Ryle, 1975), which combines the emphasis from object relations on early unconscious influences with a cognitive approach based on CBT. There are also approaches utilizing different aspects of the therapeutic relationship, for example Clarkson (2003).

Could there therefore be an integrative Jungian approach that enables other influences to be present in analysis/therapy while the Jungian flavour remains central? If so, would this be a step too far in diluting the essential qualities unique to a Jungian approach? Samuels (1985, pp. 9–10) argues:

'A list of the ways in which post-Jungian analytical psychology is in tune with various developments in psychoanalysis suggests that not only is Jung in the therapeutic mainstream but that there is a sense in which analysis and psychotherapy today are in fact "Jungian". We really need a new category: the unknowing Jungians.'

His list includes:

▸ the clinical use of countertransference, which Jung advocated

▸ the central role of the *self* in human development – found in the work of Winnicott (1960) and Kohut (2009)

▸ the extension of analytic interest to the second half of life – found in Erikson's (1950) psychoanalytic 'life stages'

▸ the idea that unresolved parental issues can be expressed in psychological problems for children – an established principle in family therapy (Gammer, 2009).

These points are not made to imply that Jung somehow secretly influenced many significant developments in psychotherapy but, rather, that a Jungian frame of mind is naturally present in the way many psychotherapists practise.

As already mentioned when discussing developmental Jungians, their approach is strongly influenced by psychodynamic thinking, and this can be seen as an 'integration' of Jungian and psychodynamic principles and practice. This approach balances amplification of symbolism with intensive transference–countertransference work as early influences are reactivated. This is now a common approach among many Jungian practitioners and training institutions.

This bears the hallmarks of a successful therapy integration where, rather than an eclectic 'pick and mix' of therapeutic tools, fundamental principles blend together well to provide a fuller array of possibilities in the therapeutic process (Norcross and Goldfried, 2005). The metaphor offered by Dunn (2002, p. 266) helps to convey what is meant by meaningful psychotherapeutic integration: 'ideas are seen as being like flour and yeast in the making of bread and not...as the oil and vinegar in salad dressing which may be shaken together but in reality do not mix'.

The blend of Jungian and object relations approaches reflects this principle. This has been further reinforced by the influence of relational psychoanalysis, a development originating in the US that prioritizes the significance of the relationship in the analytic encounter (Mitchell, 1988), and also takes into account social constructivist accounts of how we structure realities and make meaning. This involves drawing on feminist and postmodern ideas which challenge essentialist ideas, for example around gender and being a man or a woman (Harris, 2005). These sorts of questions sit well with Jung's fluid approach to interplay between different factors in psyche's life.

Finally, another example of a valued integration involves where the Jungian approach meets the Humanistic psychotherapy and counselling tradition. There is much commonality between the philosophical and attitudinal stance of 'the Two Carl's'

(Thorne, 2012) – Jung and Carl Rogers (1902–1987), who founded the person-centred approach to counselling. Both identified a fundamental tendency towards growth in the psyche: *individuation* for Jung, and the *self-actualizing tendency* for Rogers (1967). As Purton (1989) observes, they both take a stance which values the basic trustworthiness of the client/analysand, though perhaps not in quite the same way.

While Rogers emphasizes the natural tendency of the client to know what is best for them, by fostering their internal locus of evaluation (not deferring to the judgements of others about what is 'best' for them), Jung prioritizes the importance of allowing the psyche of the analysand to indicate the direction in which the analysis needs to unfold. This can often be through noticing what compensatory messages from the unconscious (via dreams, etc.) indicate. Likewise, Jung's emphasis on the importance of getting behind the *persona* corresponds with Rogers' focus on helping clients dissolve '*conditions of worth*' (Merry, 2002).

Where Thorne and Purton acknowledge differences, they also point out that these can be seen as complementary rather than problematic. A key example would be Jung's 'map' of the unconscious, arguing that this should add to the depth and quality of a person-centred approach. As Purton (1989, p. 411) puts it:

> 'I see this Jungian person-centred therapy as grounded in the Rogerian conditions of empathy, acceptance, and congruence. The additional element from the Jungian tradition is the attitude that I call "openness to the unconscious." Jungian theory comes into the picture only by way of giving some conception of what it is to which we are being open.'

There are also differences in emphasis found in therapy. A Jungian approach, for example, emphasizes how important *shadow* work is in promoting individuation, compared to the priority to fulfil potential in Rogers' use of Maslow's (2014) notion of 'self-actualization'. Also, Jungian use of a psychoanalytically influenced reading of unconscious process, and work with *complexes* that are difficult to shift, might bring differing stances on therapeutic process and relationship.

However, even here there is commonality. In terms of Jung's emphasis on the need for the analyst to put themselves fully into the process, work in the transference–countertransference (including archetypal) can be compared to the person-centred notion of working at *relational depth* (Mearns and Cooper, 2005). Although there are limited examples of syntheses between Jungian and person-centred perspectives (e.g. in Gubi, 2015), there is clearly potential for further practice and thinking towards integrating aspects of the two approaches.

Spotlight: A Humanistic and Jungian conference

The interest in developing fuller links between Humanistic and Jungian perspectives was demonstrated by the popular conference on this theme in London, October 2014. This event included a dialogue between Andrew Samuels (Jungian) and Brian Thorne (Humanistic) on the commonalities between the two approaches.

These developments also reflect a growing responsiveness to the demand for shorter-term therapeutic work rather than long-term, intensive analysis (which can often be too expensive and time-consuming for potential analysands). Here, analysts may adapt their approach to work with underlying influences on pressing 'here-and-now' issues in, say, only six or eight sessions, recognizing the limitations inherent in this but still enabling valuable gains to be made for the analysand. Contemporary Jungian analytic practice can therefore involve a combination of traditional lengthy analysis with some analysands, while offering this more targeted short-term approach to others.

A therapeutic integration to meet Jolanta's needs

As the analysis progressed and deepened, Jolanta's analyst became more aware of how deeply this work was affecting her. Liz regularly experienced feelings of anxiety and pressure in her countertransference, and wondered where these might be coming from. She explored this with her supervisor, and it became clearer how Jolanta's anxiety and uncertainty about relationships was coming through in the therapist's countertransference. She was picking up, in her feelings and bodily sensations, the presence of Jolanta's difficult feelings, which seemed to connect with what Jolanta had said about her relationship with her parents. Here, there had been a pattern of her trying to please her parents, especially her father, who Jolanta said had had very high expectations of his daughter.

Feelings of inadequacy and a difficulty in trusting her relationships had clearly fed into Jolanta's difficulties as an adult with establishing and maintaining close relationships. Her therapist found herself focusing on these transferential dynamics as well as deepening the relationship between Jolanta and her, in order to provide a reparative experience of relationship in which Jolanta could share her deeper fears, as well as hopes, about relationships.

Her therapist became the 'good object' (in psychodynamic terms), providing what Jolanta had not properly experienced as a child. She also drew on a person-centred emphasis on providing a warm and authentic presence, which enabled Jolanta to notice the way she 'needed approval', and then foster her capacity to express her fundamental needs and build up a positive self-concept and allow her 'conditions of worth' to dissolve. From a Jungian perspective, work with dream material had helped her analyst understand this dimension of the work – the dreams about the airport and being on a 'pilotless plane' (Chapter 13) in particular reflected Jolanta's lack of secure and grounded relationships as a child, generating a complex about disconnectedness from relationship/home. The combination of psychodynamic person-centred and Jungian elements helped the therapist facilitate an effective approach to tackle this.

Jolanta's analysis concluded after just under two years. The combination of image and dreamwork, transference–countertransference, and the offer of a warm, genuine relational presence from her analyst had made a real difference. She noticed that, while there were still challenges ahead and patterns of relating still remained influenced by her childhood, she now had a clearer picture of what made her 'tick': the complexes that could trip her up. However, she now had a fuller capacity to relate to others meaningfully, something manifesting itself in a new relationship, which she felt quietly confident would outlast previous ones. In Jung's terms, within the containment of the analysis, she had experimented with her nature and emerged with a sense of her reflective authority. She noticed she could be more genuinely herself with others, and was generally more settled and grounded.

Key terms

Archetypal Jungian: An approach that fosters a focus on the significance of archetypes, including working with archetypal images, with a view to fostering 'soul making' (Hillman, 2005).

Classical Jungian: An analytic approach based fully on Jung's original model, including a focus on working with the self.

Conditions of worth: Person-centred term for internalized values and rules from parents and other significant adult figures, which distort our self-image and responses to others.

Core conditions: Person-centred conditions that facilitate therapeutic change and growth: empathy ('warmth'), congruence ('authenticity') and unconditional positive regard ('respect').

Developmental Jungian: The approach initiated by the child analytic work of Michael Fordham, which placed an emphasis on object relations and the working through of early unconscious influences (and de-/re-integrative process), within a broadly Jungian framework.

Post-Jungian: Developments in theory and practice after Jung.

Relational psychoanalysis: An approach originating in the US (Mitchell, 1988). Blends object-relations, a relational/Humanistic therapeutic stance and the application of feminist and social-constructivist principles.

Dig deeper

Adler G., *Living Symbol, A Case Study in the Process of Individuation* (New York: Pantheon, 1961)

Astor, J., *Michael Fordham: Innovations in Analytical Psychology* (London: Routledge, 1995)

Clarkson, P., *The Therapeutic Relationship* (London: Whurr, 2003)

Cooper, M., *Essential Research Findings in Counselling and Psychotherapy* (London: Sage, 2008)

Corbin, H., 'Mundus Imaginalis, or the imaginary and the imaginal' in *Spring* (New York: Spring Publications, 1972)

Dobson, D. and Dobson, K., *Evidence-Based Practice of Cognitive-Behavioral Therapy* (New York: Guilford Press, 2009)

Dunn, M., 'Cognitive Analytic Therapy' in Dryden, W. (ed.), *Individual Therapy* (London: Harper & Row, 2002)

Erikson, E., *Childhood and Society* (New York: Norton, 1950)

Gammer, C., *The Child's Voice in Family Therapy: A Systemic Perspective* (New York: Norton, 2009)

Gubi, P., *Counselling and Spiritual Accompaniment: Working with Psyche and Soul,* Ch. 6 (London: Jessica Kingsley, 2015)

Harris, A., *Gender as Soft Assembly* (New York: Taylor & Francis, 2005)

Hillman, J., 'Alchemical Blue and the Unio Mentalis' in *Spring* (San Francisco: Spring Publications, 1980)

Hillman, J., and Ventura, M., *We've had a Hundred Years of Psychotherapy and the World's Getting Worse* (San Francisco: HarperCollins, 1993)

Hillman, J., *Senex & Puer* (ed. and intro. by Glen Slater) (Putnam, Conn: Spring, 2005)

Jennings, S. and Minde, N., *Art Therapy and Drama Therapy* (London: Jessica Kingsley, 1994)

Kohut, H., *Analysis of the Self: Systematic Approach to Treatment of Narcissistic Personality Disorders* (Chicago: University of Chicago Press, 2009)

Maslow, A., *Toward a Psychology of Being*, 3rd ed. (Floyd, VA: Sublime Books, 2014)

Mearns, D. and Cooper, M., *Working at Relational Depth in Counselling and Psychotherapy* (London: Sage, 2005)

Merry, T., *Learning and Being in Person-Centred Counselling* (Ross-on-Wye: PCCS, 2002)

Mitchell, S., *Relational Concepts in Psychoanalysis: An Integration* (Cambridge, MA: Harvard University Press, 1988)

Norcross, J. C. and Goldfried, M. R., *Handbook of Psychotherapy Integration* (Oxford: Oxford University Press, 2003)

Purton, C., 'The Person-centered Jungian', *Person-centered Review*, 4(4), 403–19 (1989)

Roesler, C., 'Evidence for the Effectiveness of Jungian Psychotherapy: A Review of Empirical Studies', *Behavioural Science*, 3, 562–75 (2013)

Rogers, C., *On Becoming a Person* (London: Constable and Robinson, 1967)

Rogers, N., *The Creative Connection: Expressive Arts as Healing* (Ross-on-Wye: PCCS, 2000)

Rogers-Mitchell, R. and Friedman, H., *Sandplay: Past, Present and Future* (London: Routledge, 1994)

Ryle, A., *Introducing Cognitive Analytic Psychology* (Chichester: John Wiley, 1975)

Samuels, A., *Jung and the Post-Jungians* (London: Routledge, 1985)

Sedgwick, D., *An Introduction to Jungian Psychotherapy: The Therapeutic Relationship* (London: Routledge, 2003)

Thorne, B., 'The Two Carls – Reflections on Jung and Rogers', in *Counselling and Spiritual Accompaniment: Bridging Faith and Person-Centred Therapy*, Ch. 8 (Chichester: Wiley, 2012)

Winnicott, D. W. (1960), 'Ego distortion in terms of true and false self', in Winnicott, D. W., *The Maturational Processes and the Facilitating Environment*, Ch. 12 (London: Karnac, 1965)

Fact-check (answers at the back)

1 What, according to Samuels, are the three post-Jungian schools?
- **a** The classical, the archetypal and the transcendent
- **b** The developmental, fundamental and postmodern
- **c** The classical, the developmental and the archetypal
- **d** The noumenal, the personal and the phenomenological

2 Why did Jung declare that he was 'not a Jungian'?
- **a** He did not want his psychology to become characterized as overly spiritual
- **b** He wanted to avoid being associated with uniform prescriptions about 'being Jungian'
- **c** He said this when he was very old and had got confused
- **d** He wanted to be called 'originator of analytical psychology' only

3 What does a classical Jungian approach see as the centre of analysis?
- **a** Archetypal interpretations
- **b** *The Red Book*
- **c** The place of the ego and shadow
- **d** The place of the self

4 What are the key features of archetypal psychology?
- **a** Working with archetypal images to foster the process of 'soul making'
- **b** Being able to name as many archetypes as possible
- **c** Dream work that gets us down to an archetypal level and ignores the personal
- **d** Drawing archetypal images and taking these to therapy

5 Why is a developmental Jungian approach the clearest 'post-Jungian' move?
- **a** Because it emphasizes development across the lifespan
- **b** Because it allows the therapist to choose any post-Jungian approach they wish
- **c** Because it focuses on object relations within a broader Jungian framework
- **d** Because Michael Fordham declared he was 'not a Jungian'

6 What does research into the effectiveness of Jungian analysis suggest?

   a It is very difficult to research reliably

   b It appears to be effective in addressing significant mental health needs

   c It appears to vary significantly in its effectiveness

   d It is very effective with every person it is offered to

7 What is a limitation in the research deployed in the Swiss 'PAL' study?

   a It does not take into account the ages and gender of the participants

   b It deploys statistical analyses that are not reliable or valid

   c It is naturalistic and does not deploy random controlled trials

   d It was biased in its sample selection and identification of findings

8 How did Jung's thinking influence expressive arts therapies?

   a His emphasis on symbolic expression – from dreamwork to drawing and play

   b His interest in the arts

   c His discussion of the archetypal influence of art in therapy

   d His imaginative approach to art in *The Red Book*

9 How may a post-Jungian developmental approach represent 'integration'?

   a By the way it develops Jung's thinking in new ways

   b Through its thorough incorporation of object relations thinking into analysis

   c By the way it addresses analysand needs by drawing on an eclectic range of tools

   d Through its incorporation of ideas from developmental psychology

10 How might Jungian and Humanistic principles be integrated in therapy?

   a By using typology to help understand the analysand's humanistic individuality

   b By working with imagery and using it to improve the therapeutic relationship

   c By combining Jung's approach to the unconscious with Rogers' core conditions

   d By blending self-actualization with individuation and calling it: 'self-individuation'

20

Post-Jungian thinking

This concluding chapter provides a review of contemporary ideas and approaches in the Jungian field. This includes the important critique by Giegerich of some of Jung's key ideas, as well as innovations in post-Jungian theory and practice. The chapter also offers an activity that invites you to consider your view of the Jungian model of psyche and psychotherapy, and reflect on your learning, based on what you have read.

Jung's legacy for today's world

This closing chapter explores developments in post-Jungian thinking and ponders the question of whether Jungian ideas will deepen their influence, or fade into the background. We will consider three key themes in Jung's model to help us with this, and to consolidate your understanding:

1 Meaning, individuation and spirituality

2 Archetypal figures of psyche

3 The therapeutic relationship

Meaning, individuation and spirituality

Extensive reference has been made in this book to Jung's concept of **individuation** as pivotal to the purposive nature of our journey through life, and the roles of the *self* and *ego* in facilitating us becoming more fully who we are. This, as well as Jung's emphasis on the centrality of meaning-making to our lives, and the activation of our *symbolic function* (i.e. the inbuilt capacity of our psyches to generate symbols and work with the meanings they generate) are usually seen as lynchpins to this approach, which also makes room for spirituality and religion in the individuation process.

However, although many Jungians, especially those who practise from a *classical* or *archetypal* stance, would regard such thinking as fundamental, some thinkers in the field challenge these assumptions in the light of developments in the modern, and postmodern, Westernized psyche. The most influential of these is Wolfgang Giegerich (born 1942), a German analyst who has extensively critiqued Jung's emphasis on meaning-making and on the significance of the idea of the unconscious, especially the collective unconscious and archetypes.

WOLFGANG GIEGERICH AND THE 'END OF MEANING'

Giegerich (2012) argues that we need to accept the way 'soul' as an expression of culture has moved us into a time where it is technology and physics that speak of this 'soul' more than the kind of cosmological steps forward that Jung tended to allude to, referred to in Chapter 17. For Giegerich, Westernized civilization has moved into a new era where the search for meaning and belonging (or *'in-ness'*, as he puts it) has been superseded or 'outgrown'. Humanity is now more fully conscious of itself and no longer needs to, and in fact *cannot*, defer to a 'higher power' or live a symbolic life because it is now aware that the only valid reality is the one we inhabit. We have 'woken up' from the reliance on religion and myth and are now adapting to being 'naked' to the vulnerability of our finite physical existence. We are therefore now in a state of collective 'adolescence', which involves a definitive break with the past.

Spotlight: Thinking straight about alchemy

Giegerich's approach reflects attempts by some Jungians to carefully think through Jungian ideas and apply proper intellectual rigour to them. Another example can be found in Michael Whan's (2014) critique of the ways in which alchemy might be deployed. He argues that Jungian writers can too easily slip into conflating the personal and the archetypal when working with ideas about the alchemical transference:

> *'When we identify ourselves as the central figure in the alchemical opus, we ignore what Jung meant by the "objective psyche".'*
> Whan, in Mathers ed., 2014, p. 182

He warns against interpreting alchemical images and thought in terms of our self-development: *'analytical psychology errs... (by sometimes) adorning and inflating our all-too-human inner life with the fetish of alchemical meaning.'* (op. cit.)

Giegerich's ideas have drawn counter-argument from other Jungian-influenced thinkers such as Drob (2005), who suggests he too easily overlooks a thinker's subjectivity in trying to apply 'mind' to seeing what is happening in 'soul'. Beebe (2004a) suggests that, when Giegerich writes about the end of *'in-ness'* and the futility of the search for deeper meaning, he does not have to throw the baby out with the bathwater. Giegerich's skilful efforts to apply thinking that keeps Jungians in line with contemporary consciousness does not mean we have to rule out the value of the framework developed by Jung, and those who have followed on from him.

The significant claims Giegerich makes for a shift in consciousness, asserting that what 'was' no longer 'is', could be countered. We may now be learning to oscillate between the older 'grand narratives', which still carry meaning, and a newer individualized set of meanings. From a more classical Jungian position, it might be argued that Giegerich overlooks the indeterminable workings of the *numinous* and *synchronicity* in generating unexpected but still significant routes to fresh meaning-making. There are also ways of looking at his argument about the loss of meaning in archetypal terms. Jung (1963) refers to the oscillation between archetypal poles of meaning and meaninglessness, which we all struggle with. Perhaps this can be applied collectively as well. We may currently be in an era where fresh, shared meanings are less available, but could the pendulum swing back the other way? Some would also assert 'the symbolic life' still has meaning for many.

Giegerich argues that the 'Gods' have gone from the contemporary human psyche but the proliferation of alternative spiritual practices and frameworks (e.g. Wilbur, 2007) suggests that the religious/spiritual impulse still operates somewhere. It will not easily disappear from human consciousness. However, Giegerich's observation that 'the sugar cube cannot be got back from out of the coffee in which it has been dissolved...' (2004, p. 22) suggests that religion as substance has been 'dissolved' within the logical life of humanity and presents an important challenge to conventional Jungian thinking. Other post-Jungians have carefully dissected ways in which Jung's ideas about meaning, purpose and individuation can be applied to life's realities. Dale Mathers (2003), for example, argues that we can evince meaning and purpose from the extraordinary we find in ordinary life, and from personal reflection, while Christopher Hauke has pointed out Jung's relevance to postmodernism (2000).

Spotlight: Jungian influence in universities

Jungian ideas have struggled to make a significant mark in higher education, despite their wider popularity in Westernized societies. David Tacey, an Australian academic with a long-standing interest in Jung, recounts his own efforts to establish Jungian studies as an academic discipline at La Trobe University, Melbourne. He was teaching in the English department, and his colleague, Robert Farrell, was based in Philosophy. They managed to demonstrate psychological validity for the interdisciplinary studies courses they developed, arguing against protests from the Psychology department they were invading their territory (Tacey, 2007 p. 56):

'I responded to their protest with a brief lecture on the etymology of the word <u>psychology</u>, pointing out its true meaning as the logos of the psyche or soul, and suggesting to the Psychology department that they had left psyche out of the study of human behaviour.'

Tacey reports that the protest was dropped and eventually psychology students were given the option to study Jungian ideas as part of their science degree.

This achievement is an unusual one in relation to Jungian studies. Tacey argues that there needs to be a better recognition of the ways in which Jung tends to be taught, describing how this can vary from conforming with the institution, trying to update institutional values or provide Jungian personal development, or trying to remain aloof and 'pure'. Tacey describes how such approaches can isolate Jungian thinking, for example by trying to overturn conventional academic thinking in favour of, say, alchemical or Neoplatonic perspectives. He also argues how powerful it can be to introduce Jungian insights on human development and archetypal influences into wider curricula, deepening learning and awakening student interest (sometimes via the activation of the *numinous* in the classroom).

Compared to the fruitful connections already described between Jungian and other therapeutic concepts and clinical interventions, the integration of Jungian thinking into conventional education, especially university teaching, has a long way to go. There are exceptions, such as the establishment of popular postgraduate programmes in Jungian studies at Essex University (UK) and at Pacifica University, California. As Tacey says, academics and clinicians keen to further this enterprise need to let go of approaches that are too rigid to meet the competitive demands of twenty-first-century higher education:

> *'we serve Jung best not by turning his work into a fixed ideology, but by playfully deconstructing it for the new era. We have to deconstruct his ideas about the numinous, but we cannot eradicate the numinous to suit the needs of a secular academy.'*
>
> Tacey, 2007, p. 69

Key idea: The International Association for Jungian Studies (IAJS)

The IAJS was founded in 2002 with the aim of providing a discussion forum for those teaching Jungian ideas in universities, as well as other interested academics, clinicians and students. It has proved to be a robust and flourishing international network debating applications to the arts, humanities, sciences, religious studies, politics and education. For more information see: http://jungianstudies.org

Archetypal figures of psyche

As we have seen, Jung's 'map' of the human psyche contains some key figures which strongly influence how we function: **Ego, Persona, Shadow, Anima/Animus** and **Self.** So how have post-Jungian thinkers and practitioners taken forward this model? Most Jungians and post-Jungians still pay considerable heed to the value of these figures as a way of characterizing, and playing with, dynamics within the human psyche and interpersonal relations. There have been some interesting and creative applications to thinking about *Shadow,* and *Anima/Animus* in particular.

SHADOW, AND TYPOLOGICAL APPLICATIONS

Shadow remains a very influential concept, which therapists from other modalities have adopted (e.g. Rogers, 2000) to help make sense of the presence of repressed, hidden and overlooked aspects of the psyche. Identification of *shadow* in processes arising from difficult early dynamics can be found, for example, in the child analytic work of Sidoli (2000, see Chapter 14). She has theorized about how powerful *shadow* influences can become rooted in the body in infancy, with long-term consequences, as a result of persecutory, neglectful and chaotic attachment patterns.

In Chapter 9, we explored Jung's framework for typology. John Beebe (2004b) has further developed this, based on careful observation of the operation of typology and complexes in his practice. From this he has constructed a framework for understanding how different *shadow* functions, and archetypal influences, influence the individual. This involves a juxtaposition of archetypal figures with their *shadow* versions, as follows:

Archetypal figure   Shadow

Hero/heroine – Opposing personality*

Father or mother – Senex or witch

Puer or puella – Trickster

Anima/animus – Demonic/daimonic personality

(*Note: This takes the opposite attitude to the hero/heroine, e.g. passive rather than heroically 'active'. Each 'shadow' figure takes the opposite attitude to the archetypal figure.)

With this arrangement, it becomes possible to map eight rather than four functions at work in the individual – four in *shadow* and four not. So, for example, if someone had *introverted* thinking as their superior function and *extraverted* sensation as their auxiliary (secondary) function, then they will have *extraverted* thinking and *introverted* sensation strongly in shadow. It also then becomes possible to identify possible links to complexes, which may show through their *shadow* functions (e.g. if *introverted* feeling was their tertiary (third) *shadow* function, then a *trickster* complex is suggested, which could be explored via their *introverted* feeling). As with all other Jungian frameworks, it is important not to apply this in a formulaic way but, rather, hold the individuality of the analysand/patient in mind at all times. However, as Beebe observes:

> 'Recognizing correlations between functions and complexes can be very helpful to the therapist, especially when encountering markedly altered states of mind in patients. At such times the therapist can often help to re-establish ego-strength in the patient by speaking the language of the patient's superior function rather than mirroring the typological idiom of the possessing complex...'
>
> Beebe, in Papadopoulos, 2006, p. 144

ANIMA AND *ANIMUS* IN THE TWENTY-FIRST CENTURY

Perhaps the archetypal figures of the Jungian psyche that have generated the most critique and attempts to update them are *anima* and *animus*. Here, as Polly Young-Eisendrath (2006, p. 136) observes (and as noted in Chapter 7), Jung's formulation was both a gift and a problem for the post-Jungian field:

> 'By recognizing that the experience of being a person consists of multiple subjectivities, Jung has been prescient in providing contemporary psychoanalysis with an understanding of the projection-making factors of oppositeness in sex and gender. Still, Jung's cultural biases and tendencies to universalize gender differences need to be revised in the light of contemporary findings of developmental and anthropological research on the sexes.'

In her writing on contra-sexuality and gender, she helpfully describes the ways in which this area can be worked with: first, seeing gender as thoroughly flexible so women and men both carry *anima* and *animus* as representative of the feminine and masculine in all of us (as subscribed to by some Jungian writers such as Mathers, 2003); second, assuming biological sex is fixed and contra-sexual gender is a substrate of this, thereby assigning *anima* to men and *animus* to women as biologically present, or third (which she subscribes to), seeing biological sex as fixed, but seeing *anima* in men and *animus* in women as specific *complexes* of the 'opposite sex', which generate versions of contra-sexual 'otherness' in us.

These ways of looking at, and working with, *anima* and *animus* do not intend to perpetuate unhelpful gender stereotypes but rather challenge them, often by drawing on feminist perspectives (e.g. Rowland, 2002). This is not to say there is no post-Jungian exploration of subtle instinctual and developmental differences between 'being a woman' and 'being a man'. Considering possible distinct influences on how men and women operate, such as early attachment patterns (Goss, 2010), is part of the contemporary post-Jungian debate in this area.

There is also a growing focus on the nature and dynamics of differing sexualities, and valuable explorations of lesbian, gay, bisexual and transgender (LGBT) sexualities through a post-Jungian lens (McKenzie, 2006). Here, applying *anima* and *animus* flexibly, and in a way that counters essentialist tendencies, involves drawing on LGBT studies and helping analysts think about how the powerful but fluid nature of sexuality can be worked with. All trainings in this field challenge the risk of homophobic attitudes, however unconsciously based, creeping into practice (as they also do with regard to racist, sexist, disablist and ageist assumptions coming into the work).

Post-Jungian thinking and practice is a fertile arena for original and insightful ideas and practice around gender and sexuality, carrying the potential to influence wider understanding and debate about this important, but sometimes contentious, area.

The therapeutic relationship

The creativity and responsiveness of Jungian practitioners and thinkers continues to deepen and broaden the relevance of analytical psychology. Margaret Wilkinson (see also Chapter 15) is a Jungian analyst with expertise in the impact of neuroscience on attachment patterns and the therapeutic relationship. She describes how this operates in practice, and how the principles arising can be worked with to promote healing and healthy development (Wilkinson, 2012). She refers to the important neuroimaging work carried out within neuroscience, which shows the intimate interconnection of the activity of neurons.

In turn, Wilkinson demonstrates the impact on early experience of trauma or other experiences of disruption or lack; the individual's attachment, communication and reflective styles will likewise be affected. She advocates the importance of taking care of every aspect of analytic interaction, from the positioning of the chairs (so the analysand can be facilitated into 'look – look away – look' sequences which may have been missed in early life), to the tone or musicality of the analyst's voice. As she notes:

> 'These recent imaging studies are of course confirming just why as Jungian analysts we concentrate on the mood and affect that underpin mind as revealed in the consulting room, and the relation of this to the patient's emotional life and ways of relating.'
>
> Wilkinson, 2007, p. 340

Spotlight: A Story of Jungian analysis

Unusually for this field, Naomi Lloyd's book *The Knife and the Butterfly* (2014) tells the detailed story of an analysis. Her analyst gave permission for eight months of their sessions to be audio recorded. This allows for detailed dialogue to be included in the book, and provides valuable insights into how the dynamics of a Jungian analysis unfold, and how principles are applied.

Approaches to supervision from a Jungian perspective have also been developed and these are representative of the archetypal, classical and developmental strands within the field discussed in the previous chapter (Mathers, 2009). There is also ongoing publication of innovative approaches to post-Jungian thinking and practice, such as the *Research in Analytical Psychology and Jungian Studies* series (Samuels, 2013–present), while journals such as the *Journal of Analytical Psychology* showcase cutting-edge clinical and theoretical insights (see Meredith-Owen et al.). The examples of innovation in Jungian analytic thinking and practice in this chapter underline how post-Jungian ideas continue to extend their relevance for twenty-first-century psychotherapy.

Your reflective journal

In the Introduction to this book it was suggested that you keep some form of reflective journal in which you recorded your responses to the ideas in this book. Have you done this, even partly? If so, you are invited to spend time (in a quiet space by yourself) looking back through your journal, with this book to hand, so that you can check and further reflect on anything that strikes you. If you did not keep a journal, you could use any notes you have made, or even just sit with this book and do this exercise.

Here are some prompt questions to support you in this task, which is designed to help you notice and evaluate what you have learned from this book.

1 Which ideas of Jung's have had the most impact on you, and why? (What implications does this have for your way of looking at things?)
2 Which ones have had the least impact, and why? (Do you need to revisit them?)
3 Which ideas of Jung's have been the easiest to understand, and why? (How could you build further on this?)
4 Which ones have been the hardest to understand, and why? (Do you need to revisit them?)
5 Has this book sparked or strengthened your interest in Jung, or not? (Either way, what further reading might be helpful?)

Finally, take a piece of paper and some coloured pens, and spontaneously draw an image reflecting your experience of reading this book. If you want to add words that come up spontaneously, and/or elaborate the image, do so. Either way, when you are ready, spend some time with the picture, have another look at the questions above, and see if anything further springs to mind.

This activity should have helped you notice and consolidate your learning and reflections arising from reading this book. Just as the individuation process never ends, neither does our learning. The creative energy of the unconscious wills us towards self-knowledge, and I hope this book encourages you to keep digging deeper into the insights that Jung, and many others, have made available for this purpose.

The Brazilian Jungian analyst Roberto Gambini summarizes well the lasting value of Jung's legacy:

'Jung was an inspiration, a bunch of seeds spread out by a strong wind over the vast land of rational thought. Jung was an attitude... his discoveries and working hypotheses were a gift to culture, were his individual response to the paradoxes of reality, the uncertainties of knowledge and the pain and the glory of life itself.'

Gambini, 2007, p. 362

The individuality of Jung's response to reality invites the same from each of us.

Dig deeper

Beebe, J., 'Response to Wolfgang Giegerich's "The End of Meaning and the Birth of Man"', *Journal of Jungian Theory and Practice*, (1) (2004a)

Beebe, J., 'Understanding consciousness through the theory of psychological types', in Cambray, J. and Carter, L. (eds.), *Analytical Psychology* (Hove and New York: Brunner Routledge, 2004b), pp. 83–115

Casement, A. (ed.), *Who Owns Jung?* (London: Karnac, 2007)

Drob, S., 'Response to Beebe and Giegerich', *Journal of Jungian Theory and Practice*, 7(1) (2005)

Gambini, R., 'Epilogue – Who owns the air?' in Casement, A. (ed.), *Who Owns Jung?* (London: Karnac, 2007)

Giegerich, W., 'The End of Meaning and the Birth of Man: An essay about the state reached in the history of consciousness and an analysis of C. G. Jung's psychology project', *Journal of Jungian Theory and Practice*, 6(1), 1–66 (2004)

Giegerich, W., *What is Soul?* (New Orleans: Spring Journal Books, 2012)

Goss, P., *Men, Women and Relationships, A post-Jungian Approach: Gender Electrics and Magic Beans* (Hove: Routledge, 2010)

Hauke, C., *Jung and the Postmodern: The Interpretation of Realities* (Hove: Routledge, 2000)

Lloyd, N., *The Knife and the Butterfly: A Story of Jungian Analysis* (London: Karnac, 2014)

McKenzie, S., 'Queering gender: anima/animus and the paradigm of emergence', *Journal of Analytical Psychology*, vol. 51(3), 401–21 (2006)

Mathers, D., *Meaning and Purpose in Analytical Psychology* (London: Routledge, 2003)

Mathers, D. (ed.), *Vision and Supervision: Jungian and Post-Jungian Perspectives* (London: Routledge, 2009)

Mathers, D., *Alchemy and Psychotherapy: Post-Jungian Perspectives* (London: Routledge, 2014)

Meredith-Owen, W., Wright, S. and Carter, L. (eds.), *Journal of Analytical Psychology* (London: Society for Analytical Psychology, 1955–present)

Papadopoulos, R., *The Handbook of Jungian Psychology: Theory, Practice and Applications* (London: Routledge, 2006)

Rogers, N., *The Creative Connection: Expressive Arts as Healing* (Ross-on-Wye: PCCS Books, 2000)

Rowland, S., *Jung, A Feminist Revision* (Cambridge: Polity Press, 2002)

Samuels, A., *Research in Analytical Psychology and Jungian Studies* (London: Routledge, 2013)

Tacey, D., 'The Challenge of Teaching Jung in the University' in Casement, A. (ed.), *Who Owns Jung?* (London: Karnac, 2007)

Whan, M., 'Aurum Vulgi: Alchemy in Analysis, A Critique of a Simulated Phenomenon' in Mathers, D. (ed.), *Alchemy and Psychotherapy: Post-Jungian Perspectives* (London: Routledge, 2014)

Wilbur, K., *The Integral Vision: A Very Short Introduction to the Revolutionary Integral Approach to Life, God, the Universe, and Everything* (Boston, MA: Shambhala, 2007)

Wilkinson, M., 'Jung and neuroscience: the making of mind', in Casement, A. (ed.), *Who Owns Jung?* (London: Karnac, 2007)

Wilkinson, M., *Coming into Mind: The Mind–Brain Relationship: A Jungian Clinical Perspective* (Hove: Routledge, 2012)

Young-Eisendrath, P., *Subject to Change, Self, Gender Psychoanalysis* (London: Brunner-Routledge, 2006)

Fact-check (answers at the back)

1 What is the symbolic function?
  a The ways symbols function in cultural and religious imagery
  b Another name for the transcendent function
  c An inbuilt capacity to generate symbols and work with the meanings they represent
  d The main link between the analyst and the analysand

2 With what argument does Giegerich critique Jung's ideas about meaning and individuation?
  a Jung's ideas are generally not meaningful to individuals
  b The search for deeper meaning is futile because humanity has awoken to its absence
  c Jung does not clearly enough explain the link between meaning and individuation
  d The search for deeper meaning should be left to religious thinkers, not psychologists

3 In what way can Giegerich's position be challenged?
  a Not being rigorous enough
  b Misinterpreting Jung's ideas
  c Overlooking the way some may take Jungian archetypes to be real in a literal sense
  d Overlooking the still-present interest in spirituality, and the influence of the numinous

4 What has Whan warned against?
  a Using alchemical ideas for our self-development
  b Taking alchemy literally
  c Using alchemical ideas for self-promotion
  d Trying to turn base metal into gold

5 How can Jungian studies at universities make a fuller impact?
  a By imposing a Jungian perspective on established academic disciplines
  b By trying to fit Jungian ideas into established academic disciplines
  c By deconstructing Jungian ideas while allowing the numinous spirit of them into studies
  d By offering all academic staff discounted places on courses about Jungian ideas

6 How can shadow work in analysis be linked to typology?

   a By identifying shadow typological functions at work in the analysand to build a fuller picture

   b By asking the analysand if they inherited any shadow character traits from their parents

   c By the analyst telling the analysand all about their shadow development

   d By keeping a record of how the analysand talks about their shadow and how that changes

7 Why are anima and animus still relevant to analytic work?

   a All analysts subscribe fully to what Jung said about them

   b Jungian thinkers have updated this to take into account biology, gender and sexuality

   c Analysis only works if anima and animus are both present

   d Jungian thinkers have replaced Jung's model with a completely new model

8 What have applications of Jungian theory on contra-sexuality diversified to include?

   a Insights into diverse sexualities as well as what may be particular to women and men

   b Contradictory perspectives on gender and sexuality

   c Insights into the influence of gender on choice of analyst

   d Perspectives from cognitive psychology

9 Why is neuroscience relevant for Jungian practice?

   a It demonstrates where Jungian thinking is not coherent

   b It provides new ways to bring the transcendent function to bear on the analysand

   c It helps to more fully understand underlying influences and clinical dynamics

   d It has helped Jungian ideas be accepted by neuro-biologists

10 Why can active imagination be viewed as relevant psychodynamically?

   a It can be used a tool in the countertransference

   b It usually reflects envy and guilt

   c It is often used by psychodynamic therapists

   d It is helpful to imagine the object relationships of the analysand at the start of therapy

Answers

CHAPTER 1   1 c; 2 b; 3 a; 4 c; 5 d; 6 c; 7 b; 8 a; 9 d; 10 c

CHAPTER 2   1 b; 2 d; 3 c; 4 a; 5 b; 6 c; 7 d; 8 b; 9 a; 10 b

CHAPTER 3   1 c; 2 d; 3 a; 4 c; 5 b; 6 b; 7 d; 8 b; 9 c; 10 b

CHAPTER 4   1 a; 2 d; 3 c; 4 a; 5 b; 6 d; 7 c; 8 d; 9 d; 10 b

CHAPTER 5   1 d; 2 b; 3 c; 4 a; 5 c; 6 b; 7 a; 8 b; 9 d; 10 a

CHAPTER 6   1 c; 2 b; 3 a; 4 c; 5 d; 6 a; 7 c; 8 b; 9 d; 10 c

CHAPTER 7   1 d; 2 b; 3 c; 4 a; 5 c; 6 b; 7 a; 8 d; 9 c; 10 b

CHAPTER 8   1 b; 2 c; 3 a; 4 d; 5 c; 6 b; 7 a; 8 d; 9 b; 10 a

CHAPTER 9   1 c; 2 b; 3 a; 4 b; 5 d; 6 a; 7 c; 8 b; 9 d; 10 b

CHAPTER 10   1 d; 2 c; 3 b; 4 a; 5 b; 6 c; 7 a; 8 c; 9 a; 10 b

CHAPTER 11   1 c; 2 a; 3 d; 4 c; 5 c; 6 a; 7 b; 8 d; 9 a; 10 b

CHAPTER 12   1 b; 2 c; 3 d; 4 a; 5 d; 6 c; 7 b; 8 a; 9 b; 10 d

CHAPTER 13   1 c; 2 d; 3 b; 4 a; 5 b; 6 d; 7 b; 8 a; 9 c; 10 a

CHAPTER 14   1 b; 2 d; 3 a; 4 d; 5 b; 6 c; 7 a; 8 c; 9 a; 10 b

CHAPTER 15   1 c; 2 a; 3 b; 4 c; 5 d; 6 a; 7 d; 8 b; 9 c; 10 d

CHAPTER 16   1 b; 2 c; 3 a; 4 c; 5 d; 6 a; 7 b; 8 d; 9 b; 10 c

CHAPTER 17   1 c; 2 d; 3 a; 4 d; 5 b; 6 a; 7 b; 8 c; 9 a; 10 d

CHAPTER 18   1 c; 2 b; 3 a; 4 c; 5 d; 6 a; 7 b; 8 a; 9 c; 10 b

CHAPTER 19   1 c; 2 b; 3 d; 4 a; 5 c; 6 b; 7 c; 8 a; 9 b; 10 c

CHAPTER 20   1 c; 2 b; 3 d; 4 c; 5 c; 6 a; 7 b; 8 a; 9 c; 10 a

Index

Acknowledgements

I would like to thank Ann Casement, Oliver Goss and Lesley Wilson for proof corrections, and Professor Andrew Samuels for helping me with some of the more sensitive material in the book.

My analytic practice has helped me make connections between concepts and applications, so thank you to all I have worked with. Thank you too, to students at UCLan who have challenged Jungian ideas and helped me clarify my thinking. Likewise to the Lancaster Jungian Reading Group. My appreciation too, to colleagues in the Counselling and Psychological Therapies Division, School of Health, UCLan, for helping me find time to write this.

Finally, thank you and love to my family, for once again putting up with my head being somewhere else during the many hours of work on this book.